1.00

1923
Atlas of the World
and
Gazetteer

Containing

NEW MAPS OF THE PRINCIPAL COUNTRIES OF THE WORLD
AND SEPARATE MAPS OF EACH AMERICAN STATE AND TERRITORY
THE CANADIAN PROVINCES, ETC., ETC.

ACCOMPANIED BY INDIVIDUAL INDEXES OF EACH STATE, PROVINCE, ETC.
AND A DESCRIPTIVE GAZETTEER OF THE PRINCIPAL
COUNTRIES OF THE WORLD

FUNK AND WAGNALLS COMPANY
NEW YORK AND LONDON
1923

CONTENTS
MAPS

GAZETTEER, INDEXES, ETC.

Printed in U. S. A.
Copyright C. S. Hammond & Co., New York

STATISTICAL GAZETTEER OF THE WORLD

This alphabetical list of grand divisions, countries, states, colonial possessions, etc., gives area, population and capital or seat of government. The mother country of colonial possessions is indicated in Italic abbreviations enclosed within parentheses.

ABBREVIATIONS

Br.	= British or British Empire	N. S.	= Nova Scotia
Dan.	= Danish or Denmark	N. Z.	= New Zealand
Domin.	= Dominion	Port.	= Portugal or Portuguese
Dutch	= The Netherlands	Rep.	= Republic
Fr.	= France or French	Rus.	= Russia or Russian
Ger.	= German or Germany	Sov. Rep.	= Soviet Republic
Gr.	= Greece or Greek	Sp.	= Spain or Spanish
I.	= Island	sq. m.	= square miles
Is.	= Islands	St.	= States
It.	= Italian or Italy	U. K.	= United Kingdom of
Jap.	= Japan or Japanese		Great Britain
L. of N.	= League of Nations	U. S. A.	= United States of America
	Territory	U. of So. Africa	= Union of South Africa
Mand.	= Mandate		

NEW CENSUS

The statistics of population are based on the latest official census reports or recent official estimates and include, among other reports, the new government census figures of dates as follows:

Austria................1920	France and dependencies 1921	Philippine Islands.......1921
Belgium................1921	Germany................1919	Poland................1921
Brazil................1920	Greece................1920	Spain................1920
British Empire, except	Guatemala............1921	Sweden................1920
Ireland............1921	Hungary................1921	Switzerland............1920
Bulgaria................1920	Japan................1920	United States and insular
Chosen................1920	Latvia................1920	possessions except Virgin Islands...........1920
Columbia................1918	Netherlands and dependencies................1920	Uruguay................1920
Cuba................1919	Nicaragua..............1920	Venezuela................1921
Czecho-Slovakia.......1921	Norway................1920	Virgin Islands..........1917
Denmark................1921	Panama................1920	
Finland................1920		

Country	Area (Sq. Miles)	Population	Capital
Abyssinia..............	350,000	8,000,000	Addis Abeba
Aden (*Br.*)..............	75	54,923	Aden
Afghanistan............	245,000	6,380,500	Kabul
Africa................	11,515,000	180,000,000	....
Alabama, U.S.A........	51,998	2,348,174	Montgomery
Alaska (*U.S.A.*)........	590,884	54,899	Juneau
Albania................	11,000	850,000	Durazzo
Alberta, Canada........	255,285	588,454	Edmonton
Algeria (*Fr.*)...........	222,180	5,800,974	Algiers
Andorra................	191	5,231	Andorra
Anglo-Egyptian Sudan (*Br.*)................	1,014,000	3,400,000	Khartum
Angola (*Port.*)..........	484,800	4,119,000	Loanda
Antarctic Regions.......	....	....	....
Antigua (*Br.*)..........	170	32,269	St. John
Arabia (pen.)..........	1,200,000	5,000,000	....
Arctic Regions..........	....	....	....
Argentina..............	1,153,119	8,533,332	Buenos Aires
Arizona, U.S.A..........	113,956	334,162	Phoenix
Arkansas, U.S.A........	53,335	1,752,204	Little Rock
Armenia................	71,900	2,470,900	Erivan
Ascension Island (*Br.*)...	34	200	Georgetown
Asia...................	17,057,000	920,000,000	....
Australasia............	3,188,405	7,207,676	....
Australia, Commonwealth of (*Br.*)........	2,974,581	5,436,794	Melbourne
Austria................	30,766	6,131,445	Vienna
Azerbaijan (Rus. Sov. Rep.)	33,970	2,096,973	Baku
Azores Islands (*Port.*)...	922	242,613	....
Bahama Islands (*Br.*)...	4,404	60,000	Nassau
Baluchistan............	134,638	800,678	Khelat
Barbados (*Br.*).........	166	187,000	Bridgetown
Basutoland (*Br.*)......	11,716	499,311	Maseru
Bechuanaland (*Br.*).....	275,000	152,983	Mafeking
Belgian Kongo..........	909,654	15,500,000	Boma
Belgium................	11,373	7,478,840	Brussels

Country	Area (Sq. Miles)	Population	Capital
Belize (Br. Honduras)...	8,598	45,317	Belize
Bermuda Islands (Br.)...	19	22,000	Hamilton
Bhutan.................	20,000	250,000	Punakha
Bokhara...............	79,440	3,000,000	Bokhara
Bolivia...............	514,155	2,889,970	La Paz
Borneo (British)........	31,106	208,183	Sandakan
Borneo (Dutch).........	212,737	1,625,453	....
Brazil.................	3,275,510	30,635,605	Rio de Janeiro
British Columbia, Canada	355,855	523,369	Victoria
British Honduras (Belize)	8,598	45,317	Belize
British Isles............	121,633	47,307,601	....
Brunei (Br.)............	4,000	25,454	Brunei
Bulgaria...............	40,656	4,861,439	Sofia
Burma (Br.)............	230,839	13,205,564	....
California, U.S.A.......	158,297	3,426,861	Sacramento
Cambodia,Fr.Indo-China	45,000	1,634,252	Pnom-Penh
Canada, Domin. of (Br.).	3,729,665	8,769,489	Ottawa
Canal Zone (U.S.A.)....	502	22,858	Ancon
Canary Islands (Sp.)....	3,342	506,414	....
Cape Breton Island, N.S.	3,975	131,495	....
Cape of Good Hope, U. of So. Africa............	276,966	2,781,185	Cape Town
Cape Verde Is. (Port.)....	1,480	149,793	Porto Praya
Caroline Is. (Jap. Mand.)	560	39,000	....
Caucasia (Rus. region)..	181,173	13,500,000	
Cayman Islands (Br.)...	89	5,253	Georgetown
Celebes (Dutch)........	72,070	3,089,263	Menado
Central America........	212,998	5,634,652	....
Ceylon (Br.)...........	25,481	4,504,283	Colombo
Channel Islands (U. K.).	75	89,614	....
Chile..................	289,829	3,754,723	Santiago
China, Chinese Rep......	1,532,420	302,110,000	Peking
Chinese Republic........	4,277,170	320,650,000	....
Chosen [Korea] (Jap.)...	84,738	17,284,207	Seoul
Colombia...............	440,846	5,855,077	Bogota
Colorado, U.S.A........	103,948	939,629	Denver
Connecticut, U.S.A.....	4,965	1,380,631	Hartford
Costa Rica.............	23,000	476,581	San Jose
Crete, Greece...........	3,330	310,400	....
Cuba..................	44,215	2,889,004	Havana
Curacao (Dutch)........	210	32,709	Willemstad
Cyprus (Br.)...........	3,584	310,808	Nicosia
Czecho-Slovakia........	54,264	13,595,816	Prague
Dahomey (Fr.).........	42,460	841,705	Porto Novo
Dalmatia, Jugo-Slavia (region)..............	5,090	621,503	....
Danzig, Free City of (L. of N.)............	794	330,252	Danzig
Delaware, U.S.A........	2,370	223,003	Dover
Denmark...............	16,609	3,267,831	Copenhagen
Dist. of Columbia, U.S.A.	70	437,571	....
Dominica (Br.).........	305	37,059	Roseau
Dominican Republic.....	19,332	897,405	Santo Domingo
East India Islands......	....	....	....
East Indies, Dutch......	683,000	49,161,047	....
Ecuador...............	116,000	2,000,000	Quito
Egypt.................	350,000	12,710,000	Cairo
England, U. K..........	58,340	35,678,530	London
Eritrea................	45,800	450,000	Asmara
Esthonia...............	23,160	1,750,000	Reval
Europe................	3,879,000	400,000,000	....
Europe, Southeastern....	......	3,240	Port Stanley
Falkland Islands (Br.)...	6,500	3,240	Port Stanley
Faroe Islands (Dan.).....	540	21,364	Thornshawn
Federal Territory, Australia (Br.)............	940	2,572	....
FederatedMalaySt.(Br.).	27,506	1,037,000	....
Fiji Islands (Br.)	7,083	154,584	Suva
Finland................	149,586	3,367,542	Helsingfors

Country	Area (Sq. Miles)	Population	Capital
Fiume, Free State.......	8	49,806	Fiume
Florida, U.S.A..........	58,668	968,470	Tallahassee
Formosa [Taiwan] (Jap.).	13,944	3,654,398	Taiwan
France.................	212,659	39,402,739	Paris
Franz Josef Land.......	......	......	....
French Equatorial Africa	982,049	9,000,000	Brazzaville
French Soudan.........	617,600	2,473,606	Banako
Fren h West Africa.....	1,800,566	12,275,307	Dakar
Galapagos Is. (Ecuador)..	2,400	400	....
Gambia (Br.)...........	4,500	208,000	Bathurst
Georgia (Rus. Sov. Rep.).	25,760	2,372,403	Tiflis
Georgia, U.S.A........	59,265	2,895,832	Atlanta
Germany..............	183,381	59,857,283	Berlin
Gibraltar (Br.).........	2	17,690	....
Gold Coast (Br.)........	80,000	1,500,000	Akkra
Greece.................	41,933	5,535,240	Athens
Greenland (Dan.).......	826,000	13,459	Godhaven
Grenada (Br.)..........	133	75,663	St. George
Guadeloupe (Fr.).......	722	212,430	Basse Terre
Guam (U.S.A.)........	225	13,275	Agaña
Guatemala.............	48,290	2,119,000	New Guatemala
Guiana, British........	89,500	297,691	Georgetown
Guiana, Dutch	46,060	113,181	Paramaribo
Guiana, French	32,000	49,000	Cayenne
Guinea, French........	95,218	1,875,996	Konakry
Guinea, Portuguese.....	13,940	289,000	Bulama
Haiti.................	10,204	2,500,000	Port au Prince
Hawaii (U.S.A.)........	6,449	255,912	Honolulu
Hejaz.................	170,000	900,000	Mecca
Holland (Netherlands)....	15,760	6,841,155	Hague
Honduras.............	44,275	637,114	Tegucigalpa
Honduras, Br. (Belize)...	8,598	45,317	Belize
Hong Kong (Br.).......	391	625,166	Victoria
Hungary..............	35,654	7,840,832	Budapest
Iceland................	39,709	94,690	Reikiavik
Idaho, U.S.A...........	83,888	431,866	Boise
Ifni (Sp.)..............	965	20,000	Ifni
Illinois, U.S.A..........	56,665	6,485,280	Springfield
India and Dependencies..	1,802,629	319,075,132	Delhi
Indiana, U.S.A.........	36,354	2,930,390	Indianapolis
Indo-China, French.....	256,000	16,990,229	....
Iowa, U.S.A............	56,147	2,404,021	Des Moines
Irak [Mesopotamia] (Br. Mand.)...............	143,250	2,849,282	Bagdad
Ireland, Northern, U. K.	8,613	1,581,696	Belfast
Irish Free State (Br.)....	23,973	2,808,523	Dublin
Isle of Man, U. K.......	227	60,238	Douglas
Italy..................	117,982	37,528,414	Rome
Ivory Coast (Fr.).......	121,976	1,544,845	Bingerville
Jamaica (Br.)..........	4,207	857,921	Kingston
Japan.................	148,756	56,961,140	Tokyo
Java (Dutch)...........	48,857	33,417,204	Batavia
Jugo-Slavia............	95,628	11,337,686	Belgrade
Kamerun (Br.&Fr.Mand.)	191,300	2,541,871	Buëa
Kansas, U.S.A..........	82,158	1,769,257	Topeka
Karafutu [Sakhalin] (Jap.)	13,253	105,765	....
Kentucky, U.S.A.......	40,598	2,416,630	Frankfort
Kenya (Br.)............	245,060	2,630,000	Neirobi
Khiva.................	24,310	519,438	Khiva
Kongo, Belgian.........	909,654	15,500,000	Boma
Korea [Chosen] (Jap.)...	84,738	17,284,207	Seoul
Labrador (Br.).........	120,000	3,647	....
Latvia.................	24,440	1,503,193	Riga
Leeward Islands (Br.)...	715	128,000	....
Liberia................	40,000	1,500,000	Monrovia
Liechtenstein...........	65	10,716	Vaduz
Lithuania.............	31,700	2,671,000	Kovno
Louisiana, U.S.A........	48,506	1,798,509	Baton Rouge
Luxemburg.............	998	263,824	Luxemburg

Country	Area (Sq. Miles)	Population	Capital
Macao (*Port.*)..........	4	74,866	....
Madagascar (*Fr.*).......	228,000	3,512,690	Tananarivo
Madeira Islands (*Port.*)..	314	170,000	Funchal
Madura (*Dutch*)........	1,700	1,600,000	....
Maine, U.S.A...........	33,040	768,014	Augusta
Malta (*Br.*)............	118	224,500	Valetta
Manchuria, Chinese Rep.	363,610	12,740,000	Mukden
Manitoba, Canada......	251,832	610,118	Winnipeg
Mariana Islands (*Jap. Mand.*)	250	10,000	....
Marshall Islands (*Jap. Mand.*)	150	16,500	....
Martinique (*Fr.*)........	385	193,000	Fort de France
Maryland, U.S.A........	12,327	1,449,661	Annapolis
Massachusetts, U.S.A....	8,266	3,852,356	Boston
Mauretania (*Fr.*).......	347,400	261,532	....
Memel (*L. of N.*).......	1,057	140,746	Memel
Mesopotamia [Irak] (*Br. Mand.*)...............	143,250	2,849,282	Bagdad
Mexico..............	767,198	15,501,684	Mexico
Michigan, U.S.A........	57,980	3,668,412	Lansing
Midway Island (*U.S.A.*)	....	....	....
Minnesota, U.S.A.......	84,682	2,387,125	St. Paul
Miquelon (*Fr.*).........	83	443	St. Pierre
Mississippi, U.S.A.......	46,865	1,790,618	Jackson
Missouri, U.S.A........	69,420	3,404,055	Jefferson City
Molucca Islands (*Dutch*).	22,781	392,784	....
Monaco..............	8	22,956	Monaco
Mongolia, Chinese Rep...	1,367,600	1,800,000	Urga
Montana, U.S.A........	146,997	548,889	Helena
Montserrat (*Br.*).......	32	12,120	Plymouth
Morocco, French Zone...	231,500	5,400,000	Fez
Morocco, Spanish Zone .	8,665	620,000	Tetuan
Mozambique (Port. E. Africa)..............	428,132	3,120,000	LourencoMarques
Natal, Union of So. Africa	35,284	1,194,043	
Nebraska, U.S.A........	77,520	1,296,372	Lincoln
Nepal.................	54,000	5,000,000	Khatmandu
Netherlands [Holland]....	15,760	6,841,155	Hague
Nevada, U.S.A..........	110,690	77,407	Carson City
New Britain Archipelago (*Australia Mand.*)...	18,200	188,000	....
New Brunswick, Canada	27,985	387,876	Fredericton
New Caledonia (*Fr.*)....	7,650	50,600	Noumea
Newfoundland (*Br.*).....	42,734	263,683	St. Johns
New Guinea (*Br. Mand.*)	70,000	110,000	Port Moresby
New Guinea (*Dutch*)....	121,339	Unknown	....
New Hampshire, U.S.A..	9,341	443,083	Concord
New Hebrides Islands (*Br. & Fr.*)..........	5,500	60,000	....
New Jersey, U.S.A......	8,224	3,155,900	Trenton
New Mexico, U.S.A......	122,634	360,350	Santa Fe
New South Wales, Australia................	310,700	2,099,763	Sydney
New York, U.S.A.......	49,204	10,385,227	Albany
New Zealand, Dominion of (*Br.*)............	104,751	1,218,913	Wellington
Nicaragua..............	49,200	638,119	Managua
Nigeria (*Br.*)............	336,000	16,500,000	Lagos
Niger Territory (*Fr.*)....	347,400	1,083,827	....
North America..........	9,323,000	145,000,000	
North Carolina, U.S.A....	52,426	2,559,123	Raleigh
North Dakota, U.S.A....	70,837	646,872	Bismarck
Northern Rhodesia (*Br.*).	291,000	931,500	Livingstone
Northern Territory, Australia................	523,620	3,870	....
Northwest Territories, Canada..............	18,481	6,684	....
Norway................	124,964	2,646,306	Christiania
Nova Scotia, Canada....	2,184	523,837	Halifax
Nyasaland (*Br.*)........	39,573	1,200,000	Zomba

Country	Area (Sq. Miles)	Population	Capital
Ohio, U.S.A.............	41,040	5,759,394	Columbus
Oklahoma, U.S.A........	70,057	2,028,283	Oklahoma City
Oman.................	82,000	500,000	Maskat
Ontario, Canada........	407,262	2,933,662	Toronto
Orange Free State, U. of So. Africa............	50,389	628,360	Bloemfontein
Oregon, U.S.A..........	96,699	783,389	Salem
Palestine (Br. Mand.)...	9,000	761,796	Jerusalem
Panama...............	32,380	401,428	Panama
Papua Territory [New Guinea] (Br.).........	90,540	251,000	Port Moresby
Paraguay.............	97,722	636,000	Asuncion
Pelew Islands (Jap.Mand.)	560	3,200	....
Pemba Island (Br.).....	380	83,109	....
Pennsylvania, U.S.A....	45,126	8,720,017	Harrisburg
Persia.................	628,000	9,500,000	Teheran
Peru..................	709,871	4,569,752	Lima
Philippine Islands(U.S.A.)	114,400	10,350,640	Manila
Poland................	150,267	27,778,068	Warsaw
Porto Rico (U.S.A.)....	3,435	1,299,809	San Juan
Portugal..............	35,490	5,957,985	Lisbon
Portuguese East Africa (Mozambique)........	428,132	3,120,000	Lourenço Marques
Prince Edward Island, Canada..............	2,184	88,615	Charlottetown
Quebec, Canada	706,834	2,361,199	Quebec
Queensland, Australia...	670,500	757,634	Brisbane
Rhode Island, U.S.A.....	1,248	604,397	Providence
Rhodesia (Br.).........	440,000	1,741,500	....
Rio de Oro (Sp.)........	109,200	800,000	Villa Cisneros
Rio Muni (Sp.).........	9,470	89,130	Santa Isabel
Rumania..............	122,282	17,393,149	Bukharest
Russia................	1,488,240	93,387,923	Moscow
Sakhalin [Karafutu](Jap.)	13,253	105,765	....
Salvador..............	13,183	1,500,000	San Salvador
Samoa (N.Z.Mand.).....	1,250	37,000	....
Samoa (U.S.A.)........	102	8,056	....
San Marino............	38	12,027	San Marino
Sarawak (Br.).........	42,000	600,000	Kuching
Sarre (L. of N.)........	751	657,870	....
Saskatchewan, Canada..	251,700	757,510	Regina
Scotland, U. K..........	30,405	4,882,288	Edinburgh
Senegal (Fr.)...........	74,112	1,225,523	St. Louis
Shetland Islands (Br.)...	551	25,520	....
Siam.................	198,900	9,121,000	Bangkok
Siberia, Russia.........	4,831,882	10,377,900	....
Sierra Leone (Br.)......	31,000	1,400,000	Freetown
Sinkiang, Chinese Rep...	550,340	2,000,000	Urumchi
Society Islands (Fr.)....	700	28,000	Papeete
Solomon Islands (Austra-lia Mand.)...........	3,800	17,000	....
Solomon Islands (Br.)...	11,000	150,000	....
Somali Coast, French....	5,790	208,000	Djibouti
Somaliland, British......	68,000	300,000	Berbera
Somaliland, Italian......	139,430	650,000	Mogdishu
South America..........	6,889,000	50,000,000	
South Australia, Australia	380,070	495,336	Adelaide
South Carolina, U.S.A...	30,989	1,683,724	Columbia
South Dakota, U.S.A....	77,615	636,547	Pierre
Southern Rhodesia (Br.)	149,000	810,000	Salisbury
South Georgia (Br.).....	1,000	1,000	....
Southwest Africa (U. So. Africa Mand.)........	322,400	237,237	Windhoek
Spain.................	194,783	20,783,844	Madrid
Spitzbergen (Norway)...	25,000	300	....
St. Croix Island, Virgin Is. (U. S. A.)........	84	14,901	....
St. Helena Island (Br.) .	47	3,747	....

Country	Area (Sq. Miles)	Population	Capital
St. John Island, Virgin Is. (U.S.A)	32	959	....
St. Lucia (Br.)	233	51,505	Castries
St. Pierre Island (Fr.)	10	4,209	....
Straits Settlements (Br.)	1,600	821,000	....
St. Thomas Island, Virgin Is. (U.S.A.)	33	10,191	....
St. Vincent (Br.)	150	44,447	Kingstown
Sumatra (Dutch)	160,736	5,848,872	....
Swaziland (Br.)	6,678	100,000	Embabaan
Sweden	173,035	5,903,762	Stockholm
Switzerland	15,976	3,880,320	Bern
Syria (Fr. Mand.)	60,000	3,000,000	....
Taiwan [Formosa] (Jap.)	13,944	3,654,398	Taiwan
Tanganyika Territory (Br. Mand.)	365,000	4,000,000	Dar-es-Salaam
Tasmania (Br.)	26,215	213,877	Hobart
Tennessee, U.S.A.	42,022	2,337,885	Nashville
Texas, U.S.A.	265,896	4,663,228	Austin
Tibet, Chinese Rep.	463,000	2,000,000	Lassa
Timor (Port.)	7,330	377,815	....
Timor Archipelago (Dutch)	17,698	1,146,657	....
Tobago (Br.)	114	12,465	....
Togo (Br. & Fr. Mand.)	33,700	1,032,088	Lome
Tongking, French Indo-China	46,400	6,119,720	....
Transvaal, Union of So. Africa	110,450	2,085,837	Pretoria
Trinidad (Br.)	1,863	391,279	Port of Spain
Tripoli (It.)	406,000	1,000,000	Tripoli
Tunis (Fr.)	50,000	2,093,939	Tunis
Turkestan (Rus. Sov. Rep.)	420,807	6,684,400	....
Turkey	174,900	8,000,000	Angora
Uganda (Br.)	109,119	3,361,000	Entebbe
Ukraine (Rus. Sov. Rep.)	174,510	26,001,802	Kief
Union of South Africa (Br.)	473,089	6,922,813	Cape Town
United States of America	3,026,791	105,710,620	Washington
Upper Volta, French W. Africa	154,400	2,973,951	Ouaga-dougou
Uruguay	72,153	1,494,953	Montevideo
Utah, U.S.A.	84,990	449,396	Salt Lake City
Venezuela	398,594	2,411,952	Caracas
Vermont, U.S.A.	9,564	352,428	Montpelier
Victoria, Australia	87,884	1,531,529	Melbourne
Virgin Islands (U.S.A)	132	26,051	St. Thomas
Virginia, U.S.A.	42,627	2,309,187	Richmond
Wales, U. K.	7,466	2,206,712	....
Walfisch Bay (Br.)	430	4,398	....
Washington, U.S.A.	69,127	1,356,621	Olympia
Weihaiwei (Br.)	285	147,177	....
West Africa, French	1,800,566	12,283,962	Dakar
Western Australia, Australia	975,920	332,213	Perth
West Indies	85,699	8,132,795	....
West Virginia, U.S.A.	24,170	1,463,701	Charleston
Windward Islands (Br.)	519	178,000	....
Wisconsin, U.S.A.	56,066	2,632,067	Madison
World	196,872,000	1,700,000,000	....
Wyoming, U.S.A.	97,914	194,402	Cheyenne
Yap (Jap. Mand.)	79	8,613	....
Yukon, Canada	207,076	4.162	Dawson
Zanzibar, (Br.)	640	113,624	Zanzibar

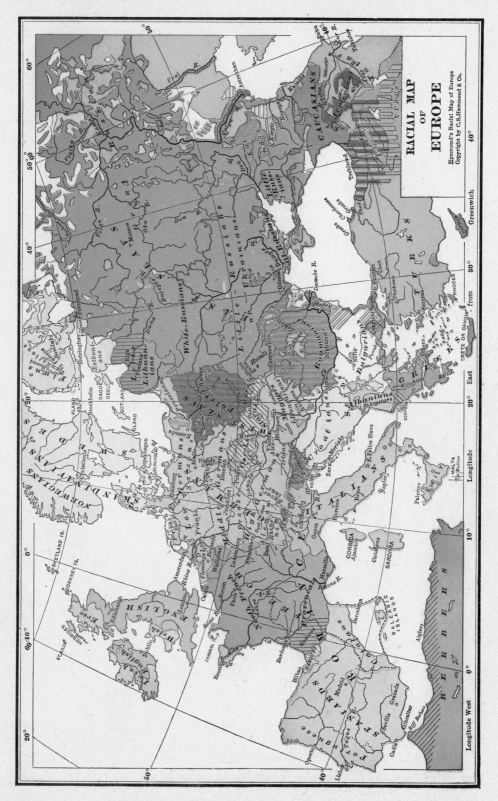

RACIAL MAP
OF
EUROPE

Hammond's Racial Map of Europe
Copyright by C.S.Hammond & Co.

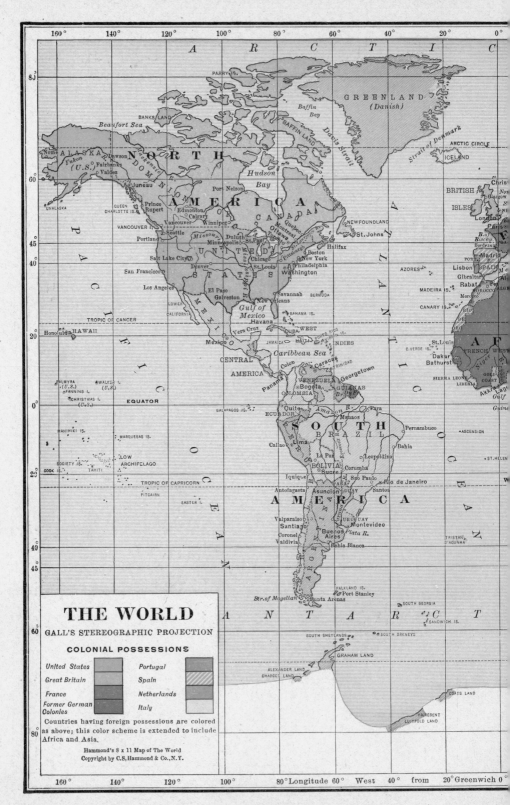

THE WORLD

GALL'S STEREOGRAPHIC PROJECTION

COLONIAL POSSESSIONS

United States

Great Britain

France

Former German Colonies

Portugal

Spain

Netherlands

Italy

Countries having foreign possessions are colored as above; this color scheme is extended to include Africa and Asia.

Hammond's 8 x 11 Map of The World
Copyright by C.S. Hammond & Co., N.Y.

O   C   E   A   N

FRANZ JOSEF
LAND

RGEN (Nor.)

Barents Sea

NOVA ZEMLA

Kara Sea

Nordenskiold Sea

NEW SIBERIA

80°

Alexandrovsk

White Sea

FINLAND

Archangel

ARCTIC CIRCLE

60°

Petrograd

RUSSIA

Moscow

Klef

UKRAINE

Warsaw

R

Tobolsk

S   I   B   E   R   I   A

Yakutsk

Sea of
Okhotsk

Bering
Sea

Okhotsk

Yenissei R.

Lena R.

Nikolaievsk

Amur R.

MANCHURIA

KAMCHATKA

SAKHALIN

ALEUTIAN IS.

45°

Odessa

RUM.
Astrakhan

Tiflis

Orenburg

Omsk

Tomsk

Yenisselsk

Irkutsk

Kobdo

Urga

MONGOLIA

Chita

Harbin

Vladivostok

PAN KURILE IS.

Japan

40°

Black Sea

BULG.
TURKEY

Constantinople

Athens

Smyrna

Teheran

TURKESTAN

Urumtsi

CHINESE

Mukden

Peking

(KOREA)
Seoul

Yellow
Sea

Yokohama

Khiva

Tashkent

Bokhara

Sea

Damascus

Bagdad

PERSIA

AFGHAN-

Kabul

ISTAN

Kandahar

R   E   P   U   B   L   I   C

Kiaochi

Tokyo

Kobe

Cairo

EGYPT

Busra

Koweit

NEJD

Medina

Maskat

Karachi

Delhi

NEPAL

Lassa

Chingtu

Yangtze R.

Hankau

Shanghai

East
China
Sea

EMPIRE

P   A   C   I   F   I   C

Lucknow

INDIA

Yunnan

Canton

TROPIC OF CANCER

BONIN IS.
(Jap.)

MIDWAY I.
(U.S.)

20°

Bombay

Arabian

Goa

Sea

Rangoon

Bay of

SIAM

Bengal

Bangkok

INDO

S. China
Sea

Hongkong

FORMOSA

MARIANNE IS.
(Jap.)

WAKE I.
(U.S.)

WALKER I.
(U.S.)

Madras

LACCADIVE IS.

PHILIPPINE

Manila

O   C   E   A   N

GUAM
(U.S.)

JAPANESE

CAROLINE IS.
(Jap.)

MARSHALL IS.
(Jap.)

HOWLAND I.(U.S.)

CEYLON

STRAITS
SETTLEMENTS

Saigon

SULU
(U.S.)

MANDATE

GILBERT IS.

EQUATOR

BAKER I.(U.S.)

MALDIVE IS.

Singapore

E   A   S   T   I   N   D   I   A   N   A   R   C   H.

BRITISH

PHOENIX IS.

0°

Nairobi

Mombasa

SEYCHELLES

COCOS IS.

Pandang

CELEBES

Batavia

JAVA

NEW GUINEA

MANDATE

NEW BRITAIN

SOLOMON IS.

LAGOON OR
ELLICE IS.

Dar es Salaam

I   N   D   I   A   N

Palmerston

SAMOA IS.

MADAGASCAR

Tananarivo

MAURITIUS

REUNION

TROPIC OF CAPRICORN

Coral Sea

Townsville

NEW HEBRIDES

FIJI IS.

20°

O   C   E   A   N

Rockhampton

Brisbane

NORFOLK I.

NEW
CALEDONIA

KERMADEC IS.

AUSTRALIA

Fremantle

Perth

LORD HOWE I.

Albany

Adelaide

Sydney

Canberra

Melbourne

Tasman Sea

Auckland

NEW

40°

TASMANIA

Hobart

ZEALAND

Wellington

CHATHAM I.

Invercargill

Christchurch

Dunedin

45°

KERGUELEN

CAMPBELL I.

60°

O   C   E   A   N

CIRCLE

ENDERBY LAND

QUEEN MARY
LAND

ADELIE LAND

KING GEORGE
LAND

BALLENY IS.

OATES LAND

80°

SOUTH
VICTORIA
LAND

ROSS I.

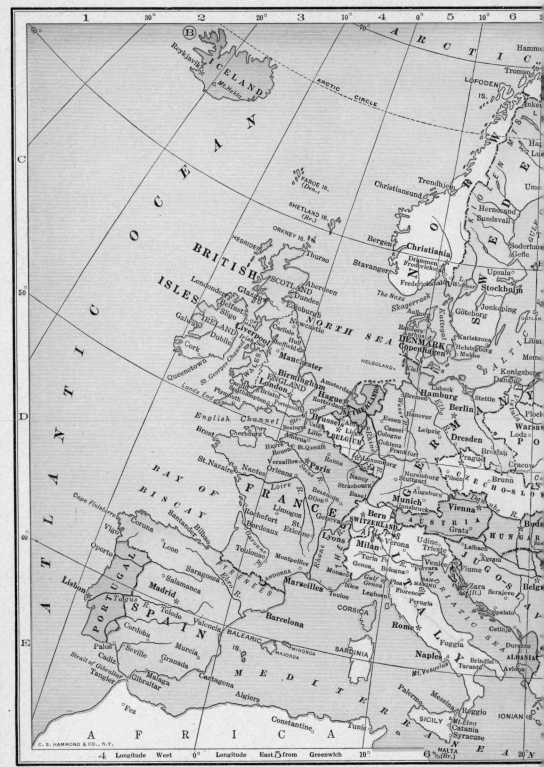

Map of Africa, Pages 44-47; Asia, 36-37.

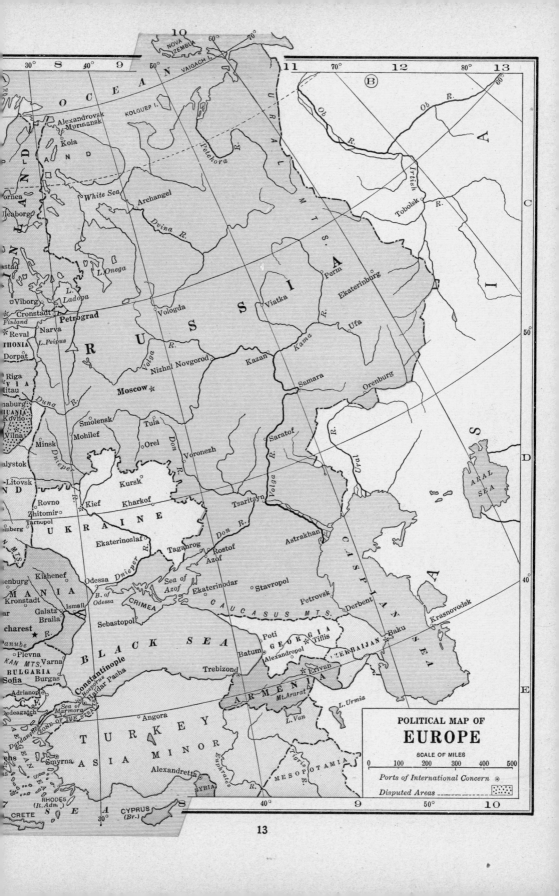

POLITICAL MAP OF
EUROPE

SCALE OF MILES

0   100   200   300   400   500

Ports of International Concern ⊙

Disputed Areas

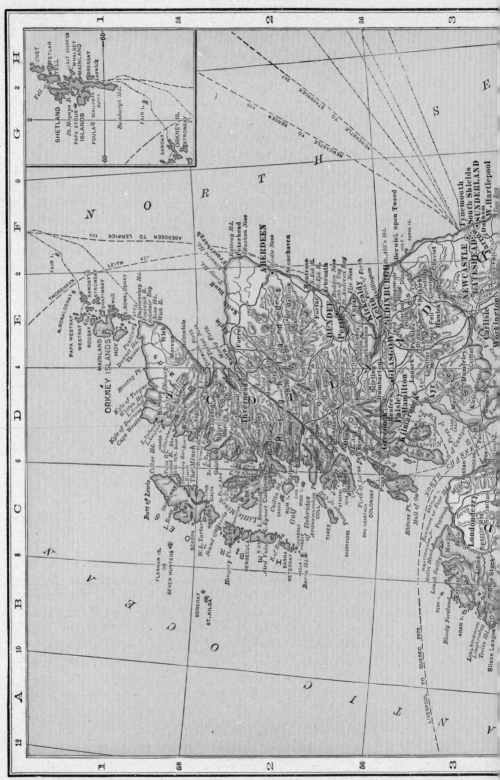

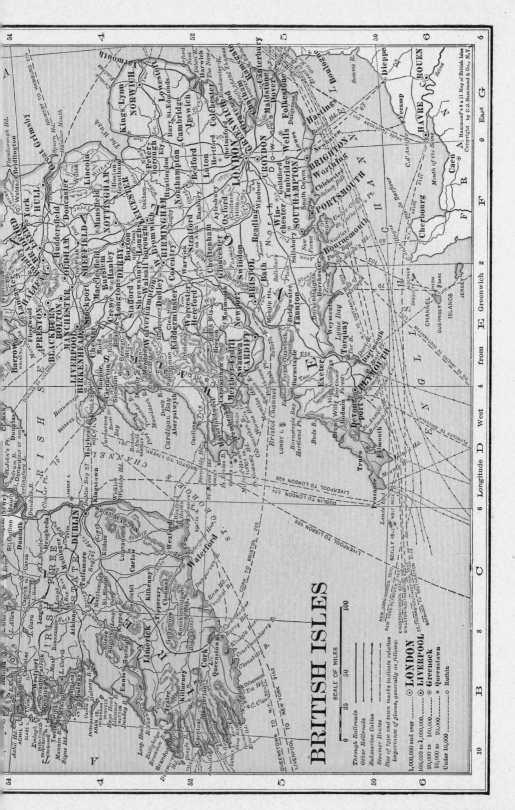

BRITISH ISLES

SCALE OF MILES

Through Railroads
Other Railroads
Submarine Cables
Steamer Routes

Size of type and town marks indicate relative
importance of places, generally as follows:

◉ **LONDON** .... 1,000,000 and over
◉ **LIVERPOOL** ... 100,000 to 1,000,000
◉ **Greenock** ...... 20,000 to 100,000
◎ Queenstown .... 10,000 to 20,000
○ Rathlin .... Under 10,000

A Hammond's 8 x 11 Map of British Isles
Copyright by C.S. Hammond & Co., N.Y.

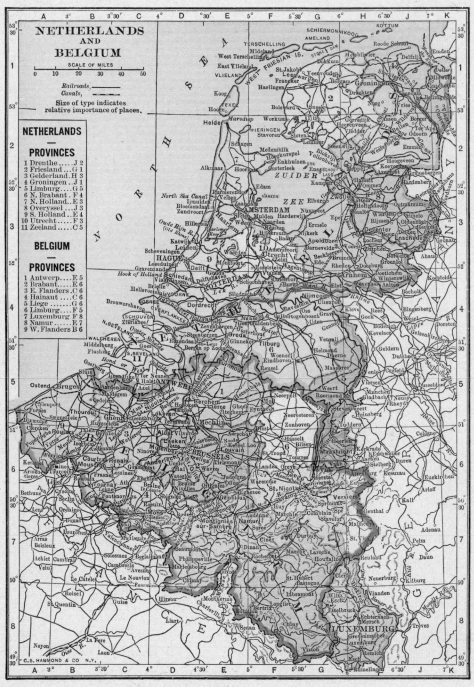

NETHERLANDS
AND
BELGIUM

SCALE OF MILES

0   10   20   30   40   50

Railroads, _____
Canals, _____
Size of type indicates
relative importance of places.

NETHERLANDS
—
PROVINCES
1 Drenthe.....J 2
2 Friesland...G 1
3 Gelderland.H 3
4 Groningen..J 1
5 Limburg....G 5
6 N. Brabant. F 4
7 N. Holland..E 3
8 Overyssel...J 3
9 S. Holland..E 4
10 Utrecht.....F 3
11 Zeeland.....C 5

BELGIUM
—
PROVINCES
1 Antwerp...E 5
2 Brabant....E 6
3 E. Flanders.C 6
4 Hainaut...C 6
5 Liege......G 6
6 Limburg...F 5
7 Luxemburg F 8
8 Namur....E 7
9 W. Flanders B 6

C. S. HAMMOND & CO. N.Y.

Map of France, Pages 18-19; Germany, 20-21.

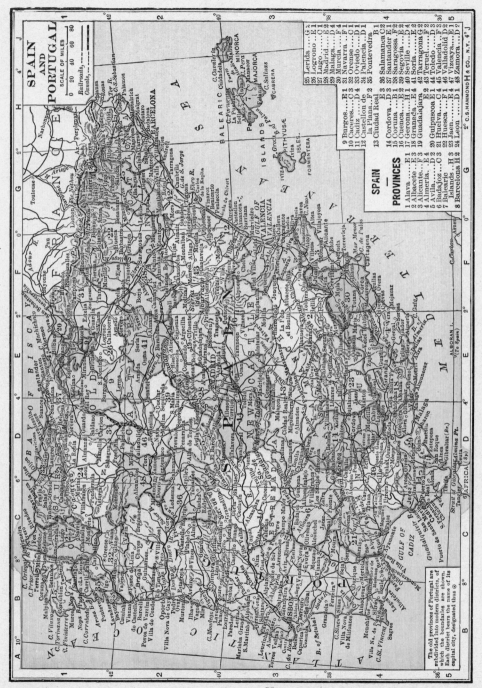

SPAIN AND PORTUGAL

SCALE OF MILES

Railroads,_____
Canals,_____

SPAIN
— —
PROVINCES

1 Alava......E3	9 Burgos......E1	25 Lerida....G2
2 Albacete...E3	10 Caceres....C3	26 Logrono...E1
3 Alicante...E4	11 Cadiz......C4	27 Lugo.......C1
4 Almeria....E4	12 Castellon de	28 Madrid....D2
5 Avila......D2	la Plana..F2	29 Malaga....D4
6 Badajoz....C3	13 Ciudad Real D3	30 Murcia....F4
7 Balearic	14 Cordova....D3	31 Navarra...F1
Islands..H3	15 Coruna.....B1	32 Orense....C1
8 Barcelona H2	16 Cuenca.....E2	33 Oviedo....D1
	17 Gerona.....H1	34 Palencia..D1
	18 Granada....D4	35 Pontevedra B1
	19 Guadalajara E2	36 Salamanca C2
	20 Guipuscoa E1	37 Santander E1
	21 Huelva.....C4	38 Saragossa F2
	22 Huesca.....F1	39 Segovia....D2
	23 Jaen.......D3	40 Seville....C3
	24 Leon.......D1	41 Soria......E2
		42 Tarragona G2
		43 Teruel.....F2
		44 Toledo....D3
		45 Valencia..F3
		46 Valladolid D2
		47 Vizcaya....E1
		48 Zamora....D2

The old provinces of Portugal are subdivided into modern districts, of which the boundaries are shown. Each district bears the name of its capital city, designated thus ⊙

Map of Africa, Pages 44-47; France, 18-19.

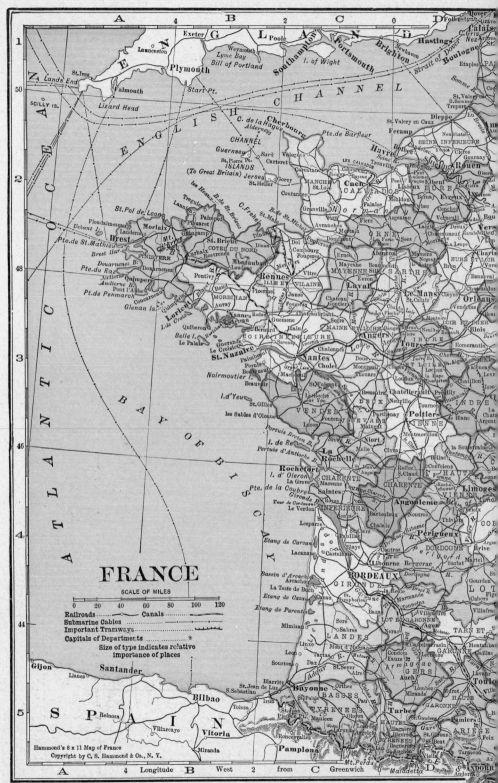

FRANCE

SCALE OF MILES

0 20 40 60 80 100 120

Railroads
Submarine Cables
Important Tramways
Capitals of Departments .... ⊙
Size of type indicates relative
importance of places

Canals

Hammond's 8 x 11 Map of France
Copyright by C. S. Hammond & Co., N. Y.

A   4   Longitude   B   West   2   from   C   Greenwich   D

Map of Belgium, Page 16; British Isles, 14-15; Germany, 20-21; Italy, 32-33; Spain, 17;

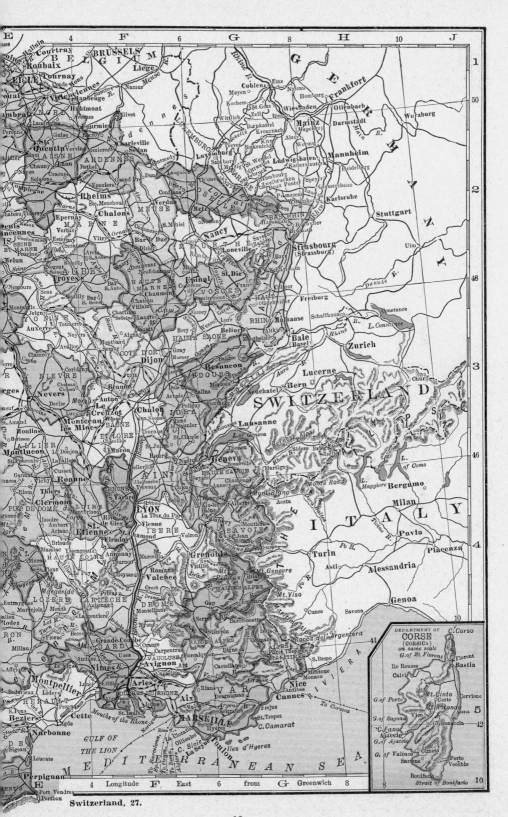

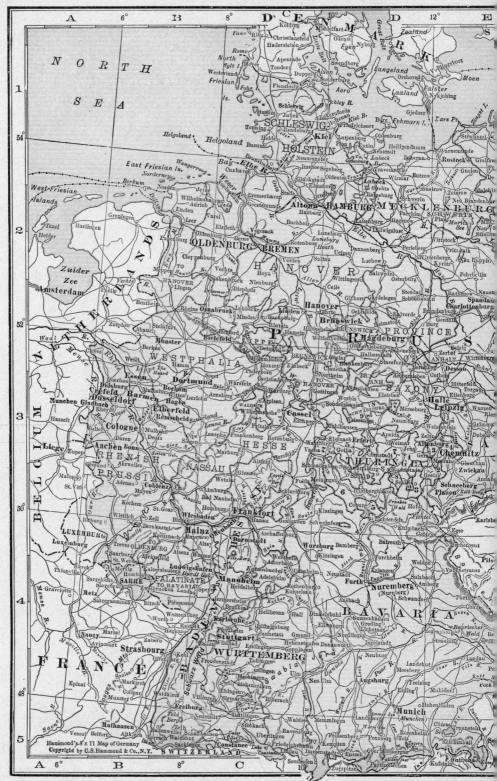

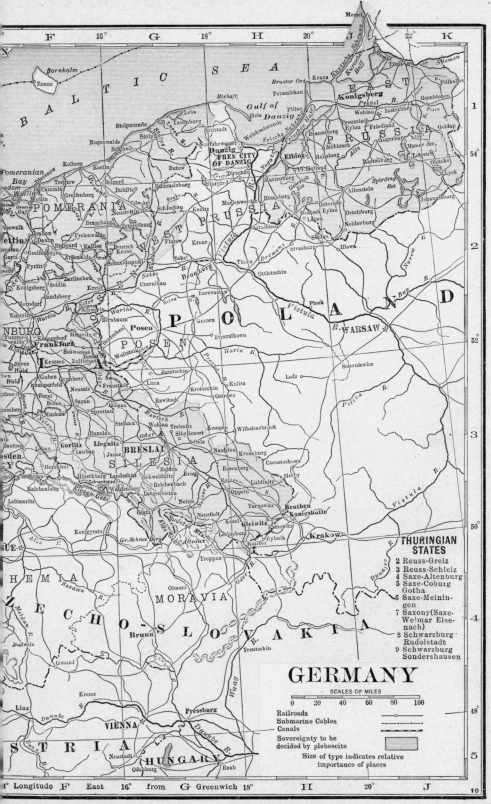

GERMANY

SCALES OF MILES

0 20 40 60 80 100

Railroads
Submarine Cables
Canals

Sovereignty to be decided by plebescite

Size of type indicates relative importance of places

THURINGIAN STATES

2 Reuss-Greiz
3 Reuss-Schleiz
4 Saxe-Altenburg
5 Saxe-Coburg Gotha
6 Saxe-Meiningen
7 Saxony(Saxe-Weimar Eisenach)
8 Schwarzburg Rudolstadt
9 Schwarzburg Sondershausen

rmania, 24; Luxemburg, 16;   Netherlands, 16;   Poland, 25; Switzerland, 27.

21

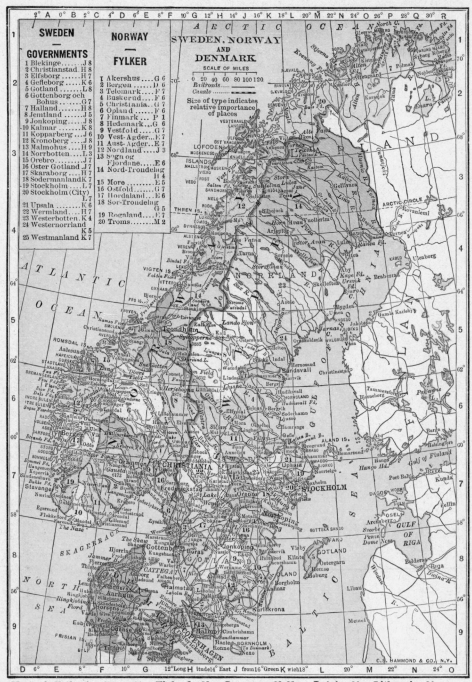

Map of Esthonia, Page 24; Finland, 23; Germany, 20-21; Latvia, 24; Lithuania, 24.

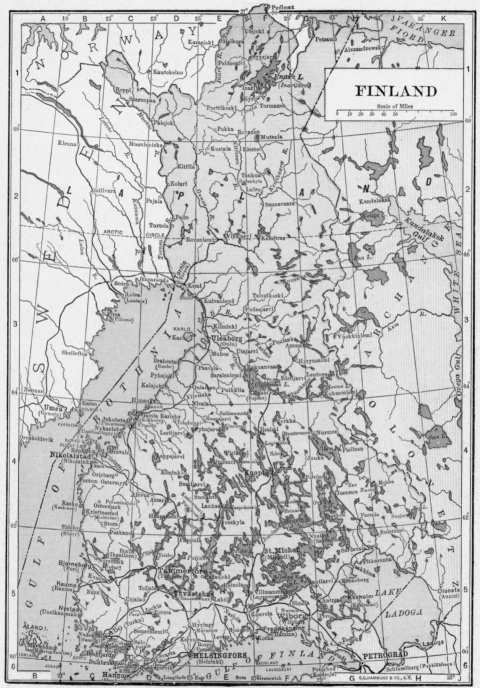

FINLAND

Scale of Miles
0 10 20 30 40 50   100

Map of Esthonia, Page 24;   Norway, 22; Russia, 26; Sweden, 22.

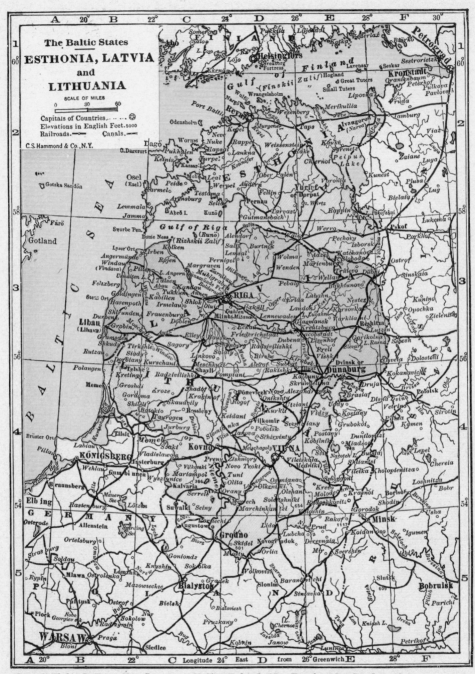

The Baltic States

ESTHONIA, LATVIA
and
LITHUANIA

SCALE OF MILES

0   30   60

Capitals of Countries......⊙
Elevations in English Feet.5000
Railroads.— Canals.—

C.S. Hammond & Co.,N.Y.

Map of Finland, Page 23; Germany, 20-21; Poland, 25; Russia, 26; Sweden, 22.

24

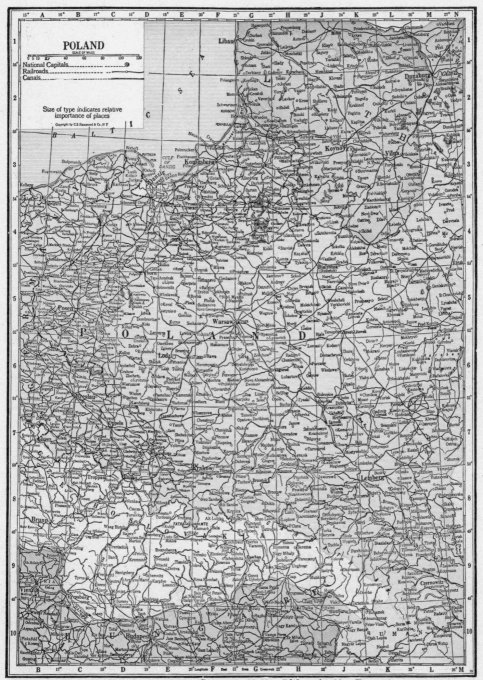

POLAND

SCALE OF MILES

National Capitals
Railroads
Canals

Size of type indicates relative importance of places

Copyright by C.S. Hammond & Co., N.Y

Map of Czecho-Slovakia, Pages, 28-29; Germany, 20-21; Lithuania, 24; Rumania, 35; Russia, 26.

25

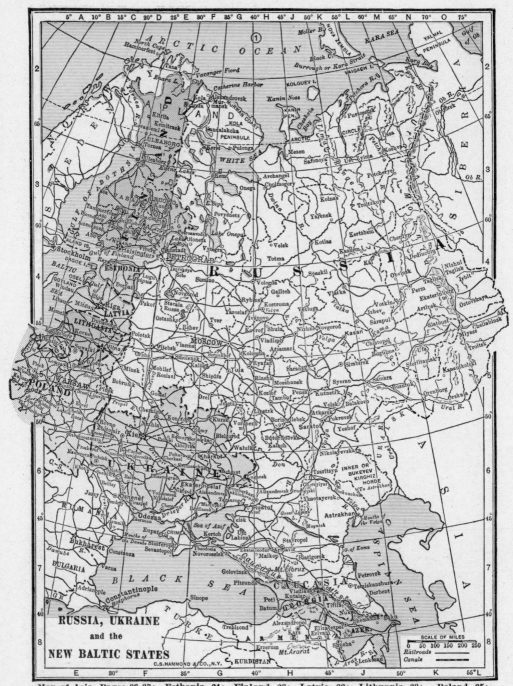

RUSSIA, UKRAINE
and the
NEW BALTIC STATES

C.S.HAMMOND & CO., N.Y.

SCALE OF MILES
0 50 100 150 200 250
Railroads
Canals

Map of Asia, Pages 36-37; Esthonia, 24; Finland, 23; Latvia, 23; Lithuania, 23; Poland, 25;
Rumania, 35.

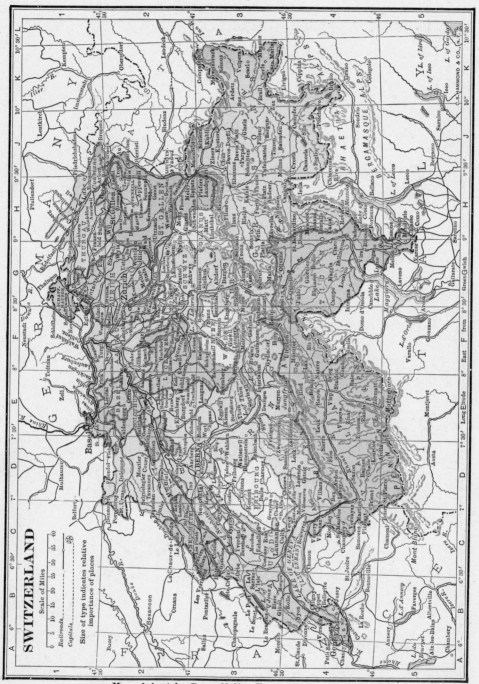

SWITZERLAND

Scale of Miles

0   5 10 15 20 25 30 35 40

Railroads..........

Capitals............ ⊛

Size of type indicates relative
importance of places

Map of Austria, Pages 30-31;   France, 18-19;   Germany, 20-21;   Italy, 32-33.

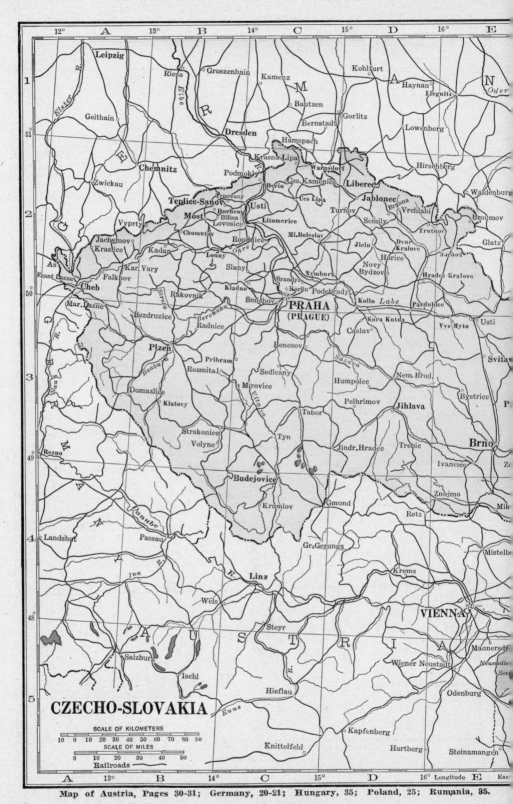

CZECHO-SLOVAKIA

SCALE OF KILOMETERS
10 0 10 20 30 40 50 60 70 80 90

SCALE OF MILES
0 10 20 30 40 50

Railroads

Map of Austria, Pages 30-31; Germany, 20-21; Hungary, 35; Poland, 25; Rumania, 35.

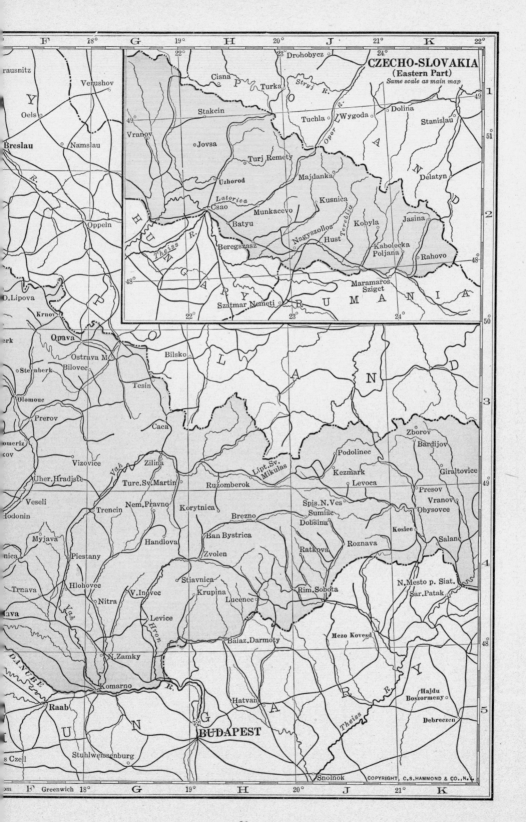

CZECHO-SLOVAKIA
(Eastern Part)
Same scale as main map

COPYRIGHT, C.S.HAMMOND & CO., N.Y.

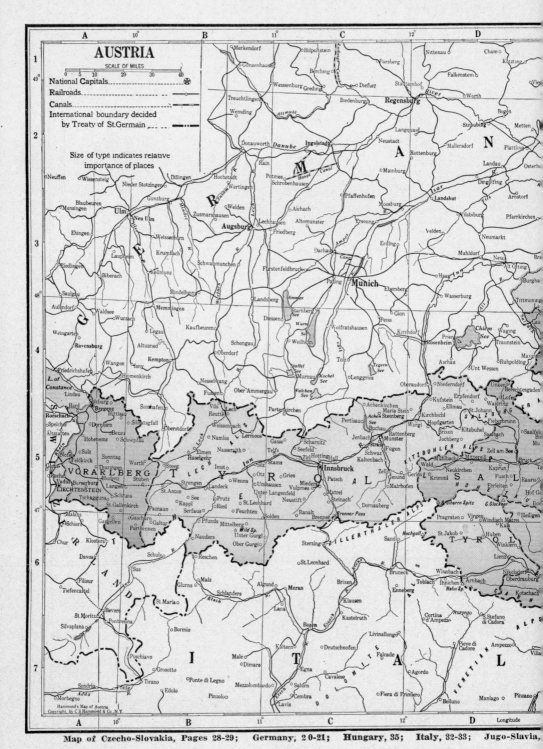

AUSTRIA

SCALE OF MILES

National Capitals............⊕
Railroads............
Canals............
International boundary decided
by Treaty of St.Germain............

Size of type indicates relative
importance of places

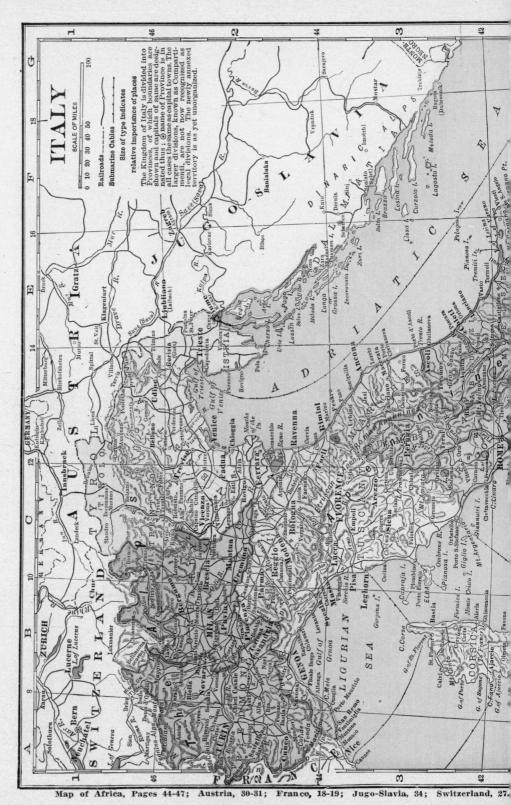

ITALY

SCALE OF MILES

0 10 20 30 40 50 ... 100

Railroads ....
Submarine Cables --------
Size of type indicates
relative importance of places

The Kingdom of Italy is divided into Provinces, of which boundaries are shown, and the capitals of same are designated thus; the name of Province is in all cases the same as capital towns. The larger divisions, known as Compartimenti, are not now recognized as legal divisions. The newly annexed territory is as yet unorganized.

Map of Africa, Pages 44-47;   Austria, 30-31;   France, 18-19;   Jugo-Slavia, 34;   Switzerland, 27.

32

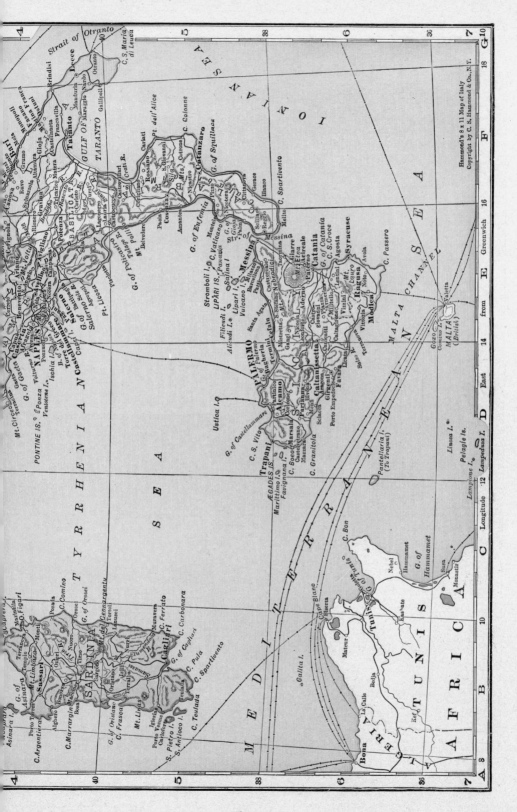

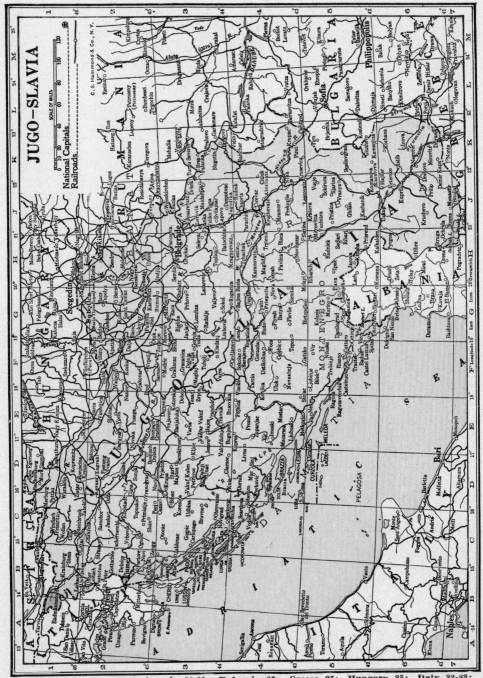

JUGO–SLAVIA

National Capitals...........
Railroads.......................

C. S. Hammond & Co., N. Y.

Map of Albania, Page 35; Austria, 30-31; Bulgaria, 35; Greece, 35; Hungary, 35; Italy, 32-33;
Rumania, 35.

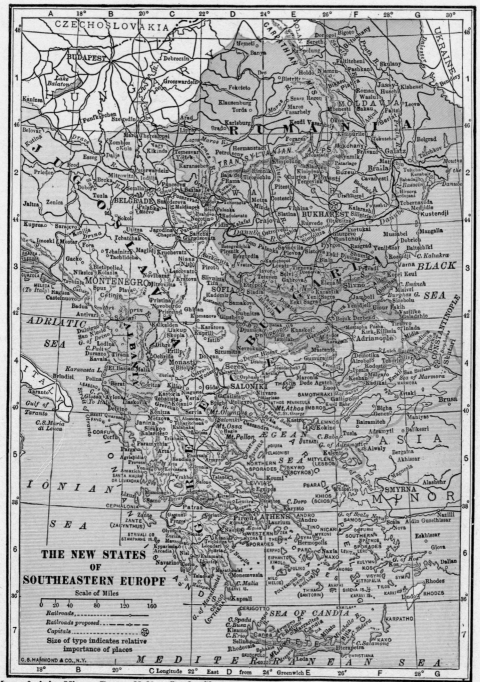

THE NEW STATES
OF
SOUTHEASTERN EUROPE

Scale of Miles

0 20 40   80   120   160

Railroads ....
Railroads proposed ....⬦⬦⬦
Capitals ....⊕
Size of type indicates relative
importance of places

C.S.HAMMOND & CO., N.Y.

Map of Asia Minor, Pages 38-39; Czecho-Slovakia, 28-29; Hungary, 25, 34; Italy, 32-33; Russia, 26.

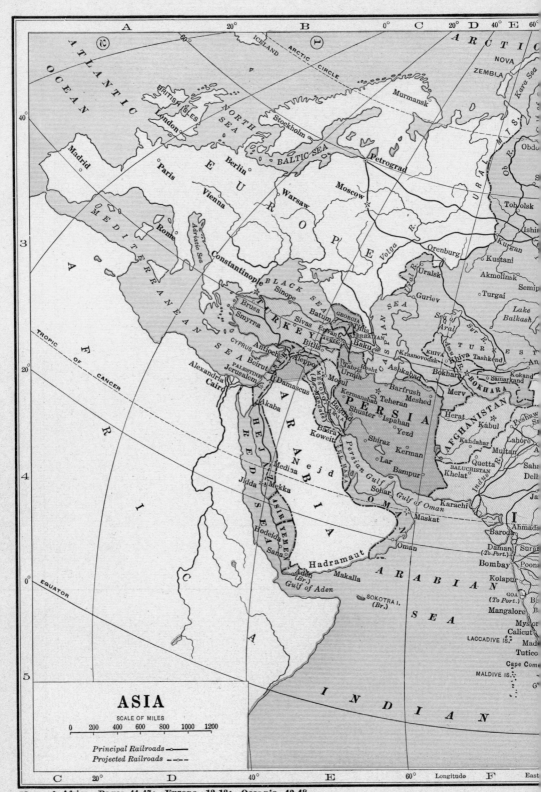

ASIA

SCALE OF MILES

0   200   400   600   800   1000   1200

Principal Railroads •——•
Projected Railroads •--•--•

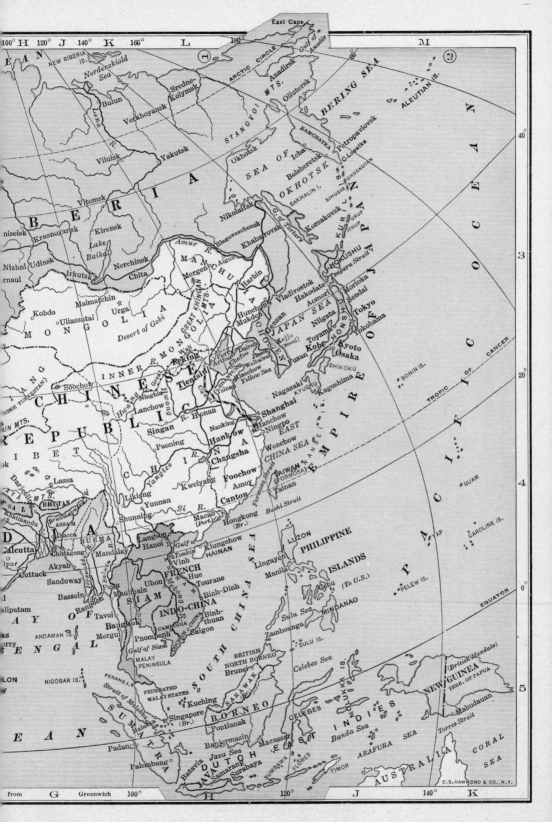

East Cape

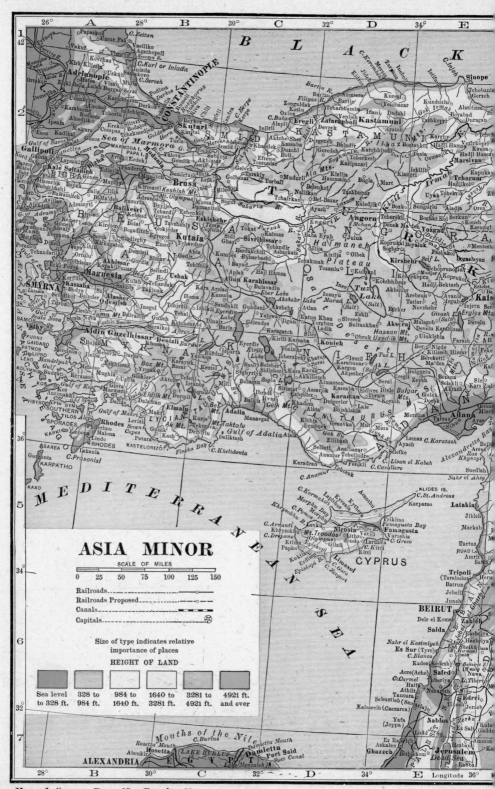

ASIA MINOR

SCALE OF MILES

0 25 50 75 100 125 150

Railroads
Railroads Proposed
Canals
Capitals

Size of type indicates relative
importance of places

HEIGHT OF LAND

| Sea level to 328 ft. | 328 to 984 ft. | 984 to 1640 ft. | 1640 to 3281 ft. | 3281 to 4921 ft. | 4921 ft. and over |

Map of Greece, Page 35; Russia, 26.

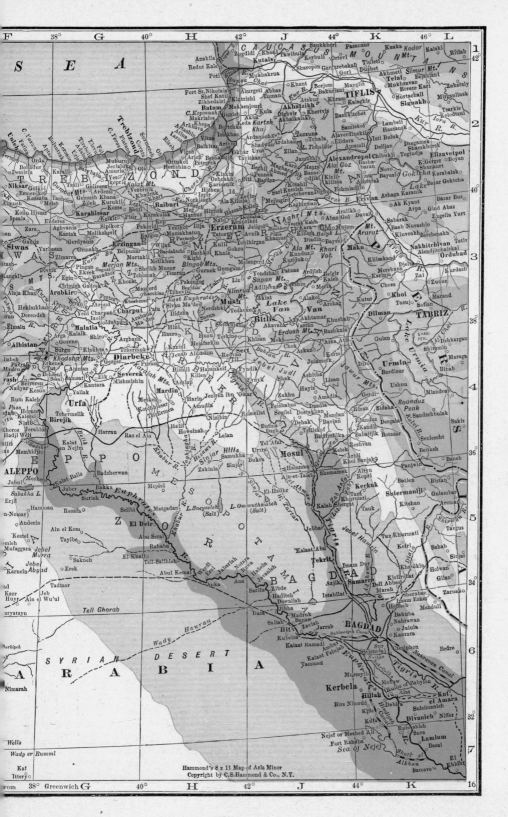

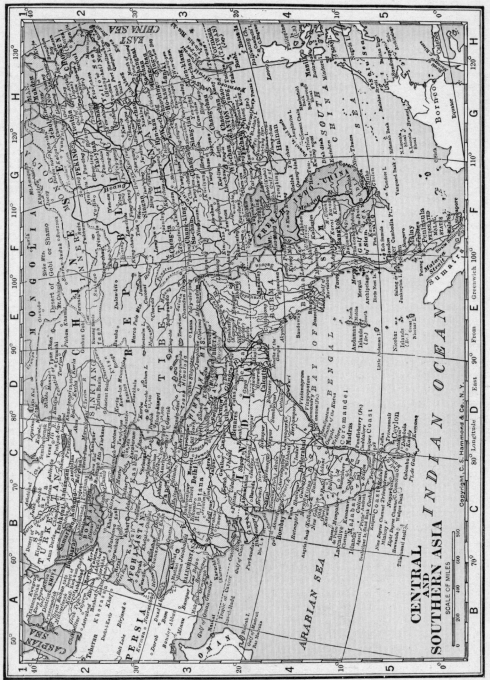

Map of Asia Minor, Pages 38-39; Borneo, 41; Philippine Islands, 42; Sumatra, 41.

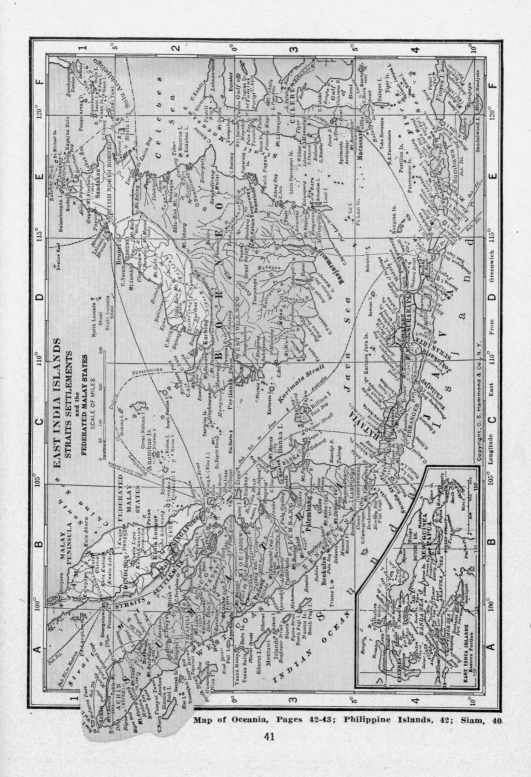

EAST INDIA ISLANDS
STRAITS SETTLEMENTS
and the
FEDERATED MALAY STATES

SCALE OF MILES

EAST INDIA ISLANDS
Eastern Portion

Copyright, C. S. Hammond & Co., N.Y.

Map of Oceania, Pages 42-43; Philippine Islands, 42; Siam, 40.

41

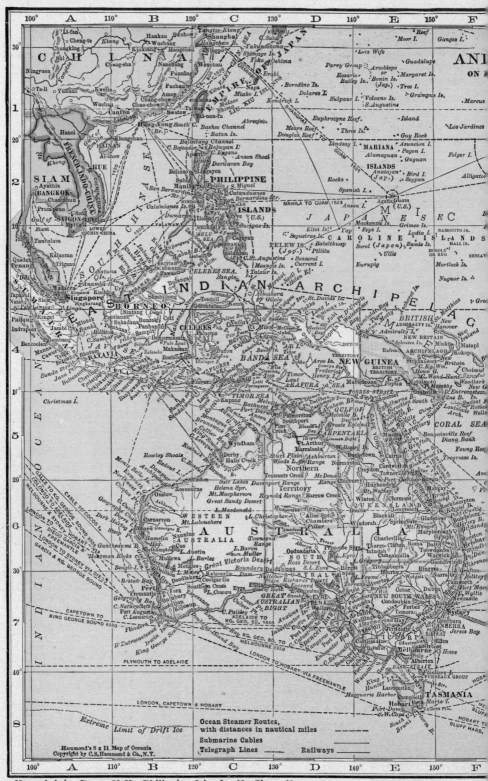

Map of Asia, Pages 36-37; Philippine Islands, 42; Siam, 40.

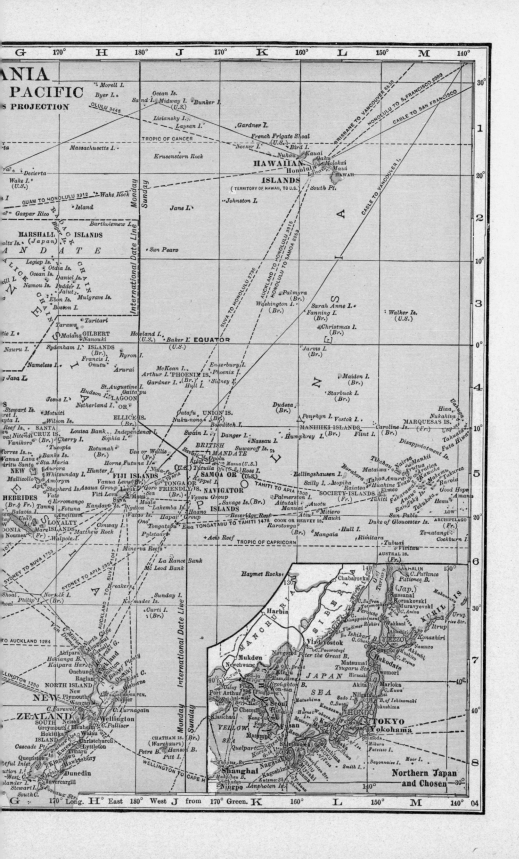

NORTHERN AFRICA

SCALE OF MILES

0   100   200   300   400   500   600

REFERENCE

British — French — Italian — Former German Colonies — Portuguese — Spanish — Belgian — Under British Control — Under French Control

Railroads — Canals

Size of type indicates relative importance of places

Hammond's 8 x 11 Map of Northern Africa

Copyright by C.S Hammond & Co., N.Y.

Map of Africa, Central and Southern, Pages 46-47; Asia, 36-37; Asia Minor, 38-39; Europe, 12-13.

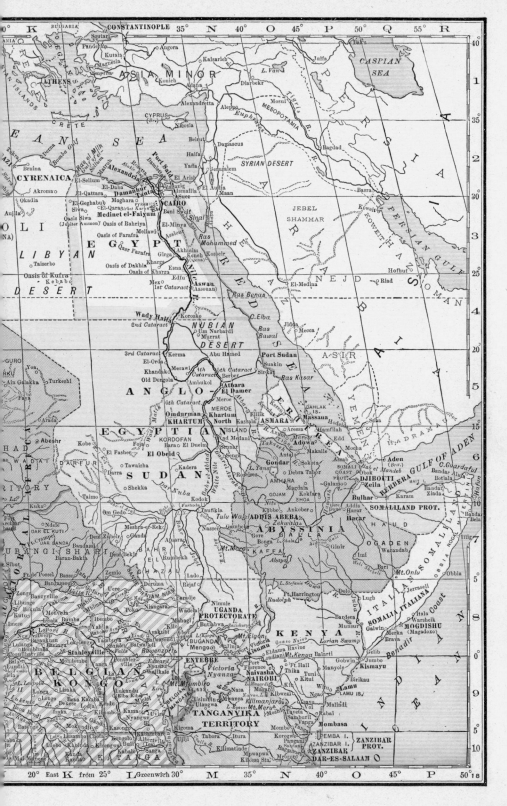

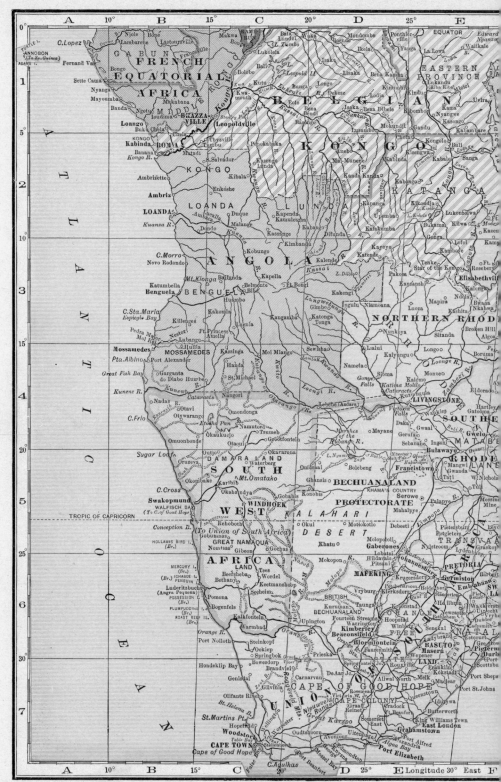

Map of Africa, Northern, Pages 44-45.

46

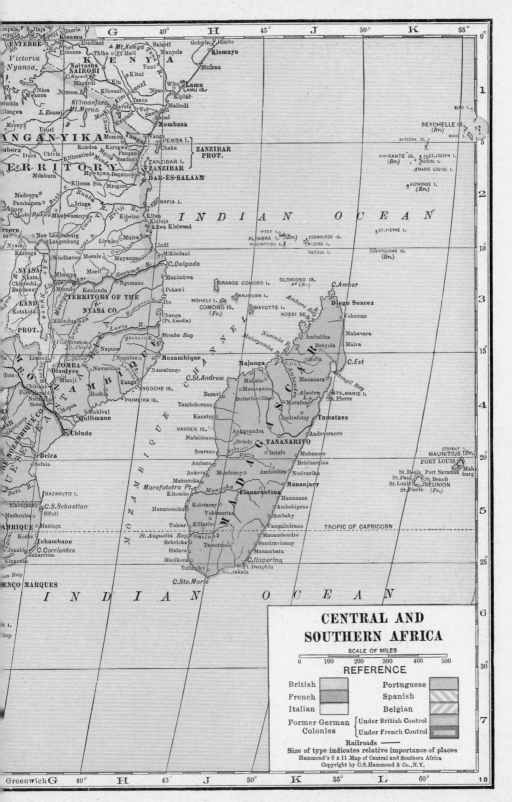

CENTRAL AND SOUTHERN AFRICA

SCALE OF MILES

0   100   200   300   400   500

REFERENCE

British		Portuguese	
French		Spanish	
Italian		Belgian	
Former German Colonies		Under British Control	
		Under French Control	

Railroads ———

Size of type indicates relative importance of places

Hammond's 8 x 11 Map of Central and Southern Africa

Copyright by C.S.Hammond & Co., N.Y.

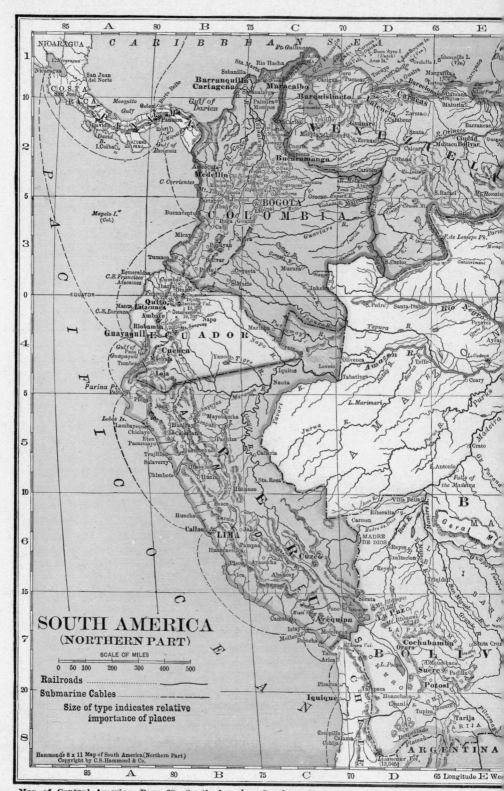

SOUTH AMERICA
(NORTHERN PART)

SCALE OF MILES

0 50 100   200   300   400   500

Railroads ....

Submarine Cables ....

**Size of type indicates relative
importance of places**

Hammond's 8 x 11 Map of South America (Northern Part)
Copyright by C.S. Hammond & Co.

Map of Central America, Page 68; South America, Southern Part, 50-51; West Indies, 69.

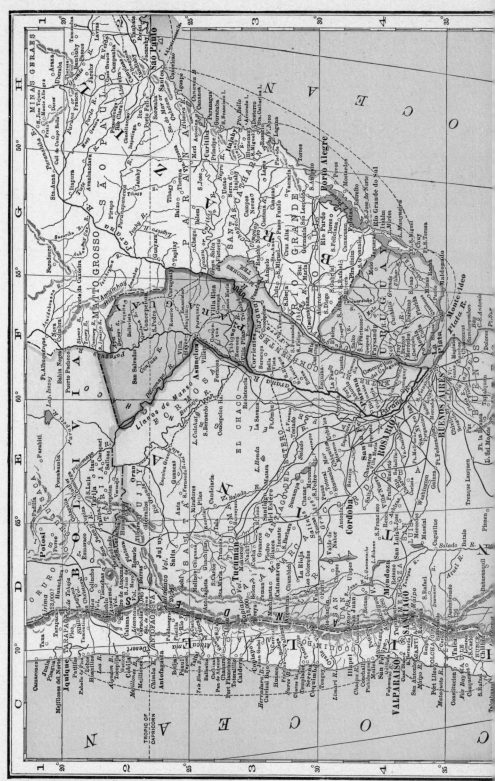

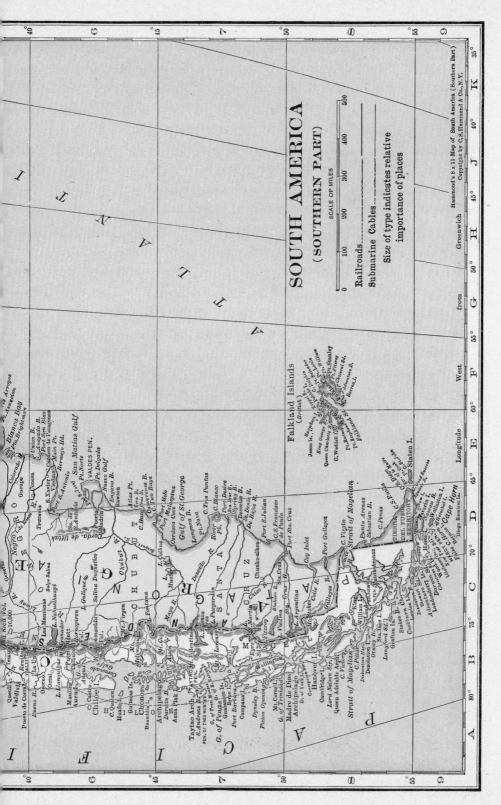

SOUTH AMERICA
(SOUTHERN PART)

SCALE OF MILES

0   100   200   300   400   500

Railroads ....
Submarine Cables ....

Size of type indicates relative
importance of places

Greenwich   from   West   Longitude

Hammond's 8 x 11 Map of South America (Southern Part)
Copyright by C. S. Hammond & Co., N.Y.

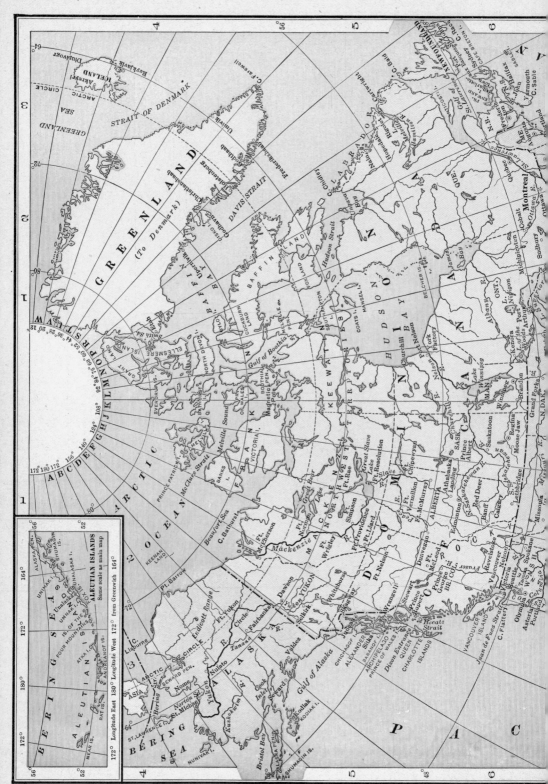

Map of Asia, Pages 36-37; South America, 44-49.

NORTH AMERICA

WINDWARD ISLANDS
Same scale as main map

SCALE OF MILES
0 100 200 300 400 500 600 700 800

C.S. HAMMOND & CO., N.Y.

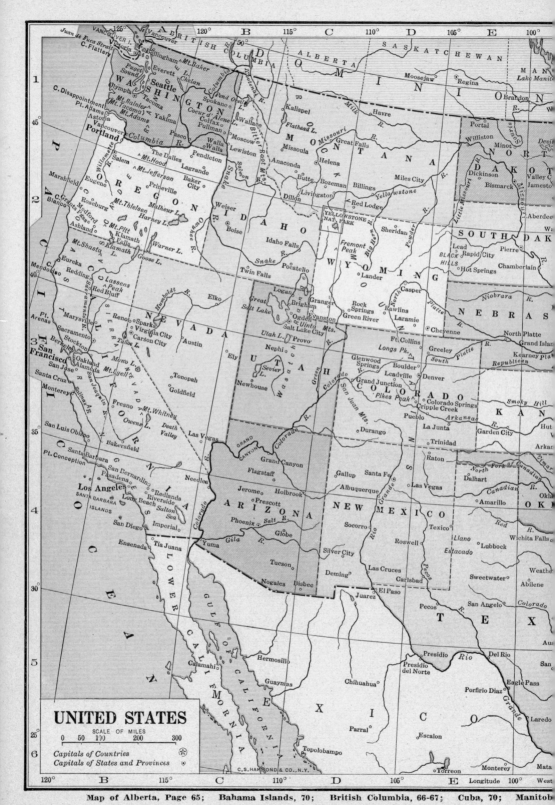

UNITED STATES

SCALE OF MILES

0   50 100   200   300

⊛ Capitals of Countries
⊙ Capitals of States and Provinces

C.S. HAMMOND & CO., N.Y.

Map of Alberta, Page 65;   Bahama Islands, 70;   British Columbia, 66-67;   Cuba, 70;   Manitob

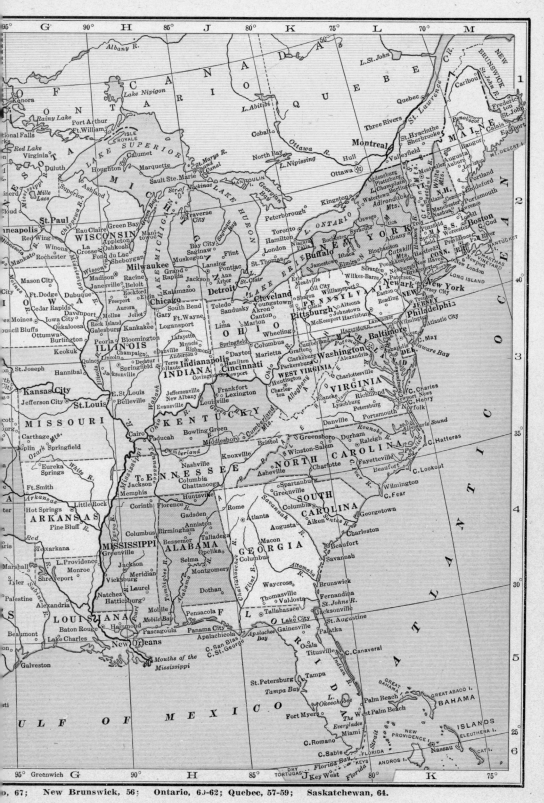

, 67;   New Brunswick, 56;   Ontario, 60-62; Quebec, 57-59;   Saskatchewan, 64.

55

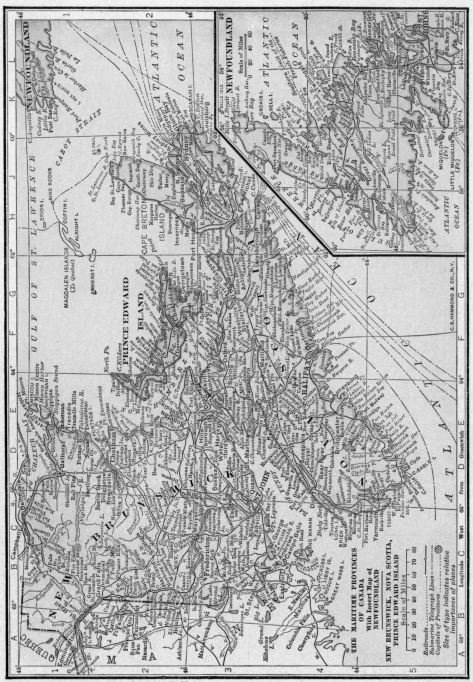

THE MARITIME PROVINCES
OF CANADA
With Insert Map of
NEWFOUNDLAND

NEW BRUNSWICK, NOVA SCOTIA,
PRINCE EDWARD ISLAND

Scale of Miles
0 10 20 30 40 50 60 70 80

Railroads _____
Submarine Telegraph Lines - - - - - -
Capitals of Provinces _____
Size of type indicates relative
importance of places

C. S. HAMMOND & CO., N.Y.

Map of Maine, Page 89;   Quebec, 57-59.

56

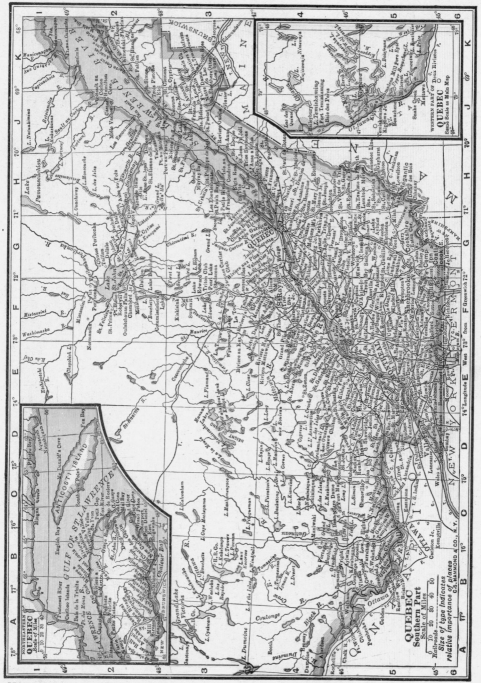

Map of Maine, Page 89; New Brunswick, 56; Ontario, 60-62; Vermont, 115. Newfoundland, 56;
New Hampshire, 99; New York, 102;

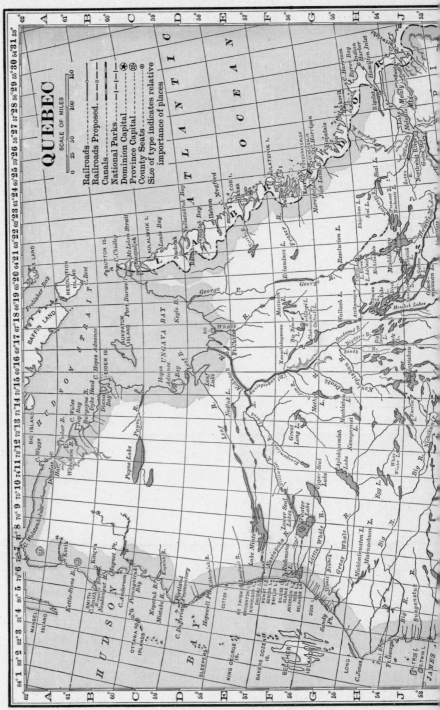

QUEBEC

SCALE OF MILES

Railroads
Railroads Proposed
Canals
National Parks
Dominion Capital
Province Capital
County Seats
Size of type indicates relative
importance of places

Map of Maine, Page 89; New Brunswick, 56; Newfoundland, 56; New Hampshire, 99;

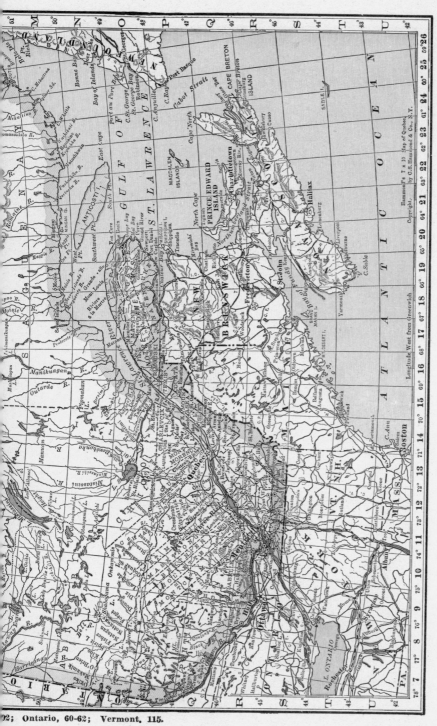

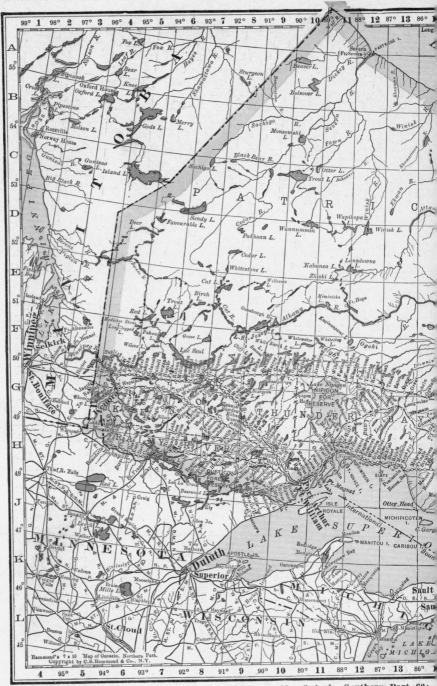

Map of Manitoba, Page 63; Michigan, 92; Minnesota, 93; Ontario, Southern Part, 62;

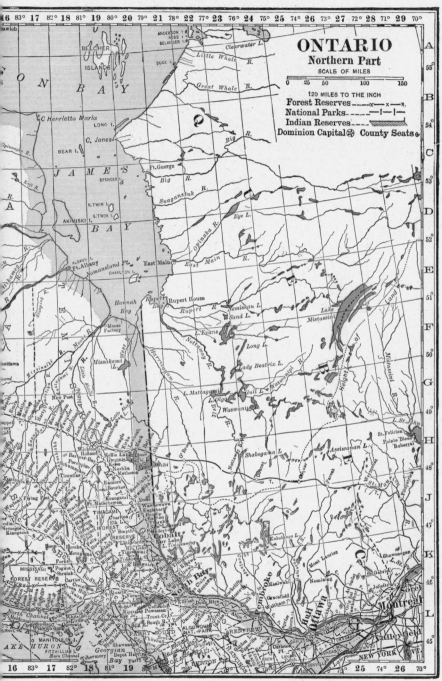

ONTARIO
Northern Part
SCALE OF MILES

0   25   50   100   150

120 MILES TO THE INCH

Forest Reserves ----x--x--x,
National Parks ----!--!--
Indian Reserves ----------
Dominion Capital ⊛   County Seats ⊙

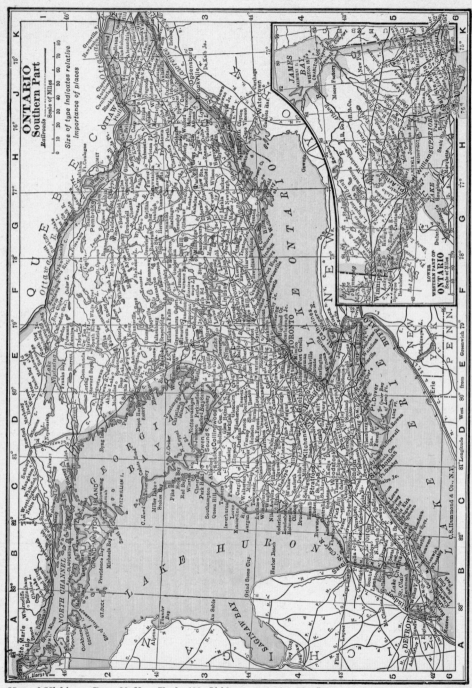

ONTARIO
Southern Part

Railroads

Scale of Miles
0 10 20 30 40 50 60 70 80

Size of type indicates relative
importance of places

LOWER
WESTERN PART OF
ONTARIO
Scale of Miles

Map of Michigan, Page 92; New York, 102; Ohio, 105; Ontario, Northern Part, 60-61; Quebec, 57-59.

62

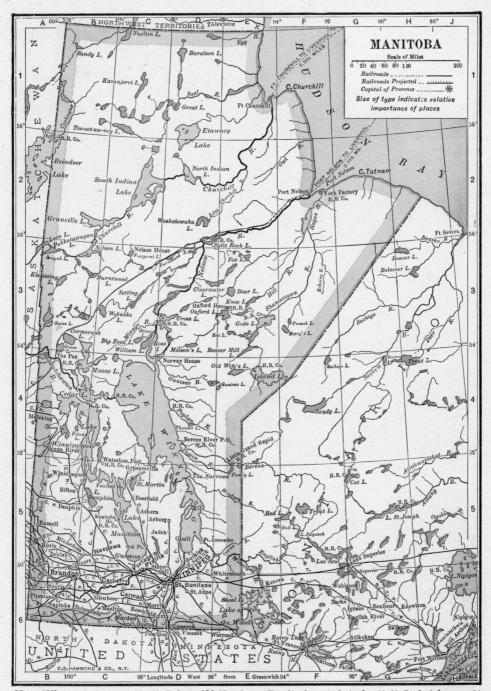

MANITOBA

Scale of Miles

0 20 40 60 80 100   200

Railroads
Railroads Projected
Capital of Province

*Size of type indicates relative
importance of places*

Map of Minnesota, Page 93; North Dakota, 104; Northwest Territories, 52; Ontario, 60-62; Saskatchewan, 64.

63

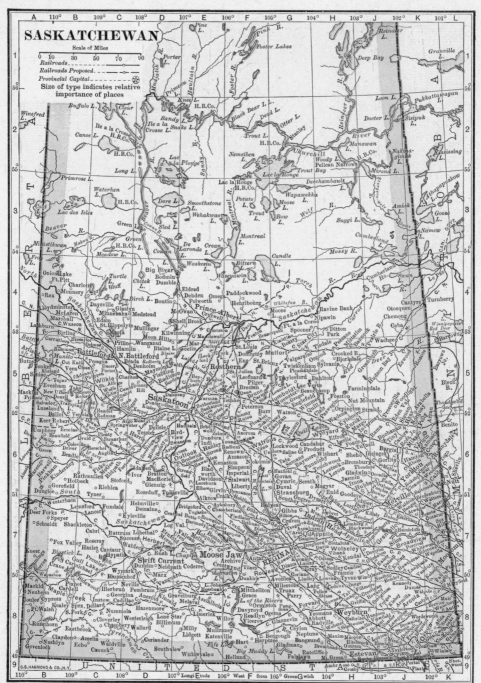

SASKATCHEWAN

Scale of Miles

0 10 30 50 70 90

Railroads .... ----------
Railroads Proposed ----------
Provincial Capital .... ⊛
Size of type indicates relative
importance of places

Map of Alberta, Page 65; Manitoba, 63; Montana, 96; North Dakota, 104; Northwest Territories, 52.

64

ALBERTA

Scale of Miles

0 10   30   50   70   90

Railroads _____
Railroads Proposed _____
Provincial Capital ⊛

Size of type indicates relative
importance of places

C.S. HAMMOND & CO., N.Y.

Map of British Columbia, Pages 66 Montana, 96; Northwest Territories, 52; Saskatchewan, 64.

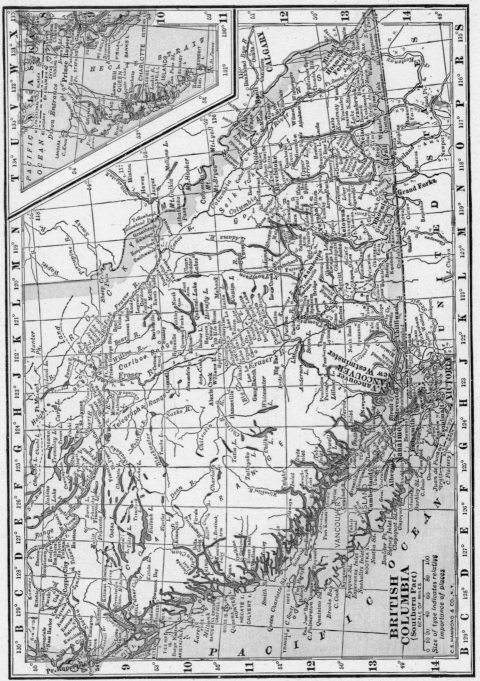

Map of Alberta, Page 65; Idaho, 82; Montana, 96; Northwest Territories, 52; Washington, 117; Yukon, 52.

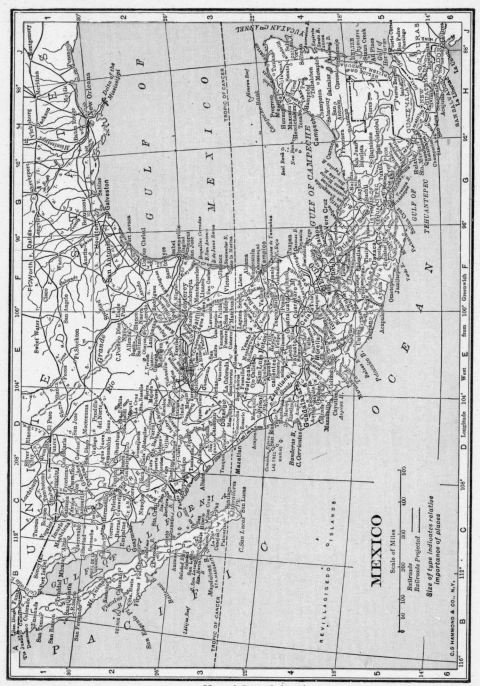

MEXICO

Scale of Miles

Railroads
Railroads Projected

Size of type indicates relative importance of places

C.S HAMMOND & CO., N.Y.

Map of Central America, Page 68; United States, 54-55.

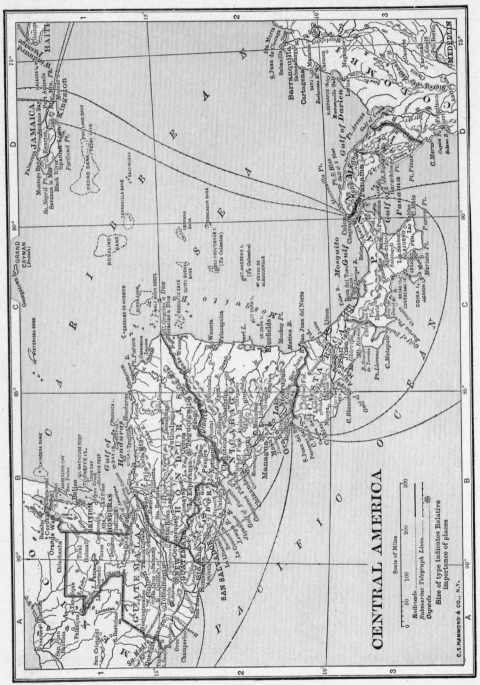

CENTRAL AMERICA

Scale of Miles

Railroads ....
Submarine Telegraph Lines ....
Cables ....

Size of type indicates Relative
importance of places

C.S.HAMMOND & CO., N.Y.

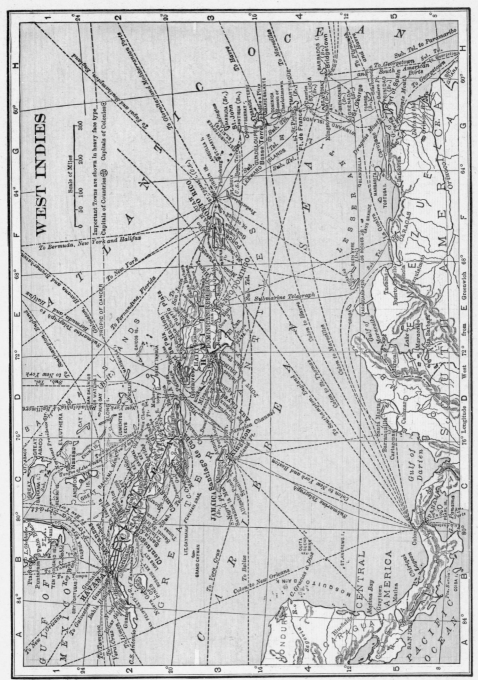

WEST INDIES

Scale of Miles

Important Towns are shown in heavy face type.
Capitals of Countries ⊛
Capitals of Colonies ⊙

Map of Central America, Page 68; United States, 54-55; South America, Northern Part, 48-49.

69

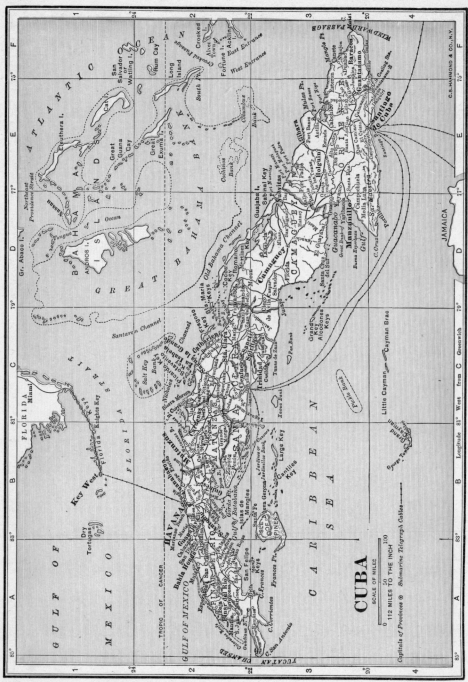

CUBA

Map of Central America, Page 68; Florida, 80; Jamaica, 68; Mexico, 67.

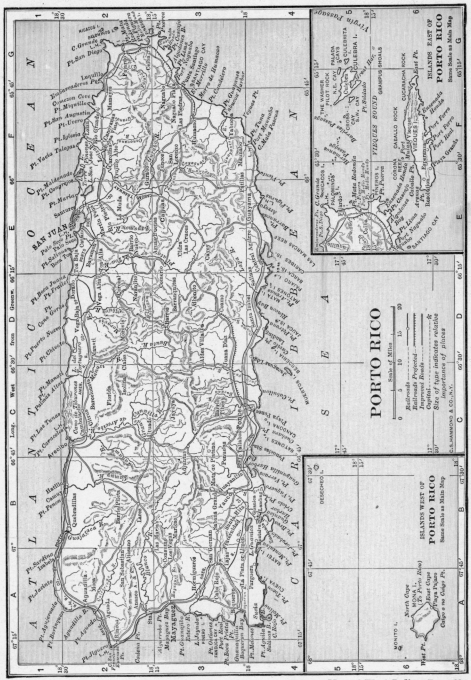

PORTO RICO

Scale of Miles

0 — 5 — 10 — 15 — 20

Railroads
Railroads Projected
Improved Roads
Capital
Size of type indicates relative importance of places

C.S. HAMMOND & CO., N.Y.

ISLANDS EAST OF PORTO RICO
Same Scale as Main Map

ISLANDS WEST OF PORTO RICO
Same Scale as Main Map

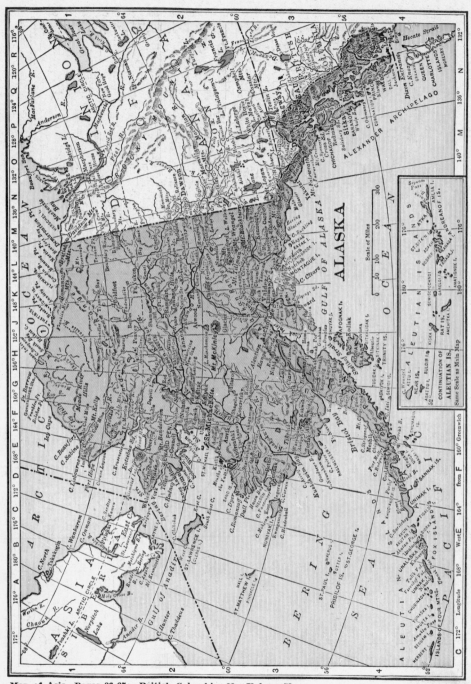

ALASKA

Map of Asia, Pages 36-37; British Columbia, 66; Yukon, 52.

THE UNITED STATES

STATE	AREA Sq. Mi.	POPULATION 1910	POPULATION 1920	Pr. Ct. Inc. 1910–1920	CAPITAL	POPU-LATION 1920	CHIEF CITY OTHER THAN CAPITAL	POPU-LATION 1920
Alabama	51,998	2,138,093	2,347,295	9.8	Montgomery	43,464	Birmingham	178,270
Arizona	113,956	204,354	333,273	63.1	Phoenix	29,053	Tucson	20,292
Arkansas	53,335	1,574,449	1,750,995	11.2	Little Rock	64,997	Fort Smith	28,811
California	158,297	2,377,549	3,426,536	44.1	Sacramento	65,857	San Francisco	506,676
Colorado	103,948	799,024	939,736	17.6	Denver	256,369	Pueblo	42,908
Connecticut	4,965	1,114,756	1,380,585	23.8	Hartford	138,036	New Haven	162,519
Delaware	2,370	202,322	223,003	10.2	Dover	4,042	Wilmington	110,168
District of Columbia	70	331,069	437,571	32.2				
Florida	58,666	752,619	966,296	28.4	Tallahassee	5,637	Jacksonville	91,543
Georgia	59,265	2,609,121	2,894,683	10.9	Atlanta	200,616	Savannah	83,252
Idaho	83,888	325,594	431,826	32.6	Boise	21,393	Pocatello	14,961
Illinois	56,665	5,638,591	6,485,098	15.0	Springfield	59,183	Chicago	2,701,212
Indiana	36,354	2,700,876	2,930,544	8.5	Indianapolis	314,194	Fort Wayne	86,549
Iowa	56,147	2,224,771	2,403,630	8.0	Des Moines	126,468	Sioux City	71,227
Kansas	82,158	1,690,949	1,769,257	4.6	Topeka	50,022	Kansas City	101,078
Kentucky	40,598	2,289,905	2,416,013	5.5	Frankfort	9,805	Louisville	234,891
Louisiana	48,505	1,656,388	1,797,798	8.5	Baton Rouge	21,782	New Orleans	387,219
Maine	33,040	742,371	768,014	3.5	Augusta	52,548	Portland	69,196
Maryland	12,327	1,295,346	1,449,610	11.9	Annapolis	11,214	Baltimore	733,826
Massachusetts	8,266	3,366,416	3,852,356	14.4	Boston	747,923	Worcester	179,741
Michigan	57,980	2,810,173	3,667,222	30.5	Lansing	57,327	Detroit	993,739
Minnesota	84,682	2,075,708	2,386,371	15.0	St. Paul	234,595	Minneapolis	380,498
Mississippi	46,865	1,797,114	1,789,384	– 0.4	Jackson	22,817	Meridian	23,399
Missouri	69,420	3,293,335	3,403,547	3.3	Jefferson City	14,067	St. Louis	772,897
Montana	146,997	376,053	547,593	45.6	Helena	12,037	Butte	41,611
Nebraska	77,520	1,192,214	1,295,502	8.7	Lincoln	54,934	Omaha	191,601
Nevada	110,690	81,875	77,407	– 5.5	Carson City	†2,750	Reno	12,016
New Hampshire	9,341	430,572	443,083	2.9	Concord	22,167	Manchester	78,200
New Jersey	8,224	2,537,167	3,155,374	24.4	Trenton	119,269	Newark	414,216
New Mexico	122,634	327,301	360,247	10.1	Santa Fe	7,236	Albuquerque	15,157
New York	49,204	9,113,614	10,384,144	13.9	Albany	113,344	New York	5,621,151
North Carolina	52,426	2,205,287	2,556,486	15.9	Raleigh	28,674	Winston-Salem	48,395
North Dakota	70,837	577,056	645,730	11.9	Bismarck	6,951	Fargo	21,961
Ohio	41,040	4,767,121	5,759,368	20.8	Columbus	237,031	Cleveland	796,†36
Oklahoma	70,057	1,657,155	2,027,564	22.4	Oklahoma	91,258	Tulsa	72,075
Oregon	96,669	672,765	783,389	16.4	Salem	17,679	Portland	258,288
Pennsylvania	45,126	7,665,111	8,720,159	13.8	Harrisburg	75,917	Philadelphia	1,823,158
Rhode Island	1,248	542,610	604,397	11.4	Providence	237,595	Pawtucket	64,248
South Carolina	30,989	1,515,400	1,683,662	11.1	Columbia	37,524	Charleston	67,957
South Dakota	77,615	583,888	635,839	8.9	Pierre	†3,600	Sioux Falls	25,176
Tennessee	42,022	2,184,789	2,337,459	7.0	Nashville	118,342	Memphis	162,351
Texas	265,896	3,896,542	4,661,027	19.6	Austin	34,876	San Antonio	161,379
Utah	84,990	373,351	419,446	20.4	Salt Lake City	118,110	Ogden	32,804
Vermont	9,564	355,956	352,421	– 1.0	Montpelier	7,125	Burlington	22,779
Virginia	42,627	2,061,612	2,306,361	11.9	Richmond	171,667	Norfolk	115,777
Washington	69,127	1,141,990	1,356,316	18.8	Olympia	8,537	Seattle	315,652
West Virginia	24,170	1,221,119	1,463,610	19.8	Charleston	39,608	Wheeling	56,208
Wisconsin	56,066	2,333,860	2,631,839	12.8	Madison	38,378	Milwaukee	457,147
Wyoming	97,914	145,965	194,402	33.2	Cheyenne	13,829	Casper	11,447
Continental U. S.	3,026,789	91,972,266	105,683,108	14.9	Washington	437,414		
Alaska	590,884	64,356	†64,356		Juneau	3,058	Ketchikan	2,458
Guam	225	12,240	13,275		Agaña	7,432		
Hawaii	6,449	191,909	255,912		Honolulu	83,327	Hilo	10,431
Panama Canal Zone	442	61,279						
Philippine Islands	114,400	8,265,348	†8,000,000		Manila	†236,940	Iloilo	†19,054
Porto Rico	3,435	1,118,012	†1,118 012		San Juan	†48,716	Ponce	†35,005
Samoa	102	7,251	†7,750		Pagopago			
St. Croix, St. John and St. Thomas Islands	138		†26,051		St. Thomas			
Persons in military and naval service stationed abroad		55,608						
Outlying possessions	716,075							
United States	3,742,864		117,933,108					

† Recent estimate. A minus sign (—) denotes decrease.

73

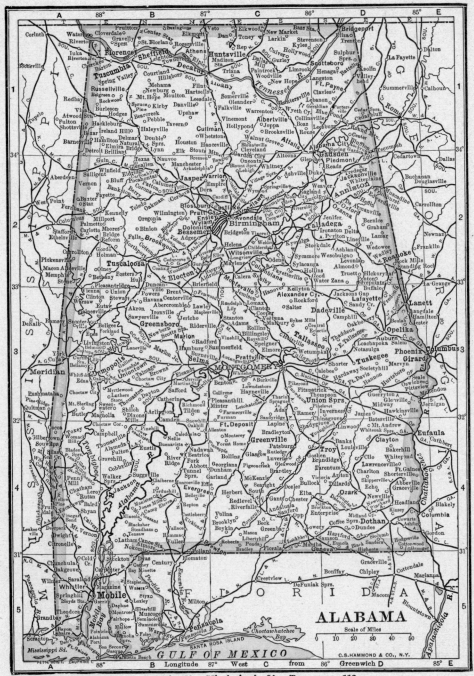

ALABAMA

Scale of Miles

C.S. HAMMOND & CO., N.Y.

Map of Florida, Page 80; Georgia, 81; Mississippi, 94; Tennessee, 112.

ARIZONA

Scale of Miles

Map of California, Page 77; Colorado, 78; Mexico, 67; Nevada, 98; New Mexico, 101; Utah, 114.

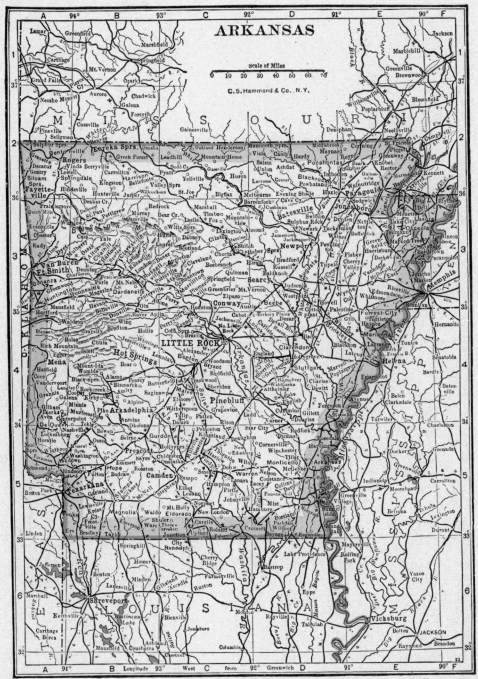

ARKANSAS

Scale of Miles

0 10 20 30 40 50 60 70

C. S. Hammond & Co., N.Y.

Map of Louisiana, Page 88; Mississippi, 94; Missouri, 95; Oklahoma, 106; Tennessee, 112. Texas, 113.

CALIFORNIA

Scale of Miles

0 10 20   40   60   80   100 120 140

Size of type indicates relative importance of places.

PART OF SOUTHEASTERN CALIFORNIA

Same Scale as Main Map

C.S. HAMMOND & CO., N.Y.   Longitude   West   from   Greenwich

Map of Arizona, Page 75;   Mexico, 67;   Nevada, 98;   Oregon, 107.

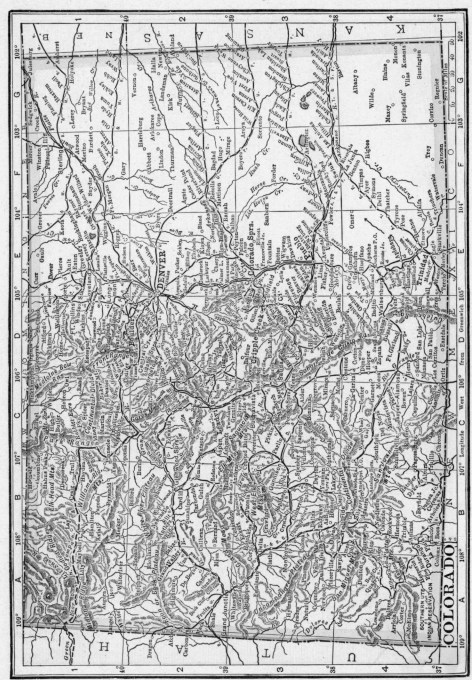

Map of Kansas, Page 86; Nebraska, 97; New Mexico, 101; Oklahoma, 106; Utah, 114; Wyoming, 120.

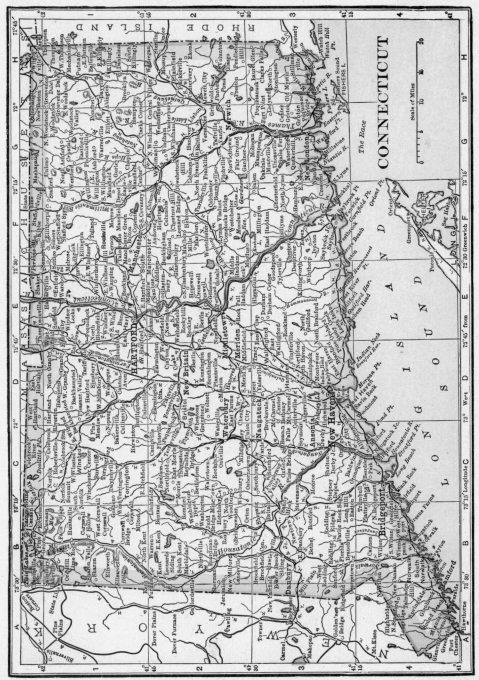

CONNECTICUT

Scale of Miles

Map of Massachusetts, Page 91; New York, 102; Rhode Island, 109.

FLORIDA

Scale of Miles

0 10 20 30 40 50 60

Size of type indicates
relative importance
of places

NORTHWESTERN PART OF
FLORIDA
Same scale as large map

C.S.HAMMOND & CO., N.Y.

Map of Alabama, Page 74; Georgia, 81.

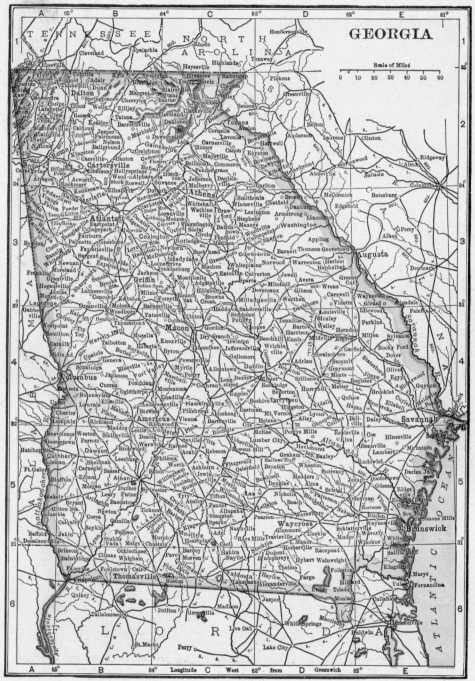

GEORGIA

Scale of Miles

0   10   20   30   40   50   60

Map of Alabama, Page 74; Florida, 80; North Carolina, 103; South Carolina, 110; Tennessee, 112.

81

IDAHO

Scale of Miles

Size of type indicates relative importance of places.

Map of British Columbia, Page 66; Montana, 96; Nevada, 98; Oregon, 107; Utah, 114; Washington, 117; Wyoming, 120.

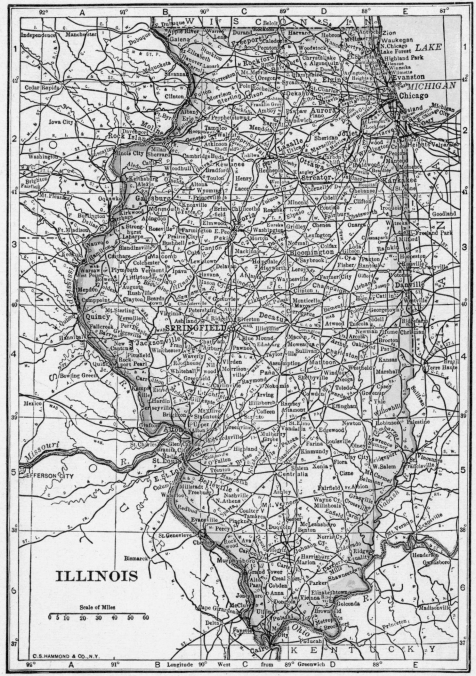

ILLINOIS

Map of Indiana, Page 84; Iowa, 85; Kentucky, 87; Missouri, 95; Wisconsin, 119.

83

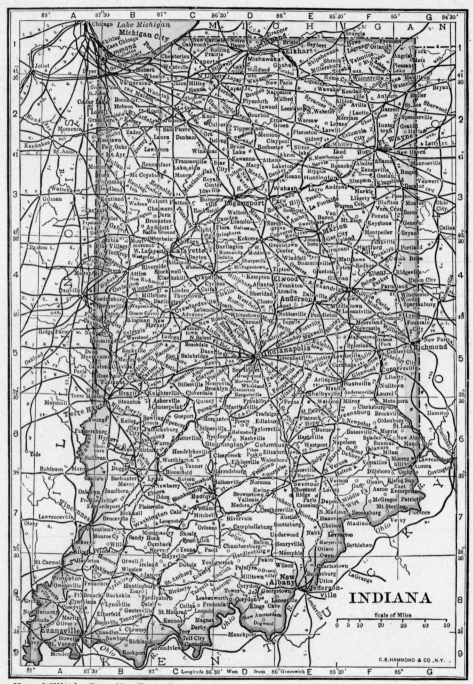

INDIANA

Scale of Miles

Map of Illinois, Page 83; Kentucky, 87; Michigan, 92; Ohio, 105.

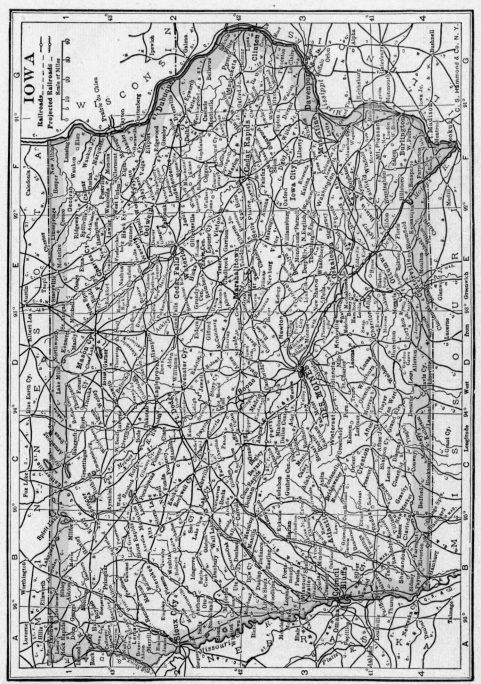

Map of Illinois, Page 83; Minnesota, 93; Missouri, 95; Nebraska, 97; South Dakota, 111; Wisconsin, 119.

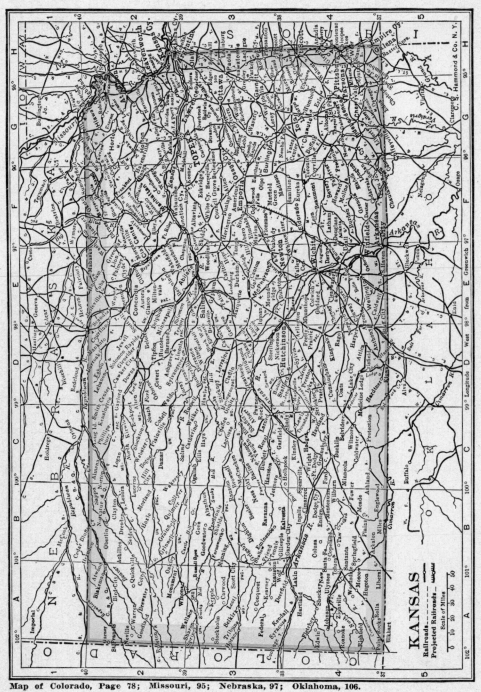

KANSAS

Railroads.————
Projected Railroads.————
Scale of Miles
0 10 20 30 40 50

Map of Colorado, Page 78; Missouri, 95; Nebraska, 97; Oklahoma, 106.

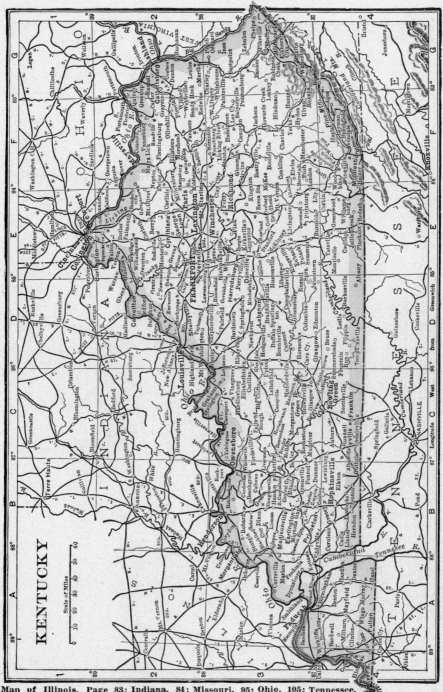

KENTUCKY

Scale of Miles

Map of Illinois, Page 83; Indiana, 84; Missouri, 95; Ohio, 105; Tennessee, 112; Virginia, 116; West Virginia, 118.

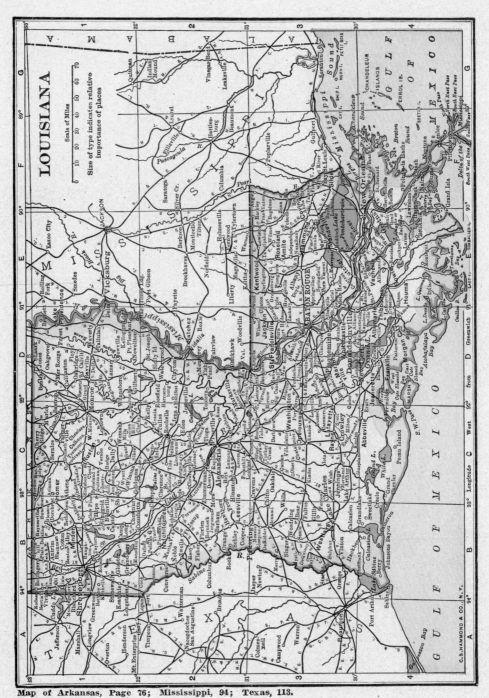

LOUISIANA

Scale of Miles

Size of type indicates relative importance of places

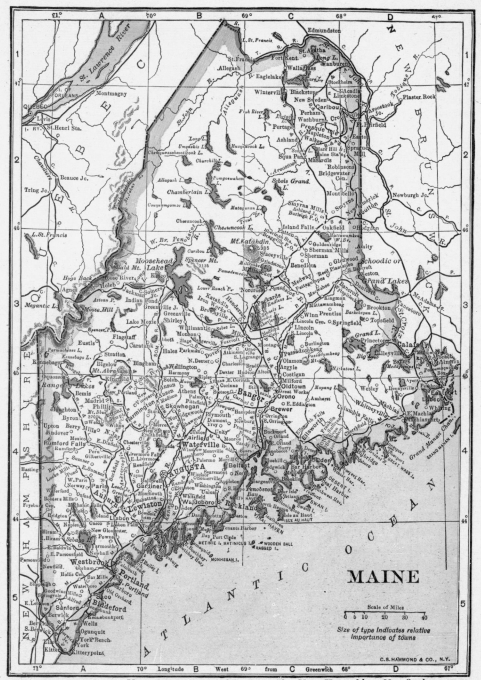

MAINE

Scale of Miles

Size of type indicates relative
importance of towns

C. S. HAMMOND & CO., N.Y.

Map of New Brunswick, Page 56; New Hampshire, 99; Quebec, 57-59.

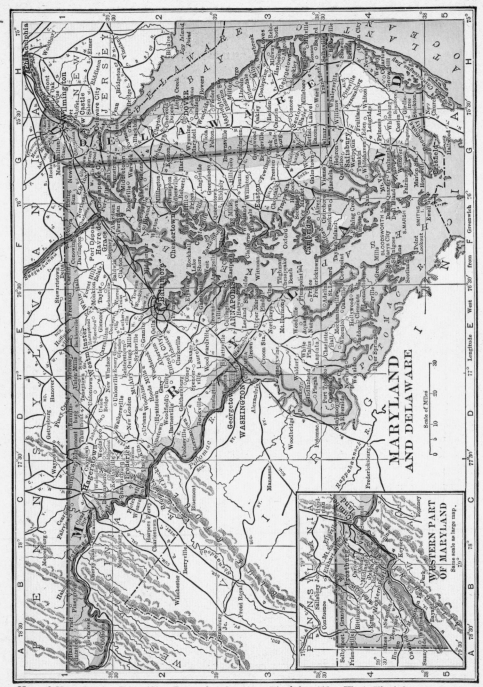

MARYLAND
AND DELAWARE

WESTERN PART
OF MARYLAND

Same scale as large map.

Map of New Jersey, Page 100; Pennsylvania, 108; Virginia, 116; West Virginia, 118.

90

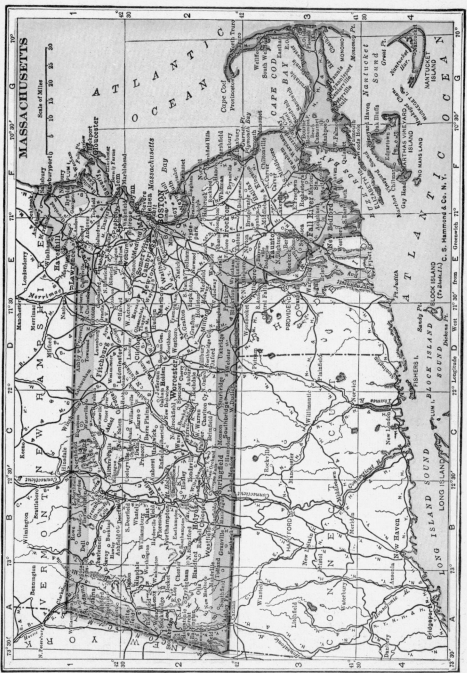

Map of Connecticut, Page 79; New Hampshire, 99; New York, 102; Rhode Island, 109; Vermont, 115.

MICHIGAN

Scale of Miles

Map of Illinois, Page 83; Indiana, 84; Ohio, 105; Ontario, 60-62; Quebec, 58-59; Wisconsin, 119.

92

Map of Iowa, Page 85; Manitoba, 63; North Dakota, 104; Ontario, 60-62; South Dakota, 111; Wisconsin, 119.

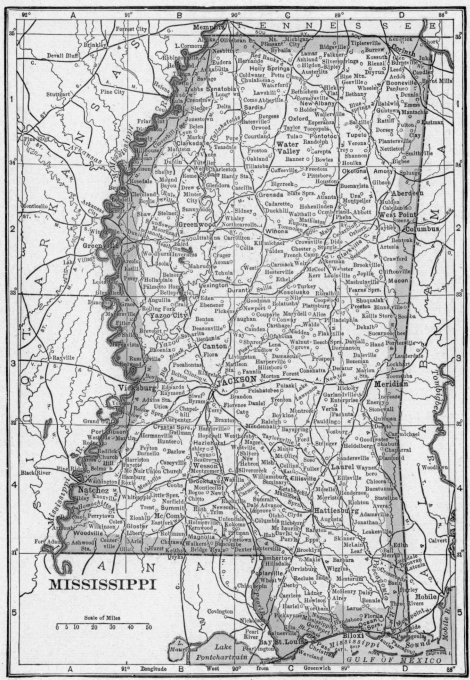

MISSISSIPPI

Scale of Miles

Map of Alabama, Page 74; Arkansas, 76; Louisiana, 88; Tennessee, 112.

94

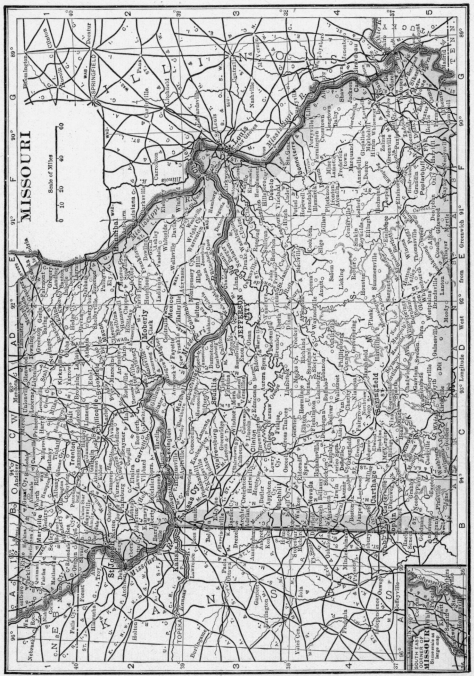

MISSOURI

Scale of Miles

0 10 20 40 60

Map of Arkansas, Page 76; Illinois, 83; Iowa, 85; Kansas, 86; Kentucky, 87; Nebraska, 97; Oklahoma, 106; Tennessee, 112.

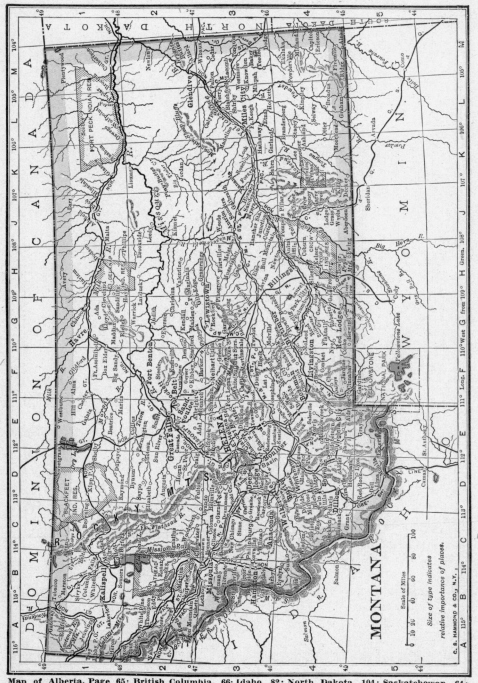

MONTANA

Map of Alberta, Page 65; British Columbia, 66; Idaho, 82; North Dakota, 104; Saskatchewan, 64; South Dakota, 111; Wyoming, 120.

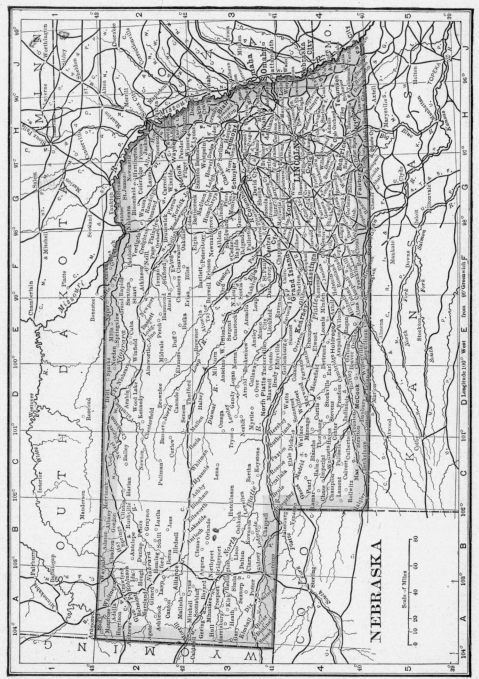

Map of Colorado, Page 78; Iowa, 85; Kansas, 86; Missouri, 95; South Dakota, 111; Wyoming, 120.

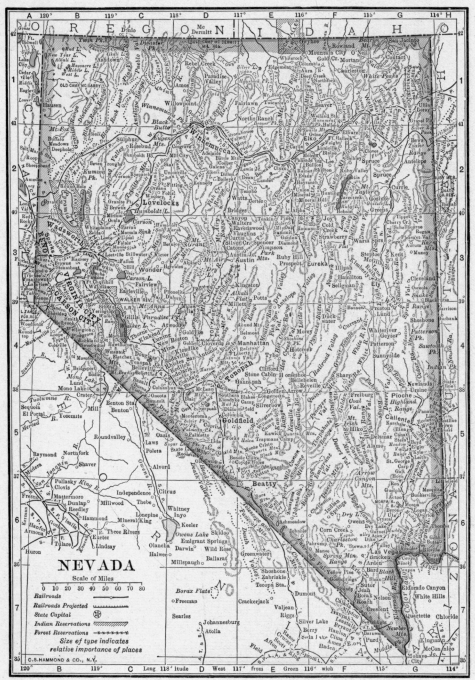

NEVADA

Scale of Miles

0 10 20 30 40 50 60 70 80

Railroads
Railroads Projected
State Capital
Indian Reservations
Forest Reservations
Size of type indicates relative importance of places

C.S. HAMMOND & CO., N.Y.

Map of Arizona, Page 75; California, 77; Idaho, 82; Oregon, 107; Utah, 114.

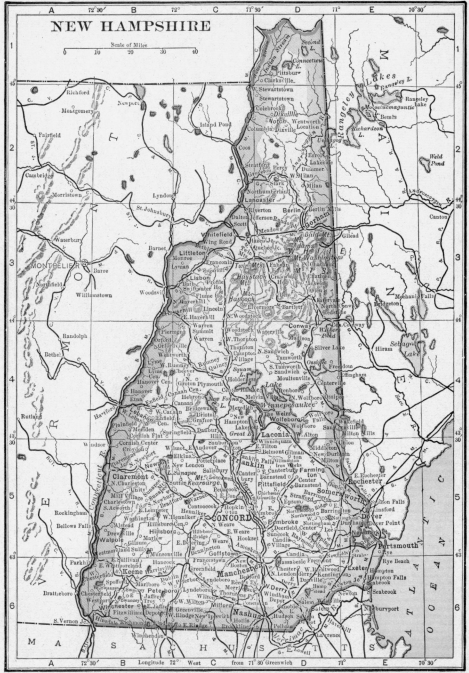

NEW HAMPSHIRE

Scale of Miles

Map of Maine, Page, 89; Massachusetts, 91; Quebec, 57-59; Vermont, 115.

99

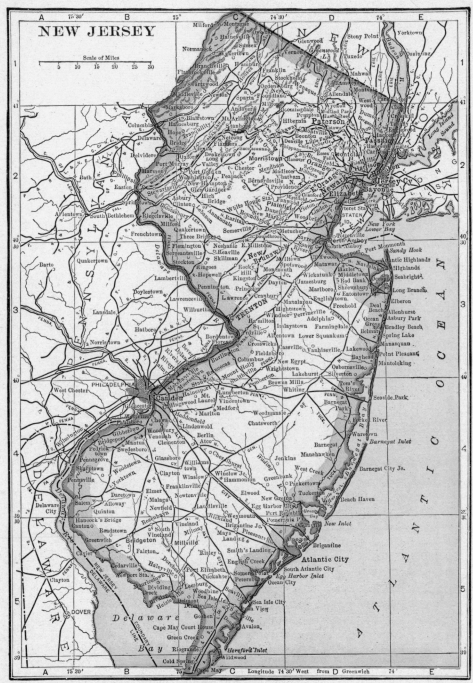

NEW JERSEY

Scale of Miles

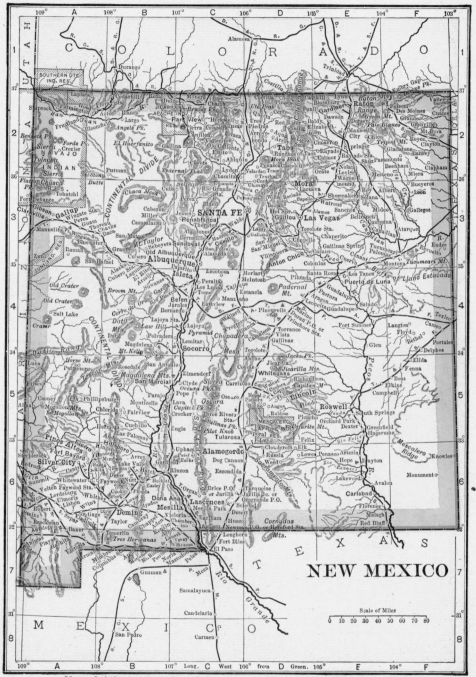

NEW MEXICO

Scale of Miles

0 10 20 30 40 50 60 70 80

Map of Arizona, Page 75; Colorado, 78; Mexico, 67; Oklahoma, 106; Texas, 113.

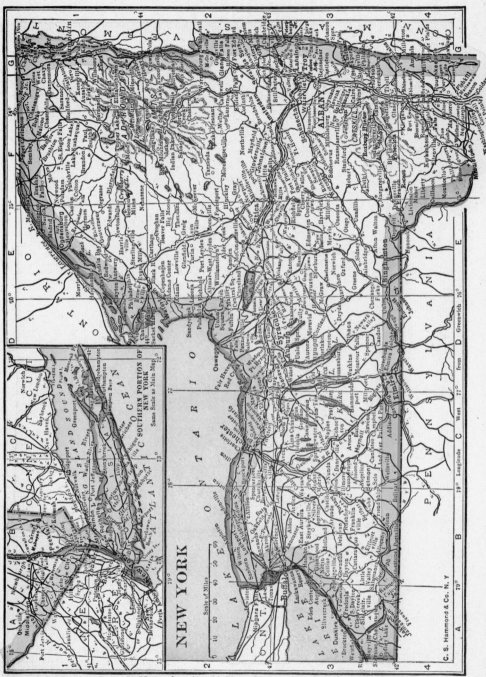

NEW YORK

SOUTHERN PORTION OF NEW YORK

Same Scale as Main Map

Scale of Miles

C. S. Hammond & Co., N. Y.

Map of Connecticut, Page 79; Massachusetts, 91; New Jersey, 100; Ontario, 60-62. Pennsylvania, 108; Quebec, 57-59; Vermont, 115.

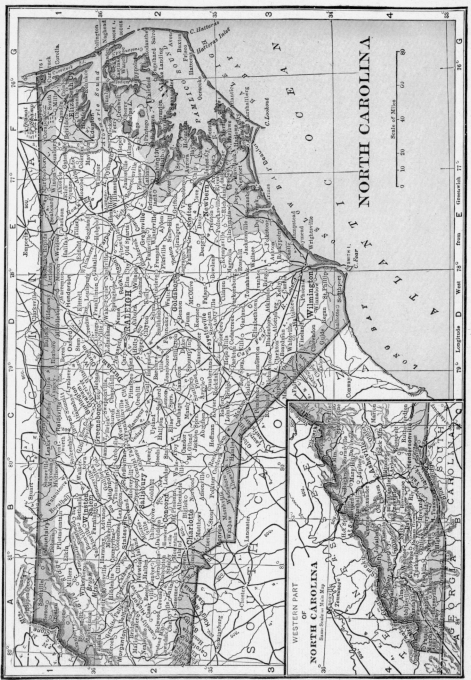

NORTH CAROLINA

Scale of Miles

WESTERN PART
OF
NORTH CAROLINA
Same Scale as Main Map

Map of Georgia, Page 81; South Carolina, 110; Tennessee, 112; Virginia, 116.

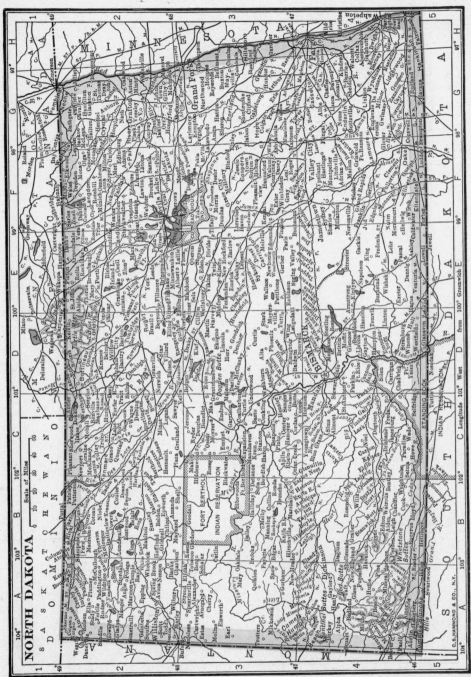

NORTH DAKOTA

Map of Manitoba, Page 63; Minnesota, 93; Montana, 96; Saskatchewan, 64; South Dakota, 111.

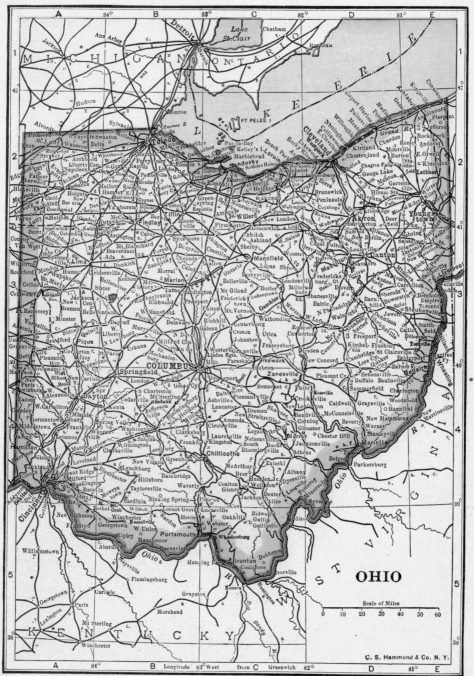

OHIO

Scale of Miles

0 10 20 30 40 50 60

C. S. Hammond & Co. N. Y.

Map of Indiana, Page 84; Kentucky, 87; Michigan, 92; Pennsylvania, 108; West Virginia, 118.

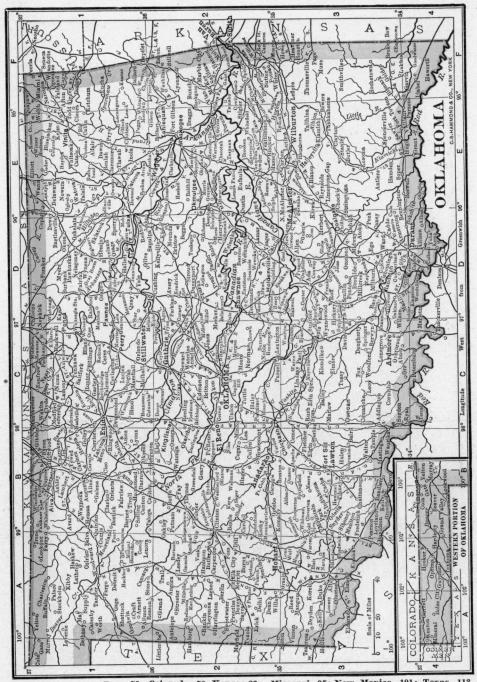

Map of Arkansas, Page 76; Colorado, 78; Kansas, 86; Missouri, 95; New Mexico, 101; Texas, 113.

106

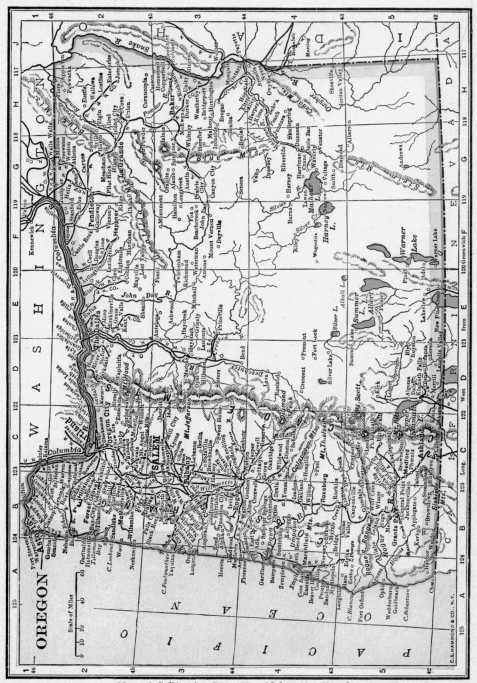

OREGON

Scale of Miles

Map of California, Page 77; Idaho, 82; Nevada, 98; Washington, 117.

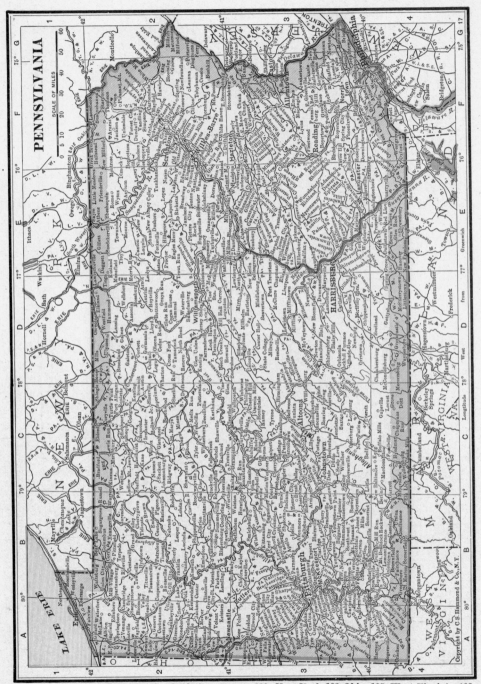

PENNSYLVANIA

SCALE OF MILES
0 5 10 20 30 40 50 60

Map of Delaware, Page 90; Maryland, 90; New Jersey, 100; New York, 102; Ohio, 105; West Virginia, 118.

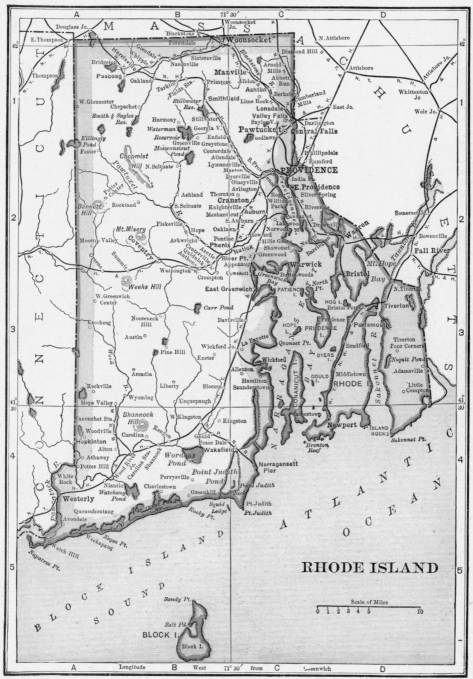

RHODE ISLAND

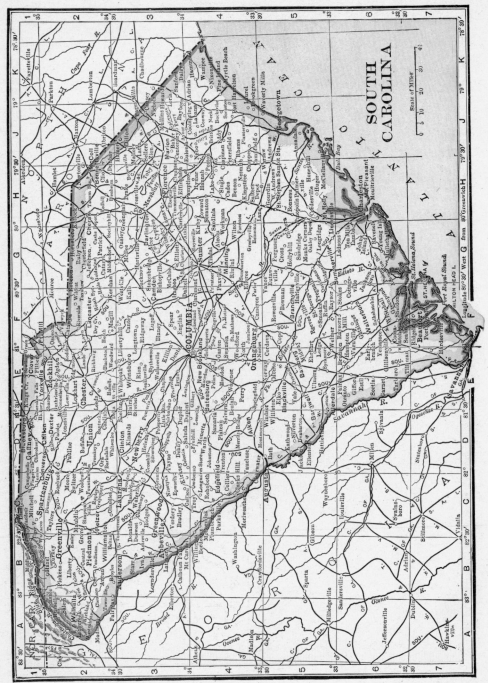

SOUTH CAROLINA

Scale of Miles

Map of Georgia, Page 81; North Carolina, 103.

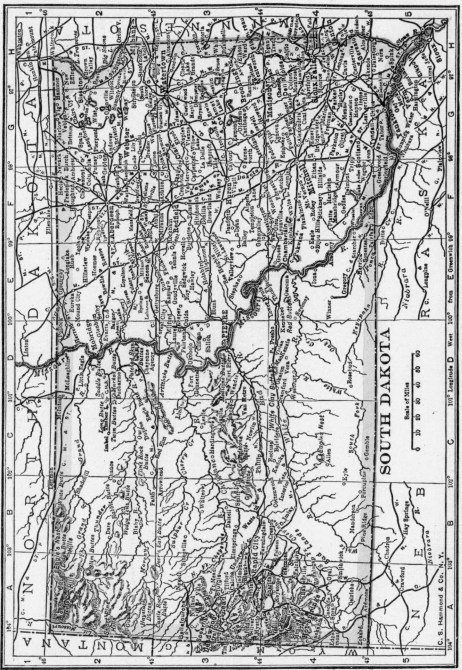

SOUTH DAKOTA

Scale of Miles
10 20 30 40 50 60

C. S. Hammond & Co., N. Y.

Map of Iowa, Page 85; Minnesota, 93; Montana, 96; Nebraska, 97; North Dakota, 104; Wyoming, 120.

111

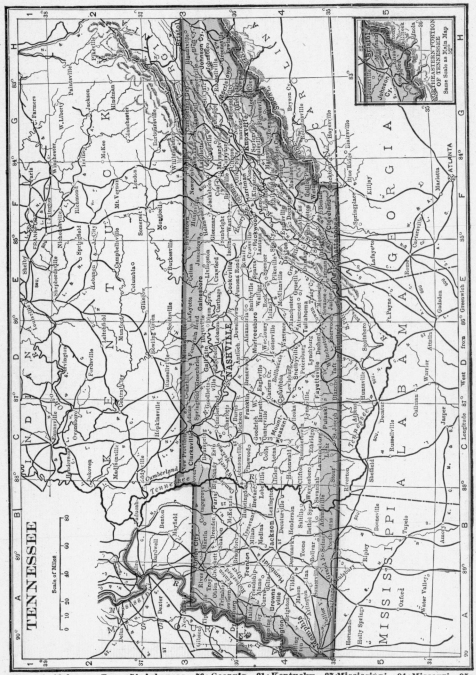

TENNESSEE

Scale of Miles

0 10 20 40 60 80

Map of Alabama, Page 74; Arkansas, 76; Georgia, 81; Kentucky, 87; Mississippi, 94; Missouri, 95; North Carolina, 103; Virginia, 116.

TEXAS

Scale of Miles

0   25   50   75   100

Size of type indicates
relative importance
of places.

C. S. HAMMOND & CO., N.Y.

WESTERN PORTION OF
TEXAS
Same Scale as Main Map

Map of Arkansas, Page 76; Louisiana, 88; Mexico, 67; New Mexico, 101; Oklahoma, 106.

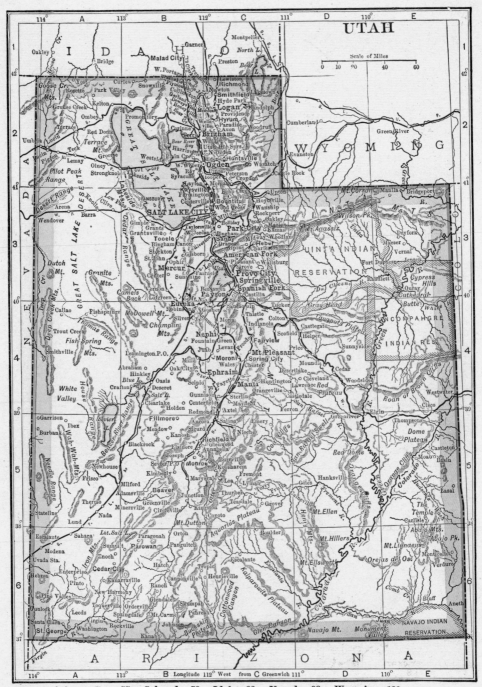

UTAH

Map of Arizona, Page 75; Colorado, 78; Idaho, 82; Nevada, 98; Wyoming, 120.

114

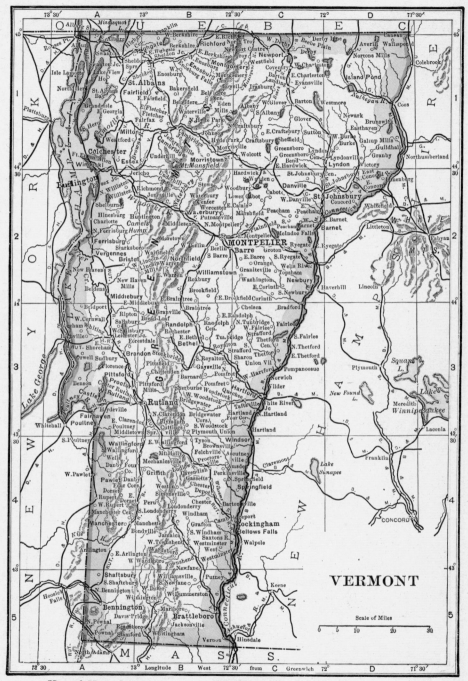

VERMONT

Scale of Miles

Map of Massachusetts, Page 91; New Hampshire, 99; New York, 102; Quebec, 57-59.

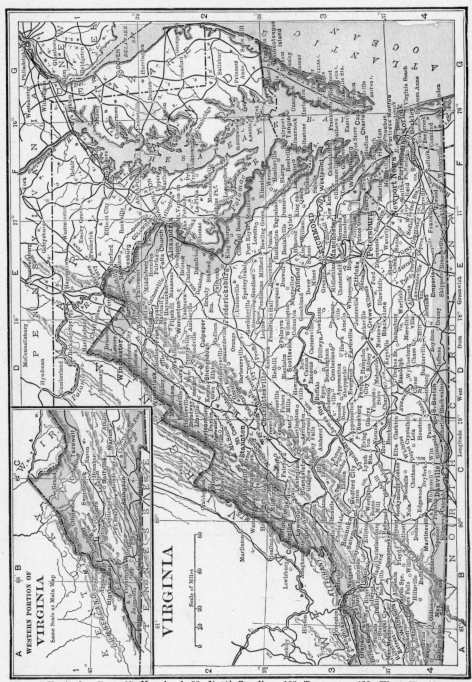

WESTERN PORTION OF
VIRGINIA
Same Scale as Main Map

VIRGINIA

Scale of Miles

Map of Kentucky, Page 87; Maryland, 90; North Carolina, 103; Tennessee, 112; West Virginia, 118.

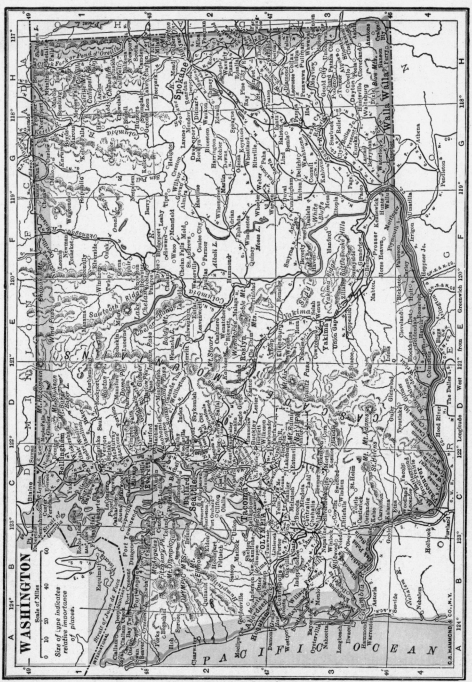

WASHINGTON

Scale of Miles

Size of type indicates
relative importance
of places.

PACIFIC OCEAN

C.S. HAMMOND & CO., N.Y.

Map of British Columbia, Page 66; Idaho, 82; Oregon, 107.

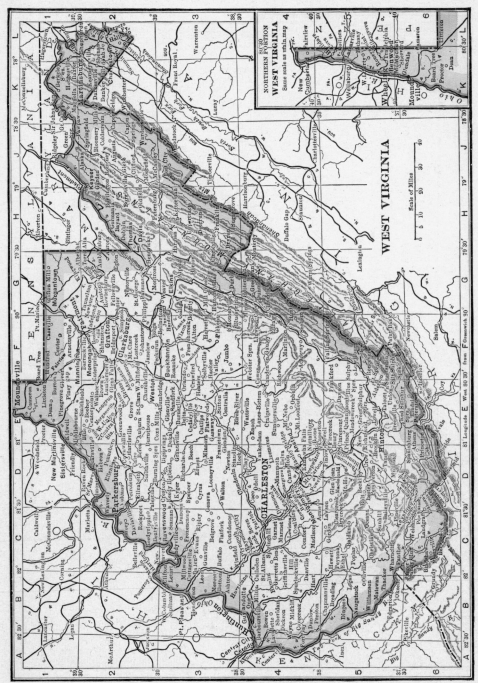

WEST VIRGINIA

NORTHERN PORTION WEST VIRGINIA
Same scale as main map

Scale of Miles

Map of Kentucky, Page 87; Maryland, 90; Ohio, 105; Pennsylvania, 108; Virginia, 116.

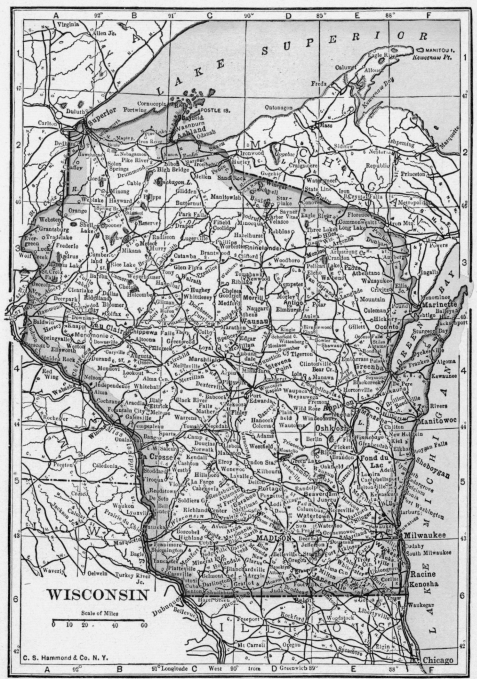

WISCONSIN

Scale of Miles

0 10 20   40   60

C. S. Hammond & Co. N. Y.

Map of Illinois, Page 83; Iowa, 85; Michigan, 92; Minnesota, 93.

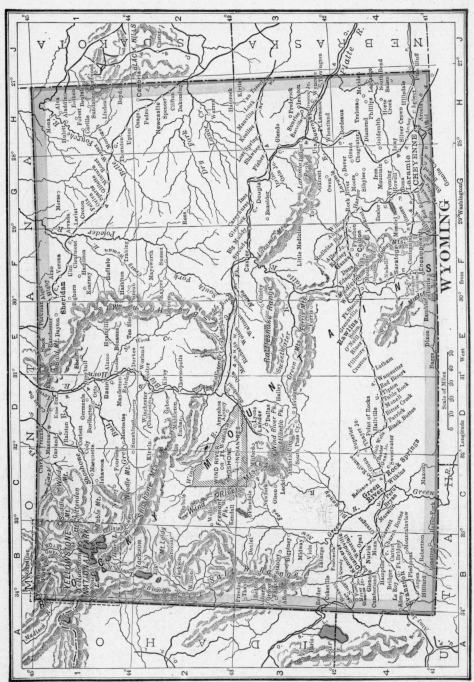

Map of Colorado, Page 78; Idaho, 82; Montana, 96; Nebraska, 97; South Dakota, 111; Utah, 114.

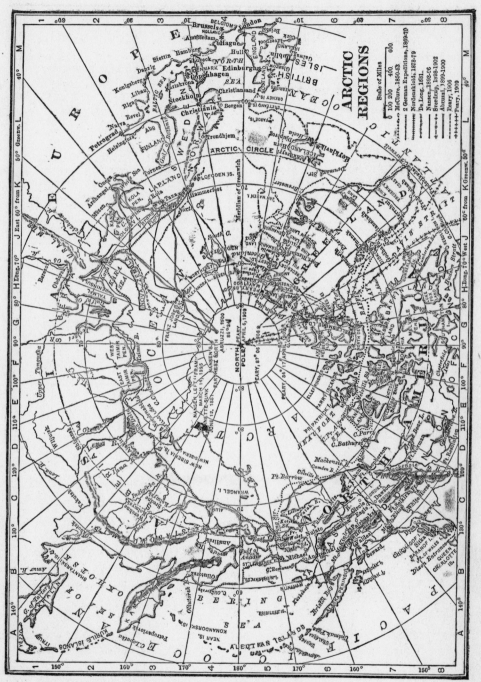

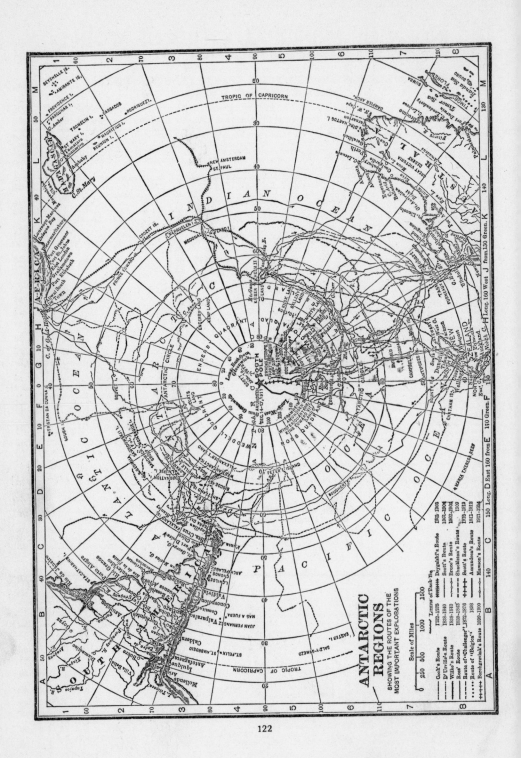

ANTARCTIC REGIONS

SHOWING THE ROUTES OF THE
MOST IMPORTANT EXPLORATIONS

Scale of Miles

122

INDEX OF PRINCIPAL CITIES OF WORLD

(Exclusive of United States of America)

WITH POPULATION FIGURES FROM LATEST CENSUS REPORTS AS EXPLAINED ON PAGE 3.

The name of the place is followed by the name of the country or state, the population, the index references and the plate number. The index references indicate the location of the place on the accompanying maps; these references show the point on the map at which lines will converge if drawn to connect the respective marginal letters upon top and bottom and the numerals on either side of map. Places known under different names or by various spellings of the same name in different forms have, to some extent, been inserted in parenthesis. Capitals of countries and states are designated by asterisks *. Populations of cities including suburbs are designated by daggers †. Index of cities and towns of United States of America will be found on pages 126 to 143, inclusive.

123

INDEX OF CITIES AND TOWNS OF UNITED STATES
1920 CENSUS

The following list names in alphabetical order approximately all places in the United States having one thousand or more inhabitants and some of smaller size, locally important. The index references enclosed in parentheses, indicate location of city or village on the accompanying maps. The numerals at the extreme right of column are the 1920 census figures or recent official estimates of population. ■ = Population of township. Capitals of States are in capital letters.

ALABAMA

Abbeville (D4)...	1,267
Acton (C2)...	1,500
Adamsville (C2)..	649
Adger (B2)...	1,200
Alabama City (D1)...	5,432
Albany (C1)...	7,652
Albertville (C1)..	1,666
Alexander City (C3)...	2,293
Aliceville (A2)...	944
Altoona (C2)...	1,078
Andalusia (C4)...	4,023
Anniston (D2)...	17,734
Ashland (D2)...	1,655
Athens (B1)...	3,323
Atmore (B4).......	1,775
Attalla (C1)...	3,462
Auburn (D3)...	2,143
Austinville (C1)...	838
Avondale (C4)...	4,500
Bay Minette (B5)..	1,092
Benton (C3)......	600
Bessemer (B2)...	18,674
Birmingham (C2)...	178,806
Blocton (B2)...	2,800
Blossburg (B2)...	2,000
Boaz (C1)...	1,369
Boyles (C2)...	1,364
Brantley (C4)...	702
Brewton (C4)...	2,682
Bridgeport (D1)	2,018
Brierfield (B2)...	2,100
Brighton (B2)...	3,665
Brilliant (B1)...	700
Brookside (C2)...	666
Brookwood (B1)...	1,550
Brundidge (D4)...	941
Calera (C2)...	852
Camden (B3)...	700
Camp Hill (D3)..	952
Capitol Heights (C3)	812
Carbonhill (B2)..	2,666
Centerville (B3)...	793
Chapman (C4)...	1,142
Citronelle (A4)...	932
Clanton (C3)...	1,411
Clayton (D4)......	989
Clio (D4)......	838
Coal City (C2)...	685
Collinsville (D1)...	793
Columbia (D4)...	860
Columbiana (C2)..	1,073
Cordova (B2)...	1,622
Corona (B2)...	1,500
Cuba (A3)......	719
Cullman (C1)...	2,467
Dadeville (D3)...	1,146
Daphne (B5)...	700
Decatur (B1)..	4,752
Demopolis (B3)...	2,779
Dolomite (B2)...	1,000
Dora (B2)...	1,117
Dothan (D4)...	10,034
East Brewton (C4)	836
East Tallassee, (D3)...	2,000
Elba (C4)...	1,681
Ensley (C2)...	8,200
Enterprise (D4)...	3,013
Eufaula (D4)...	4,939
Eutaw (B3)...	1,359
Evergreen (B4)...	1,813
Fairfield (C2)...	5,003
Fairhope (B5)...	853
Fayette (B2)...	1,741
Fivepoints (D2)..	835
Florala (C4)...	2,633
Florence (B1)...	10,529
Fort Deposit (C4).	830
Fort Payne (D1)..	2,025
Gadsden (D1)...	14,737
Gate City (C2)...	700
Geneva (D4)...	1,581
Georgiana (C4)...	1,550
Girard (D3)...	4,942
Good Water (D2)	920
Gordo (B2)......	642
Greensboro (B3)..	1,809
Greenville (C4)..	3,471
Guntersville (C1).	1,909
Gurley (C1)......	727
Haleyville (B1)...	1,404
Hartford (D4)...	1,561
Hartsells (C1)...	2,009
Headland (D4)...	1,252
Heflin (D4)......	1,026
Helena (C2)......	808
Hollins (C2)......	688
Huntsville (C1)...	8,018
Hurtsboro (D3)...	868
Inglenook (C2)...	1,590
Irondale (C2)......	809
Jackson (B4)...	1,331
Jacksonville (D2)	2,395
Jasper (B2)...	3,246
Jonesboro (C2) ..	1,979
Kimberly (B2)...	800
Lafayette (D3) ..	1,911
Lanett (D3)...	4,976
Leeds (C2)...	1,600
Lineville (D2)...	1,507
Lipscomb (C2)...	1,605
Livingston (A3)...	968
Luverne (C4)...	1,464
Lower Peachtree (B8)...	700
McFall (D2)...	1,000
Marion (B3)......	2,035
Mobile (B5)...	60,777
Monroeville (B4).	1,017
Montevallo (C2).	850
MONTGOMERY (C3)...	43,464
Mount Vernon (A4)	800
Nanafalia (B3)...	600
North Birming-ham (C2)...	5,500
Oakman (B2)...	1,083
Oneonta (C2)...	876
Opelika (D3)...	4,960
Opp (C4)...	1,556
Oxford (D3)...	1,108
Ozark (D4)......	2,518
Pell City (C2)...	825
Phoenix (D3)...	5,432
Piedmont (D2)...	2,645
Prattville (C3)...	2,316
Reform (B2)...	1,069
River Falls (C4)...	1,107
Roanoke (O2)...	3,841
Russellville (B1)..	2,269
Samson (C4)...	1,646
Sanford (C4)...	742
Sayre (C2)...	600
Scottsboro (D1)...	1,417
Searles (B2)...	700
Selma (B3)...	15,589
Sheffield (B1)...	6,682
Shelby (C2)...	750
Sulligent (A2)...	1,071
Stockton (B5)...	600
Sylacauga (C2)...	2,141
Talladega (D2)...	6,546
Tallassee (D3)...	2,034
Thomasville (B4)...	1,002
Townly (B2)...	1,554
Troy (D4)...	5,696
Trussville (C2)...	750
Tuscaloosa (B2)...	11,996
Tuscumbia (B1)	3,855
Tuskegee (D3)...	2,475
Union Springs (D3)...	4,125
Uniontown (B3)	1,359
Vincent (C2)...	1,034
Watson (C2)...	1,000
West Blocton (B2)...	1,023
Wetumpka (C3)	1,520
Whistler (A5)...	2,000
Wilsonville (C2)	815
Woodward (C2)..	1,000
Yolande (B2)...	1,000
York (A3)...	1,651

ARIZONA

Ajo (C6)...	900
Ashfork (C3)...	200
Benson (E6)...	900
Bisbee (F7)...	9,205
Blackwater (D5)..	250
Bowie (F6)...	350
Buckeye (C5)...	400
Campverde (D4)	300
Casagrande (D6) .	948
Central (F6)...	300
Chloride (A3)...	800
Clifton (F5)...	4,163
Concho (F4)...	260
Congress (B4)...	900
Constellation (C4).	100
Courtland (F7)...	500
Douglas (F7)...	9,916
Duncan (F6)...	600
Eden (F6)...	500
Flagstaff (D3)...	3,186
Florence (D6)...	1,161
Fort Apache (F5)	300
Fort Huachuca (E7)	400
Fort Thomas (E5).	150
Gleeson (F7)...	500
Glendale (C5)...	2,737
Globe (E5)...	7,044
Grand Canyon (C2).	130
Hayden (E5)...	900
Holbrook (E4)...	1,206
Humboldt (C2)...	100
Jerome (D4)...	4,030
Kelvin (D5)...	350
Kingman (B3)...	1,000
Lowell (F7)...	2,500
Mammoth (E6)...	400
Mayer (C4)...	260
Mesa (D5)...	3,036
Metcalf (F5)...	2,500
Miami (E5)...	6,689
Morenci (F5)...	5,010
Naco (F7)...	200
Nogales (D7)...	5,199
Oatman (A3)...	900
Octave (C4)...	500
Parker (A4)...	400
Patagonia (E7)...	500
Pearce (F7)...	700
PHOENIX (C5)..	29,053
Pima (F6)...	515
Pirtleville (F7)...	1,500
Prescott (C4)...	5,010
Quartzsite (B5)...	300
Ray (E5)...	900
Rice (E5)...	300
Safford (F6)...	1,336
St. David (E7)...	500
St. Johns (F4)...	1,250
San Carlos (E5)...	2,500
Seligman (B3)...	330
Silverbell (D6)...	700
Snowflake (E4)...	758
Solomonsville (F6)	750
Sonora (E5)...	800
Springerville (F4).	600
Superior (E5)...	900
Taylor (E4)...	100
Tempe (C5)...	1,963
Thatcher (F6)...	899
Tombstone (F7)	1,178
Toreva (E3)...	550
Tubac (D7)...	300
Tucson (D6)...	20,292
Twin Buttes (D7).	300
Warren (F7)...	300
Wickenburg (C5)..	527
Wilcox (F6)...	905
Williams (C3)...	1,350
Winkelman (E6)...	573
Winslow (E4)...	3,730
Yuma (A6)...	4,237

ARKANSAS

Arkadelphia (B4) .	3,311
Arkansas City (D5)...	1,482
Ashdown (A5)...	2,052
Atkins (C3)...	1,529
Augusta (D3)...	1,731
Batesville (D3)...	4,299
Benton (C4)...	2,933
Bentonville (A2)..	2,313
Blytheville (F3)...	6,447
Booneville (B3)...	2,199
Brinkley (D4)...	2,714
Camden (C5)...	3,238
Clarendon (D4)...	2,638
Clarksville (B3)...	2,127
Coalhill (B3)...	1,057
Conway (C3)...	4,564
Corning (E2)...	1,564
Cottonplant (D3)..	1,661
Crossett (D5)...	2,707
Dardanelle (B3)...	1,835
De Queen (A4)...	2,517
Dermott (D5)...	2,330
Desarc (D4)...	1,307
Earl (E3)...	2,091
Eldorado (C5)...	3,887
England (D4)...	2,408
Eureka Sprs. (B2).	2,429
Fayetteville (A2)..	5,362
Fordyce (C5)...	2,996
Foreman (A5)...	1,408
Forrest City (E4).	3,377
Fort Smith (A3)...	28,870
Greenwood (A3)..	1,374
Gurdon (B5)...	1,469
Hamburg (D5)...	1,538
Harrison (B2)...	3,477
Hartford (A3)...	2,067
Heber Sprs. (D3)..	1,675
Helena (E4)...	9,112
Hope (B5)...	4,790
Hot Springs (D4)..	11,695
Hoxie (D2)...	1,711
Huntington (A3)	1,453
Huttig (C5)...	1,261
Jonesboro (E3)...	9,384
Lake Village (D5).	1,449
Leslie (C3)...	1,472
Lewisville (B5)...	1,067
LITTLE ROCK (C4)...	65,142
Lonoke (D4)...	1,711
McGehee (D5)...	2,368
Magnolia (B5)...	2,158
Malvern (C4)...	3,864
Marianna (E4)...	5,074
Marked Tree (E3).	1,318
Mena (A4)...	3,441
Monticello (E3)...	2,378
Morrillton (C3)...	3,010
Nashville (B5)...	2,144
Newport (D3)...	3,771
North Little Rock (C4)...	14,048
Osceola (E3)...	1,755
Ozark (B3)...	1,262
Paragould (E2)...	6,306
Paris (B3)...	1,740
Piggott (E2)...	2,016
Pinebluff (C4) ...	19,280
Pocahontas (D2)	1,806
Prescott (B5)...	2,691
Rector (E2)...	1,801
Rogers (A2)...	3,318
Russellville (B3)..	4,505
Searcy (D3)...	2,836
Siloam Sprs. (A2)	2,569
Springdale (A2)...	2,263
Stamps (B5)...	2,564
Stuttgart (D4)...	4,522
Texarkana (B5)..	8,257
Trumann (E3)...	2,598
Van Buren (A3)..	5,224
Walnutridge (E2)	2,226
Warren (C5)...	2,145
West Helena (E4).	6,226
Wynne (E3)...	2,933

CALIFORNIA

Alameda (C5)...	28,806
Alhambra (G8)...	9,096
Anaheim (G9)...	5,526
Angels Camp (E4)	3,900
Antioch (D4)...	1,936
Arcadia (G8)...	2,239
Arcata (A2)...	1,486
Auburn (E4)...	2,289
Azusa (G8)...	2,460
Bakersfield (G7)..	18,639
Benicia (D4)...	2,693
Berkeley (C5)...	56,036

126

CALIFORNIA, Cont'd

Bishop (G5)...... 1,304
Brawley (H4)..... 5,389
Brea (H8)........ 1,037
Burbank (G8).... 2,913
Burlingame (C5).. 4,107
Calexico (H4).... 6,223
Chico (D3)....... 9,339
Chino (H9)....... 2,132
Chula Vista (H10). 1,718
Claremont (G8)... 1,728
Coalinga (E6).... 2,934
Colma (C5)....... 1,950
Colton (H9)...... 4,282
Colusa (D3)...... 1,846
Corona (H9)...... 4,129
Coronado (H10) .. 3,289
Covina (G8)...... 1,999
Crockett (C4).... 1,800
Daly City (C5)... 3,779
Dunsmuir (C1)... 2,528
Eagle Rock (G9).. 2,256
E. San Diego (H10) 4,148
El Centro (H4)... 5,464
El Cerrito (C5)... 1,505
El Monte (G8).... 1,283
El Segundo (G9).. 1,563
Emeryville (C5)... 2,390
Escondido (J9)... 1,789
Eureka (A2).....12,923
Exeter (F6)...... 1,852
Fillmore (G8).... 1,597
Folsom City (D4). 1,500
Fort Bragg (B3).. 2,616
Fowler (F6)...... 1,528
Fresno (F6).....45,086
Fullerton (H9)... 4,415
Gilroy (D5)...... 2,862
Glendale (G8)...13,536
Glendora (H8)... 2,028
Grass Valley (D3). 4,006
Gridley (O3)..... 1,636
Hanford (F6)..... 5,888
Hayward (D5).... 3,487
Healdsburg (B4).. 2,412
Hermosa Beach
(G9).......... 2,327
Hollister (D6)... 2,781
Huntington Park
(G9).......... 4,513
Imperial (H4)... 1,885
Inglewood (G9)... 3,286
Jackson (E4)..... 1,601
LaVerne (H8)..... 1,698
Lemoore (F6)..... 1,355
Lincoln (D4)..... 1,325
Lindsay (F6)..... 2,576
Livermore (D5)... 1,916
Lodi (D4)........ 4,850
Lompoc (E8)..... 1,876
Longbeach (G9)..55,593
Los Angles (G9) 576,673
Los Gatos (C5)... 2,317
Madera (F5)..... 3,444
Martinez (C5).... 3,858
Marysville (D3).. 5,461
Mendocino (B3) . 1,250
Merced (E5)..... 3,974
Mill Valley (C5).. 2,554
Modesto (E5).... 9,241
Monrovia (H8)... 5,480
Monterey (D6)... 5,479
Mountain View
(D5)......... 1,888
Napa (C1)...... 6,797
National Cy. (J10) 3,116
Needles (J2)..... 2,807
Nevada City (E3). 1,782
Oakdale (E5).... 1,745
Oakland (C5)..216,261
Oceanpark (G9)..3,119
Ontario (H8)..... 7,280
Orange (H9)...... 4,884

Oroville (D3)..... 3,340
Oxnard (F8)...... 4,417
Pacific Grove (C6) 2,974
Palo Alto (C5).... 5,900
Pasadena (G8)...45,354
Paso Robles (E7). 1,919
Petaluma (C4)... 6,226
Piedmont (C5)... 4,282
Pittsburg (D4)... 4,715
Placerville (E4).. 1,650
Pomona (H8).....13,505
Porterville (G6).. 4,097
Red Bluff (C2)... 3,104
Redding (C2)..... 2,962
Redlands (H8)... 9,571
Redondo Beach
(G9).......... 4,913
Redwood City (C5) 4,020
Reedley (F6)..... 2,447
Richmond (C5)..16,843
Riverside (H9)...19,341
Roseville (D4)... 4,477
SACRAMENTO
(D4).........65,908
St. Helena (C4) .. 1,346
Salinas (D6)..... 4,308
San Anselmo (C4). 2,475
San Bernardino
(H8).........18,721
San Diego (H10) .74,683
San Fernando (F8) 3,204
San Francisco
(C5).........506,676
Sanger (F6)...... 2,578
San Jose (D5)...39,642
San Leandro
(D5)..........5,703
San Luis Obispo
(E7).......... 5,895
San Mateo (C5).. 5,979
San Pedro (G9) .. 1,200
San Rafael (C5).. 5,512
Santa Ana (G9) .15,485
Santa Barbara
(F8).........19,441
Santa Clara (C5) . 5,220
Santa Cruz (C6). 10,917
Santa Maria (E8) 3,943
Santa Monica
(G9).........15,252
Santa Paula (G8). 3,967
Santa Rosa (C4) . 8,758
Sausalito (C5)... 2,790
Sawtelle (G8).... 2,143
Sebastopol (C4).. 1,493
Selma (F6)...... 3,158
Sierra Madre (H8). 2,026
Sonora (E4)..... 1,684
So. Pasadena (H8). 7,652
South San Fran-
cisco (C5)..... 4,411
Stockton (D5)...40,296
Sunnyvale (C5)... 1,675
Taft (F7)........ 3,317
Tracy (D5)....... 2,450
Truckee (E3).... 1,250
Tulare (F6)...... 3,539
Turlock (E5)..... 3,394
Ukiah (B3)....... 2,305
Upland (H8)..... 2,912
Vacaville (C4)... 1,254
Vallejo (C4).....21,107
Ventura (F8)..... 4,342
Visalia (F6)...... 5,753
Watsonville (D6). 5,013
Watts (G9)....... 4,529
Whittier (G9).... 7,997
Willits (B3)...... 1,468
Wilmington (G9).. 2,250
Woodland (D4)... 4,147
Yreka (C1)....... 1,277
Yuba City (D3)... 1,708

COLORADO

Aguilar (E4)..... 1,236
Akron (F1)...... 1,401
Alamosa (D4).... 3,171
Antonito (C4) 946
Arvada (D2)...... 915
Aspen (C2)...... 1,265
Aurora (E2)...... 983
Berthoud (E1).... 852
Boulder (D2).....11,006
Breckenridge (D2) 796
Brighton (E1).... 2,715
Brush (F1)....... 2,103
Buenavista (C3) .. 903
Canon City (D3)... 4,551
Colorado Springs
(E3).........30,105
Craig (B1)....... 1,297
Crested Butte (C3) 1,213
Cripple Creek
(D3).......... 2,325
Delagua (E4).... 1,035
Del Norte (C4) .. 1,007
Delta (A3)....... 2,623
DENVER (E2) .256,491
Durango (B4).... 4,116
Eaton (E1)....... 1,289
Edgewater (E2)... 664
Englewood (E2)... 4,356
Florence (D3)... 2,629
Fort Collins (D1). 8,755
Fort Logan (D2).. 2,500
Fort Lupton (E1). 1,014
Fort Morgan (F1). 3,818
Fowler (E3)..... 1,062
Fruita (A2)...... 1,193
Georgetown (D2) . 703
Glenwood Springs
(B2).......... 2,073
Golden (D2)..... 2,484
Goldfield (E3).... 633
Grand Junction
(A2).......... 8,665
Greeley (E1).....10,958
Gunnison (B3)... 1,329
Haxtum (G1)... 1,118
Holly (G3)....... 940
Holyoke (G1).... 1,205
Idaho Springs
(D2).......... 1,192
Julesburg (G1)... 1,320
Lafayette (E2)... 1,815
La Junta (F4)... 4,964
Lamar (G3)..... 2,512
Las Animas (F3). 2,252
La Veta (D4).... 737
Leadville (C2)... 4,959
Limon (F2)...... 1,047
Littleton (E2)... 1,636
Longmont (E1).. 5,848
Louisville (E2)... 1,799
Loveland (E1)... 5,065
Manassa (D4).... 906
Manitou (D3)... 1,129
Meeker (B1)..... 935
Montevista (C4).. 2,484
Montrose (B3)... 3,581
Ordway (F3)..... 1,186
Ouray (B3)...... 1,165
Pagosa Springs
(C4).......... 1,032
Palisades (A2)... 855
Paonia (B3)..... 925
Primero (E4).... 2,000
Pueblo (E3).....43,050
Rifle (B2)....... 885
Rockvale (D3)... 1,249
Rockyford (F3)... 3,746
Saguache (C3)... 948
Salida (D3)..... 4,689
Silverton (B4)... 1,150
South Canon (D3) 1,281
Starkville (E4)... 1,000

Steamboat Springs
(C1).......... 1,249
Sterling (F1)..... 6,415
Sugar City (F3) .. 836
Telluride (B4)... 1,618
Trinidad (E4).....10,906
Victor (D3)...... 1,777
Walsenburg (E4).. 3,565
Windsor (D1).... 1,290
Wray (G1)...... 1,538
Yuma (G1)...... 1,177

CONNECTICUT

Ansonia (C3).....17,643
Avon (D1)....... 1,100
Beacon Falls (C3) ■1,593
Berlin (D2)...... ■4,298
Bethel (B3)...... ■3,201
Bloomfield (E1)... ■2,394
Branford (D3).... 2,619
Bridgeport (C4)..143,555
Bristol (D2).....20,620
Broadbrook (F1).. 1,400
Brookfield (B3) .. ■896
Brooklyn (H1)... ■1,655
Burlington (D1).. ■1,109
Burnside (E1).... 980
Central Village
(H2).......... ■1,000
Cheshire (D2)... ■2,855
Chester (F3)..... ■1,675
Clinton (E3)..... ■1,217
Collinsville (D1).. 2,500
Cromwell (E2)... ■2,455
Danbury (B3)...19,943
Danielson (H1)... 3,130
Darien (B4)..... ■4,184
Dayville (H1).... 950
Deepriver (F3)... 1,480
Derby (C3).....11,238
Durham (E3)..... ■959
E. Haddam (F3). ■2,312
E. Hampton (F2). ■2,394
E. Hartford (E1) ■11,648
East Haven (D3). ■3,520
Easton (B3)..... ■1,017
East Port Chester
(A4).......... 2,000
Ellington (F1)... ■2,127
Enfield (E1)..... ■11,719
Essex (F3)...... ■2,815
Fairfield (C4)... ■11,475
Forestville (D2).. 3,400
Glastonbury (E2) ■5,592
Granby (D1)..... ■1,342
Greenwich (A4)... ■5,939
Griswold (H2)... ■4,220
Groton (G3)..... 4,236
Guilford (E3).... 1,612
Haddam (E2)... ■1,736
Hamden (D3)... ■8,611
HARTFORD
(E1).........138,036
Harwinton (C1).. ■2,020
Hazardville (E1).. 1,200
Higganum (E3).. 1,000
Jewett City (H2).. ■3,196
Kensington (D2).. ■1,950
Kent (B2)....... ■1,086
Killingly (H1)... ■8,178
Lebanon (G2)... ■1,343
Ledyard (H3).... ■1,161
Madison (E3).... ■1,857
Manchester (F1).■18,370
Mansfield (G1) .. ■2,574
Meriden (D2)... 29,867
Middlefield (E2). ■1,047
Middletown (E2). 13,638
Milford (C4).... 10,193
Monroe (C3).... ■1,161
Montville (G3)... ■3,411
Moodus (F2)..... 950
Moosup (H2)..... 2,300
Mystic (H3)..... 3,900

Naugatuck (C3) .15,051
New Britain (D2). 59,316
New Canaan (B4). 1,918
New Hartford
(D1).......... ■1,781
New Haven (D3) 162,537
Newington (E2).. ■2,381
New London
(G3).........25,688
New Milford (B2) ■4,781
Niantic (G3)..... 1,200
Noank (G3)..... 1,100
Norfolk (C1)..... ■1,229
North Grosvenor
Dale (H1)..... 2,500
North Haven
(D3).......... ■1,968
North Stoning-
ton (H3)...... ■1,144
Norwalk (B4)....■27,743
Norwich (G2)...■22,304
Norwichtown
(G2).......... 1,800
Oakville (C2).... 950
Old Lyme (F3)... ■946
Old Saybrook (F3)■1,463
Orange (C3).....■16,614
Oxford (C3)..... ■998
Plainfield (H2)... ■7,926
Plainville (D2)... ■4,114
Plantsville (D2).. 1,800
Plymouth (C2) .. ■5,942
Pomfret (H1).... ■1,454
Portland (E2).... ■3,644
Preston (H2).... ■2,743
Putman (H1)..... 7,711
Redding (B3).... ■1,315
Ridgefield (A3)... 1,030
Rockville (F1)... 7,726
Rockyhill (E2)... ■1,633
Rowayton (B4)... 1,150
Salisbury (B1)... ■2,497
Sandy Hook (B3) 1,000
Saybrook (F3)... ■2,325
Seymore (C3)....■6,781
Sharon (B1)..... ■1,585
Shelton (C3).... 9,475
Simsbury (D1)... ■2,958
Somers (F1)..... ■1,673
Sound Beach (A4). 1,000
Southbury (H3)... ■1,093
South Glaston-
bury (F2)..... 1,100
Southington (D2). 5,085
South Manchester
(E1).......... 9,000
Southport (B4)... 1,200
South Windsor
(E1).......... ■2,142
Stafford (F1).... ■5,407
Stafford Springs
(F1).......... 3,383
Stamford (B4)...35,096
Sterling (H2).... ■1,266
Stonington (H3) . 2,100
Stony Creek (E3). 1,200
Stratford (C4)...■12,347
Suffield (E1)..... ■4,070
Taftville (G2)... 4,500
Terryville (C2)... 2,400
Thomaston (C2). ■3,993
Thompson (H1).. ■5,055
Thompsonville
(E1).......... 6,000
Tolland (F1)..... ■1,040
Torrington (C1)..20,623
Trumbull (C4)... ■2,597
Union City (C2) . 4,000
Unionville (D1).. 2,200
Vernon (F1)..... ■8,898
Wallingford (D3). ■9,648
Warehouse Point
(E1).......... 1,250
Washington (B2). ■1,619

MAINE, Cont'd

Machias (D4).... ■2,152
Machiasport (D4).■1,117
Madawaska (C1)..■1,933
Madison (B4).... 3,729
Mapleton (C2)... ■1,128
Mars Hill (C2)... ■1,783
Mechanic Falls
 (A4).......... ■1,614
Mexico (A4).... ■3,242
Millbridge (D4).. ■1,196
Millinocket (C3).. ■4,528
Milltown (D3).... 1,000
Milo (B3)....... ■2,894
Monmouth (B4) . ■1,372
Monson (B3).... ■1,079
Monticello (B4).. ■1,268
Mt. Desert (C4).. ■1,497
New Gloucester
 (A5).......... ■1,384
Newport (B4)... ■1,709
Norridgewock
 (B4).......... ■1,532
North Anson (B4). 1,200
No. Berwick (A5) ■1,652
Norway (A4).... 2,208
Oakland (B4).... ■2,473
Old Orchard (A5) ■1,164
Oldtown (C4).... 6,956
Orono (C4)...... ■3,133
Orrington (C4)... ■1,174
Parsonsfield (A5).. ■1,062
Patten (C3)..... ■1,498
Pembroke (D4).. ■1,168
Perry (D4)...... ■1,146
Pittsfield (B4)... 2,146
Poland (A4).... ■1,399
Portland (A5)... 69,272
Presque Isle (C2).. 3,452
Princeton (D3)..... ■1,091
Randolph (B4).... ■1,145
Richmond (B4)... ■1,724
Rockland (B4).... 8,109
Rockport (B4) .. ■1,774
Rumford (A4).... 7,016
Saco (A5)....... 6,817
St. Agatha (C1).. ■1,669
St. Albans (B4)... ■1,207
St. George (B4).. ■1,654
Sanford (A5).... ■10,691
Sangerville (B3).. ■1,246
Scarboro (A5).... ■1,832
Searsport (C4)... ■1,373
Sherman (C3)... ■1,134
Skowhegan (B4).. ■5,981
Solon (B4)...... ■1,054
So. Berwick (A5).. 2,955
South Paris (A4) . ■1,793
So. Portland (A5).. 9,254
So. Windham (A5) ■1,200
Springvale (A5)... 2,300
Standish (A5)... ■1,735
Stockton Springs
 (C4).......... ■1,175
Stonington (C4)... ■1,353
Sullivan (C4).... ■1,132
Tenants Har. (B5). 1,700
Thomaston (B4) . ■2,019
Topsham (B5).... ■2,102
Tremont (C4).... ■1,029
Turner (A4)...... ■1,382
Union (B4)....... ■1,133
Vassalboro (B4)... ■1,936
Vanburen (C1)... ■4,594
Vinalhaven (C4).. ■1,965
Waldoboro (A5).. ■2,426
Wallagrass (C1).. ■1,144
Warren (B4)..... ■1,500
Washburn (C2)... 1,870
Waterville (B4)... 13,351
Wells (A5)....... ■1,943
Westbrook (A5)... 9,453
Wilton (A4)...... ■2,505

Winslow (B4).... ■3,280
Winterport (B4) . .■1,433
Winthrop (A4)... ■1,902
Wiscasset (B5)... ■1,192
Yarmouth (A5)... ■2,216
Yarmouthville
 (A5).......... 1,600
York Village (A5) . 1,100

MARYLAND

Aberdeen (F2)... 1,067
ANNAPOLIS
 (E3)...........11,214
Arlington (E2).... 1,000
Baltimore (E2) .733,826
Barton (B4)...... 765
Belair (F1)...... 1,091
Berlin (H4)...... 1,366
Boonsboro (C1)... 1,044
Brunswick (C2)... 3,905
Cambridge (F3)... 7,467
Capitol Heights
 (E3)........... 1,194
Catonsville (E2).. 4,500
Centerville (F2)... 1,765
Chestertown (F2) . 2,537
Cockeysville (E2) . 1,500
Crisfield (G5).... 4,116
Cumberland (C4) 29,837
Deal Island (G4).. 2,000
Delmar (G4)..... 1,291
Denton (G3)..... 1,570
Easton (F3)...... 3,442
Eastport (F3)..... 1,500
Eckhart Mines
 (C4).......... 1,700
Elkton (G1)..... 2,660
Ellicott City (E2) . 1,246
Emmitsburg (D1)... 940
Federalsburg (G3). 1,288
Frederick (D2)....11,066
Frostburg (B4)... 6,017
Hagerstown (C1)..28,064
Hamilton (E2)... 1,500
Hancock (B4)... 972
Havre de Grace
 (F1)........... 4,377
Hurlock (G3).... 1,075
Hyattsville (E3).. 2,675
Kitzmiller (B4)... 1,044
Laurel (E2)...... 2,239
Lonaconing (C4).. 2,054
Midland (B4)..... 910
Mt. Rainier (E3).. 2,462
Mt. Savage (C4).. 3,600
Northeast (G1)... 1,112
Oakland (A4)..... 1,225
Oxford (F3)...... 998
Pikesville (E2)... 1,200
Pocomoke City
 (G4).......... 2,444
Port Deposit (F1). 1,090
Princess Anne
 (G4).......... 968
Reisterstown (E2) 1,000
Relay (E2)...... 1,000
Rockville (D2)... 1,145
St. Michaels (F3).. 1,347
Salisbury (G4)... 7,553
Savage (E2)..... 1,000
Snow Hill (H4) .. 1,684
Sparrows Point
 (F2).......... 4,800
Takoma Park (D3) 3,168
Texas (E2)...... 1,000
Thurmont (D1)... 1,074
Towson (E2).... 3,700
Union Bridge (D1) 1,082
Western Port
 (B4).......... 3,971
Westminster (E1). 3,521
Westport (E2).... 1,000
Williamsport (C1) 1,615

MASSACHUSETTS

Abington (E2)... ■5,787
Acton (E2) .... ■2,162
Acushnet (F3)... ■3,075
Adams (A1) ....■12,967
Agawam (B2)... ■5,023
Amesbury (E1).. ■10,036
Amherst (C2)... ■5,550
Andover (E1)... ■8,268
Arlington (E2)...■18,665
Arlington Heights
 (E2)........... 2,200
Ashburnham (D1) ■2,012
Ashland (E2).... ■2,287
Athol (C1)...... ■9,792
Attleboro (E3)...19,731
Auburn (D2).... ■3,891
Auburndale (E2) . 2,500
Avon (E2)...... ■2,176
Ayer (D1)....... ■3,052
Baldwinsville (C1) 1,700
Barnstable (G3)..■4,836
Barre (C2)...... ■3,357
Bedford (E1) ... ■1,362
Belchertown (B2) ■2,058
Bellingham (D2) . ■2,102
Belmont (E2)...■10,749
Beverly (F1)....22,561
Beverly Farms
 (F1)........... 950
Billerica (E1)... ■3,646
Blackstone (E2).. ■4,299
Bondsville (C2)... 1,750
BOSTON (F2)..748,060
Bourne (F3).... ■2,530
Braintree (F2)...■10,580
Bridgewater (F3).■8,438
Brockton (E2)...66,254
Brookfield (C2).. ■2,216
Brookline (E2)...■37,748
Byfield (F1).... 880
Cambridge (E2)..109,694
Canton (E2).... ■5,945
Chatham (G3)... ■1,737
Chelmsford (E1)..■5,682
Chelsea (E2)....43,184
Cherry Valley
 (D2).......... 1,200
Cheshire (A1)... ■1,476
Chester (B2).... ■1,302
Chicopee (B2)...36,214
Chicopee Falls
 (B2).......... 8,500
Cliftondale (E2) . ■3,500
Clinton (D2)... ■12,979
Cochituate (E2)... 1,300
Cohasset (F2)... ■2,639
Colerain (B1)... ■1,607
Collinsville (E2).. 1,850
Concord (E2)... ■6,461
Concord Jct. (E2) 1,850
Dalton (A2).... ■3,752
Danvers (F1)...■11,108
Danversport (F1) 1,000
Dartmouth (E3).. ■6,493
Dedham (E2)...■10,792
Deerfield (B1)... ■2,803
Dennis (G3)..... ■1,536
Dighton (E3).... ■2,574
Douglass (D2)... ■2,181
Dracut (E1).... ■5,280
Dudley (D2).... ■3,701
Duxbury (F2).... ■1,533
E. Braintree (E2).. 1,200
East Bridgewater
 (F2).......... ■3,486
E. Dedham (E2).. 3,800
E. Douglass (D2).. 1,500
Easthampton(B2)■11,261
E. Lexington (E2) . 840
East Milton (E2).. 2,000
E. Pepperell (D1) 2,400
E. Saugus (F2).... 960

E. Taunton (E3).. 900
E. Walpole (E2)... 900
E. Weymouth (F2) 4,000
Edgartown (F4).. ■1,190
Erving (C1)..... ■1,295
Essex (F1)...... ■1,478
Everett (E2).....40,120
Fairhaven (F3)... ■7,291
Fall River (E3) . 120,485
Falmouth (F3).. ■3,500
Fiskdale (C2).... 1,200
Fitchburg (D1)...41,029
Florence (B2).... 2,400
Foxboro (E2).... ■4,136
Framingham (E2)■17,033
Franklin (E2)... ■6,497
Gardner (C1).... ■16,971
Georgetown (F1).. ■2,004
Gilbertville (C2).. 2,250
Globe Village (C2). 2,300
Gloucester (F1).. 22,947
Grafton (D2).... ■6,887
Graniteville (E1)... 1,200
Great Barrington
 (A2).......... 6,315
Greenfield (B1) . ■15,462
Groton (D1).... ■2,185
Groveland (F1).. ■2,650
Hadley (B2)..... ■2,784
Hamilton (F1)... ■1,631
Hanover (E2)... ■2,575
Hanson (F2).... ■1,900
Hardwick (C2)... ■3,085
Harvard (D1).... ■2,546
Harwich (C3).... ■1,846
Hatfield (B2)... ■2,651
Haverhill (E1)... 53,884
Haydenville (B2).. 1,100
Hingham (F2).. ■5,604
Hinsdale (A2)... ■1,065
Holbrook (F2)... ■3,161
Holden (D2).... ■2,970
Holliston (E2)... ■2,707
Holyoke (B2)... 60,203
Hopedale (D2)... ■2,777
Hopkinton (E2).. ■2,289
Housatonic (A2).. 2,200
Hudson (D2).... ■7,607
Hull (F2)....... ■1,771
Huntington (B2) ■1,425
Hyannis (G3)... 2,000
Indian Orchard
 (C2).......... 7,500
Ipswich (F1).... ■6,201
Jefferson (D2)... 900
Kingston (F3)... ■2,505
Lakeville (F3)... ■1,419
Lancaster (D2)... ■2,461
Lanesville (F1)... 1,000
Lawrence (E1)...94,270
Lee (A2)....... ■4,085
Leeds (B2)...... 1,100
Leicester (D2)... ■3,635
Lenox (A2)..... ■2,691
Leominster (D1) . 19,744
Lexington (E2)... ■6,350
Lincoln (E2)..... ■1,042
Linwood (D2)... 1,400
Littleton (D1)... ■1,277
Longmeadow (B2).■2,618
Lowell (E1)....112,759
Ludlow (C2).... ■7,470
Luenburg (D1)... ■1,634
Lynn (F2).......99,148
Malden (E2).....49,103
Manchaug (D2)... 1,600
Manchester (F1).. ■2,466
Mansfield (E2)... ■6,255
Marblehead (F1).. ■7,324
Marion (F3)..... ■1,288
Marlboro (D2)...15,028
Marshfield (F2)... ■1,379
Mattapoisett (F3).■1,277
Maynard (D2)... ■7,086

Medfield (E2).... ■3,595
Medford (E2).....39,038
Medway (E2)... ■2,956
Melrose (E2).....18,204
Merrick (B2).... 1,300
Merrimac (E1)... ■2,173
Methuen (E1).. .■15,189
Middleboro (F3)..■8,453
Middleton (E1)... ■1,195
Milford (D2).....13,471
Millbury (D2)... ■5,653
Millis (E2)...... ■1,485
Millville (D2).... 2,224
Milton (E2)..... ■9,382
Mittineague (B2) . 3,000
Monson (C2).... ■4,826
Montague (B1)... ■7,675
Nahant (F2).... ■1,318
Nantucket (G4).. ■2,797
Natick (E2).....■10,907
Needham (E2).. ■7,012
Needham Heights
 (E2).......... 1,700
New Bedford
 (E3)..........121,217
Newbury (F1)... ■1,303
Newburyport
 (F1)..........15,618
Newton (E2)....46,054
Newton Center
 (E2).......... 6,000
Newton Highlands
 (E2).......... 3,000
Newton Lower Falls
 (E2).......... 1,200
Newton Upper Falls
 (E2).......... 2,500
Newtonville (E2).. 6,200
Norfolk (E2).... ■1,159
No. Abington (F2) 2,800
No. Adams (A1) .22,282
Northampton
 (B2)..........21,951
No. Andover (E1) ■6,265
No. Attleboro (E3)■9,238
Northboro (D2)... ■1,753
Northbridge (D2)■10,174
North Brookfield
 (C2).......... ■2,610
North Chelmsford
 (E1).......... 1,700
No. Cohasset (F2). 1,400
North Dartmouth
 (F3).......... 900
No. Dighton (E3) . 900
No. Easton (E2) .. 3,200
Northfield (C1).. ■1,775
No. Grafton (D2) . 2,000
North Leominster
 (D1).......... 900
No. Plymouth (F3). 900
No. Scituate (F2). 1,100
No. Woburn (E1) . 2,000
Norton (E3)..... ■2,374
Norwell (F2)..... ■1,348
Norwood (E2)...■12,627
Oak Bluffs (F4)... ■1,047
Onset (F3)...... 1,600
Orange (C1).... ■5,393
Oxford (D2)..... ■3,820
Palmer (C2).... ■9,896
Peabody (F1)... ■19,552
Pembroke (F2) .. ■1,358
Pepperell (D1)... ■2,468
Pittsfield (A2)...41,763
Plainville (E2)... ■1,365
Plymouth (F3)...13,045
Provincetown (E3)■4,246
Quincy (E2).....47,876
Randolph (F2)... ■4,756
Raynham (E3)... ■1,695
Reading (E1).... ■7,439
Rehoboth (E3)... ■2,065
Revere (F2)......28,823

Descriptive Gazetteer

of the

Principal Countries of the World

ABYSSINIA

The Country. A native kingdom of East Africa, separated from the Red Sea by Italian, French and British colonies; area about 350,000 square miles. It is mainly a plateau varying from 4,000 ft. to 8,000 ft. high. Minerals abound, including gold, silver, iron, rock salt and coal.

Government. Abyssinia is ruled by an emperor and political institutions essentially feudal.

Commerce and Industry. Abyssinia is an agricultural and grazing country varying in climate and products. In the south, cotton does well, while further north, **coffee** is indigenous. Sugar is grown in the south and oranges, indigo and bananas are abundant. The forests produce ebony, mahogany and other hard woods, as well as acacia and bamboo. In the northwest is a district famous for **cattle.** The *exports* mainly consist of coffee, skins and hides, bees-wax, ivory, rubber, butter and herbs.

Communications. The main avenue of trade is the French-Ethiopian Railway which runs from the port of Djibouti, in French Somaliland to the Abyssinian capital, Addis Abeba, a distance of 490 miles. In the West and north, goods are exported via Khartum.

Principal Towns. The principal towns are Addis Abeba, the capital; Harar, Adowa, Gondar, Ankober and Gambela.

AFGHANISTAN

The Country. The length of Afghanistan from the Persian frontier to the Khyber Pass is about 600 miles and the extreme width north to south about 500 miles, estimated area being 245,000 square miles. It is mainly mountainous, broken by deep ravines and fertile valleys.

Government. Afghanistan is an absolute monarchy. The country is divided into provinces, each ruled by a governor responsible to the Ameer.

Commerce and Industry. Climate and products are those of temperate regions, varying in altitude, permitting cultivation in the south of tobacco, cotton and fruits. The spring crop consists of **wheat, barley** and lentils and the autumn harvest produces rice, millet, sorghum, tobacco and corn. Cotton goods, indigo, tea and sugar are the chief articles of import and the wool and skins of fat-tailed sheep, cattle, horses, timber, **fruit, silk** and drugs are the principal exports. Of manufactured articles, silk and carpets are the most important.

Communications. There are no railways in the country. The Khyber and Bolan roads are fit for light-wheeled traffic as far as Kabul and Kandahar, respectively. Merchandise is still transported on camel or pony back. Telephonic communication exists between Dakka, Jelalabad and Kabul, a distance of 136 miles, and it is being extended to Kandahar.

Principal Towns. The principal towns are Kabul, the capital, 6,396 feet above sea level; Herat, the chief town in the west, an important depot for the carpets of central Asia; Kandahar, the chief city in the south; Ghanzi, Jelalabad and Faizabad.

ALBANIA

The Country. Albania is a mountainous country on the western side of the Balkan peninsula, with an area of about 11,000 square miles. It is independent, but under the political influence of Italy. In the center, part of the plateau is cultivable and in the south there is fertile alluvial soil with grazing land on the slopes. Saseno Island, off the Albanian coast, forms the Gibraltar of the Adriatic.

Commerce and Industry. Albania has little outside trade. **Tobacco,** wool and **olive oil** are the principal products. Forests are scarce but as for minerals, Albania possesses silver, copper, gold and lead. There is little agriculture, but in a few districts, fair crops of corn are raised and olives, mulberries and other fruits are grown. Flocks and herds provide the main subsistence of the people.

Communications. Northern Albania has one road connecting Durazzo and Tirana with Scutari. Central Albania has no roads but some military roads have been constructed in the south.

Principal Towns. The principal towns are Durazzo, a port and the provisional capital; Scutari, Elbassan, Tirana, the port Avlona (Valona) and Goritza (Korytsa.)

ANDORRA

The Country. A small republic in the eastern Pyrenees, with an area of about 190 square miles.

Government. Andorra is under the joint suzerainty of the president of France and the bishop of Urgel and its government is intrusted to a council of twenty-four members, holding office for four years, who elect the first and second syndic to preside. The executive power rests with the first syndic while the civil judge and two magistrats alternately exercise judicial power.

Commerce and Industry. Agriculture thrives where the soil is suited to tillage, rye, barley, vines and **tobacco** being cultivated. There is also some mineral wealth, especially iron and lead. Transport difficulties make exploitation doubtful. The inhabitants pay much attention to stock-breeding. **Principal Town:** Andorra la Vieja.

ARGENTINA

The Country. A South American republic with an area of about 1,153,119 square miles. The republic measures about twenty-three hundred miles from north to south. It is mountainous toward the west and the mountains extend to the Western Andes. The remainder of the surface consists of grassy plains, forested hills, drained by the Parana, Plata, Colorado and other rivers flowing into the Atlantic.

Government. The constitution of the Argentine Confederation resembles that of the United States. The republic consists of 14 provinces, 10 territories and one federal district. The provinces elect their own governors and legislatures. The territories are under governors appointed by the president. The executive power, which is practically independent of the legislature, is in the hands of a president elected for six years by electors appointed by the provinces. The national congress consists of a senate and a house of deputies. There are 30 senators, two elected by each province and two by the capital; one-third of the senate is renewed every three years. The 120 deputies are elected directly by the people for four years, but half the house retires every two years. Justice is administered by a federal court of five judges which sits at Buenos Aires, four appeal courts with three judges each at Buenos Aires, La Plata, Cordoba and Parana, and provincial and a number of minor courts. Each province has formulated its own judicial system.

Commerce and Industry. Argentina is in the forefront among the countries in exporting food and raw materials such as **wheat, corn, linseed,** oats, **alfalfa,** wool, chilled or **frozen meat** and hides. Tobacco-growing is not inconsiderable and cotton-growing is increasing. The northern forests supply hard quebracho, excellent for building but also exported for use in tanning. Textiles, food-stuffs, iron, glassware and oil are the chief articles of import. The metric system of weights and measures is compulsory.

Communications. There are about 25,000 miles of railways in operation, about one-third of which are owned by the government. The rivers Parana, Plata, and Uruguay also form important means of communication. There is an excellent postal, telegraph and telephone system and cable communication with all parts of the world.

Principal Towns. Buenos Aires, the capital; Rosario, Cordoba, Tucuman, Santa Fe, Mendoza, La Plata, and Bahia Blanca.

AUSTRALIA

The Country. Australia may be considered the largest island and the smallest continent in the world. It is the greatest isolated mass of land south of the equator. Its total area, including the island of Tasmania, is 2,974,581 square miles, with a coastline of about 8,800 miles. Its extreme measurements are from Cape York in the north to Wilson's Promontory in the south, about 2,000 miles and from Steep Point in the west to Cape Byron in the east, 2,450 miles. Its climate is partly temperate and partly sub-tropical. Tasmania, the island of the southeast, is the most temperate area, with a climate similar to that of Ireland. A series of highlands runs along the eastern and northeastern shores of Australia; coastal plains are the feature of the southeastern littoral, which broaden out in the eastern half of the interior into a great plain through which flow the main rivers of New South Wales, Victoria and South Australia—the Darling, Murrumbidgee and Murray. This plain covers nearly the whole of New South Wales and adjacent parts of Queensland and Victoria. Another large plain stretches inland along the Great Bight in the south, but both middle and southern plains give way to the western plateau, which reaches from the Indian Ocean to the Eyria Peninsula and comprises over half the continent. Although the Darling, Murrumbidgee and Murray water the great area of the

eastern plains, and are both navigable and irrigable for hundreds of miles, the western half of the continent is almost waterless. The soil is generally fertile—even in the most arid districts a heavy rainfall favors a rapid growth of vegetation—but while the eastern shores are washed by a warm ocean current from the north, the western shores are washed by a cold current from the Antarctic Ocean. The eastern half is visited at intervals of every few years by droughts causing heavy loss and suffering. In the northern tropical belt, where several short but torrential rivers run into the sea, growth is again luxuriant; but the whole of this great district, potentially wealthy in minerals as well as in pasture and arable land, awaits development. The eastern plains form one of the great stock-raising districts of the world.

Government. The Commonwealth of Australia is divided politically into five states: New South Wales, Western Australia, Southern Australia, Victoria and Queensland and two territories, the Northern Territory and the Federal Capital Territory, which, with Tasmania, constitute the Commonwealth. Australia is a self-governing dominion of the British Empire and its constitution is defined by the Commonwealth of Australia Constitution Act as "an indissoluble Federal Commonwealth under the Crown of the United Kingdom." It is governed, like other British dominions, by a governor-general appointed by and responsible to the crown; the governor-general is assisted by an advisory federal executive council—in practice, the commonwealth cabinet of the day. The Australian parliament consists of two houses, called the senate and the house of representatives. In the theory of the constitution the senate represents the states, and the house of representatives the people, as in the U. S. A.; but the senators in Australia are elected directly by the people.

Commerce and Industry. There are no native cattle, sheep, horses, or pigs. The main industry is the production of **wool.** General agriculture has long been the second industry, and **wheat** is grown for export. In recent years wines have become an important subsidiary industry. The soil of many districts, particularly in South Australia, Victoria and New South Wales, is suitable to the grape. The discovery of gold in Victoria first called attention to Australian minerals. Before this, copper and coal had been mined to some extent, but it was the sensational finds of gold in Victoria that induced the great stream of immigration. Since then large quantities of gold have been found in Western Australia, enormous deposits of silver at Broken Hill in New South Wales, and other metals elsewhere. Australia is now one of the great metal-producing countries of the world, both for precious and base, and the extent of the deposits, particularly in Queensland and the Northern Territory, is still imperfectly known. *Agricultural products:* **wheat,** oats, barley, corn, hay, potatoes, sugarcane, beet sugar, wine and fruit. *Mineral output:* **gold,** lead, **silver,** copper, zinc and tin. *Imports:* textiles, yarns, woolen, all other apparel (including boots), bags and sacks, cotton piece goods and other textiles, manufactures of metal, agricultural machinery, other machinery, iron and steel, plate and sheet, tinned plates, vehicles and parts, paper and paper boards, drugs, chemicals and fertilizers, oils and waxes, tobacco, alcoholic liquors, and sugar. *Exports:* wool, wheat, flour, skins and hides, tinned meat, butter, **beef,** copper ingots and bars, leather products, tallow, silver, jams and jellies, metal products, mutton and lamb, dry chemicals and fertilisers, milk, tin ingots, coal and zinc concentrates.

Communications. Government railways, miles open 23,295. Private railways in commonwealth, open for general traffic, 968 miles.

Principal Towns. Melbourne, present capital until the Canberra site is ready for the new capital; Ballarat, gold field center; Bendigo, quartz crushing; Sydney, capital of New South Wales with Port Jackson, one of the world's most convenient harbors; Parramatta, in the orange district; Newcastle, coal-mining town and place of coal export; Brisbane, capital of Queensland, important port; Adelaide, one of chief ports and capital of South Australia; Perth, capital of Western Australia; Fremantle, port for Perth; Albany, port; Hobart, capital of Tasmania, important port.

AUSTRIA

The Country. The Austrian republic consists roughly of the German-speaking portion of what was Austria in the dual monarchy of Austria-Hungary. The approximate area of the country is about 30,766 square miles. A large part of the Alps lies in that part of western Austria called the Tyrol. Eastern Austria is in the valley of the Danube river and its branches.

Government. A national constitutional assembly consisting of a single chamber, is elected by universal suffrage. In each of the seven provinces, there is a provincial assembly consisting likewise of one chamber which is elected on the basis of the same suffrage as the national assembly.

Commerce and Industry. Agriculture predominates, but there is some forestry and stockbreeding. Manufactures include cottons, woollens, glass, woodwork, pianos, motor cars, etc. The country has not been deprived of all minerals and is producing lignite, anthracite, and iron ore in considerable quantities. Some copper, zinc, silver and gold ore, lead and salt are also produced. Chief *imports* are coal, iron and food stuffs. Weights and measures—metric system.

Communications. Although now a land-locked state, Austria was accorded free access by rail to the Adriatic. The Danube river is internationalized from the Ulm to the Black Sea. There are about 4,000 miles of railroads and an elaborate telephone system.

Principal Towns. Vienna, the capital; Gratz, Linz, Innsbruck, Salzburg, Wiener-Neustadt and Klagenfurt.

BELGIUM

The Country. Belgium is the most densely populated country in Europe, occupying an area of 11,373 square miles. In the Ardennes, which include parts of the provinces of Namur, Luxemburg and Liege, the average elevation is about 500 feet while the highest points attain an altitude of little over 2,000 feet. The country is well watered, but its two principal rivers, the Schelde and the Meuse, are Belgian only in part. Their affluents, however, are for the greater part held by Belgium and those of the Schelde are the more important of the two. Four-fifths of the land is under cultivation and more people are employed on the land than in all the trades, including mines.

Government. Belgium is a constitutional and hereditary monarchy. The legislative power is vested in the chamber of representatives and the senate, whose members are elected partly directly and partly indirectly.

Commerce and Industry. While Belgium is a great agricultural country, its prosperity is in scarcely less degree the result of industrial activity. The principal manufactures are **lace, iron work,** locomotives and steam engines, motor cars, **arms,** bronze, **porcelain,** glass, etc. Belgium is rich in minerals including valuable zinc and coal mines. Metric weights and measures.

Communications. The railway system is the oldest on the continent, total mileage 6,600. With few exceptions all railways are owned by the state. There are more than fifty canals, with a total length of over 3,000 miles, and five ship canals.

Principal Towns. Brussels, the capital; Antwerp, Liege, and Ghent.

Dependencies. *Belgian Kongo* in central Africa, with an area of 909,654 square miles. This colony is of great importance to the mother country owing to its great yield of rubber, palm nuts and palm oil. Principal towns are Leopoldville and Boma, the capital and seaport.

BOLIVIA

The Country. The area of the republic of Bolivia is estimated at about 514,155 square miles. Cut off from direct access to the sea, it is the most sparsely populated of any of the South American republics. The northern part is the more inhabited, as it contains the Lake of Titicaca and many well-watered valleys around it. The southern and lower tableland is chiefly a desert.

Government. The president is elected by direct popular vote for four years; the chamber of deputies, 68 in number, also for four years, one-half the deputies retiring every two years; the senators, 16 in number, two for each department, are elected for six years, one-third retiring every two years. There are two capitals, an arrangement due to early local rivalries. La Paz is the seat of the executive and legislature. The supreme tribunal sits at Sucre, which is also the seat of the archbishop.

Commerce and Industry. The chief *imports* are provisions, hardware, wines and spirits, cotton, woolen, linen and silk goods, and ready-made clothes. The chief *exports* are silver, tin and rubber. There is scarcely any food export. The metric system of weights and measures is in use.

Communications. Three railways descend from the highlands to the Chilean ports of Antofagasta and Arica and to the Peruvian port of Mollendo, the total railway mileage being about 1,500 miles. Rubber and timber of the eastern forests are carried to the Amazon and Atlantic by Brazilian rail and river. Southern Bolivia has an outlet by way of Tupiza to the Argentine railway system. Notwithstanding the extensive navigable waters and a considerable extent of roads, partly admitting slow motor traffic, internal communication is very defective.

Principal Towns. La Paz, the actual seat of government; Sucre, the capital; Cochabamba, Potosi, Oruro, Santa Cruz, and Trinidad.

BRAZIL

The Country. Brazil occupies more than half of the South American continent, an area of 3,275,510 square miles and is the largest of the South American republics. From north to south, the extreme measure of her territory is 2,630 miles; from east to west it is even greater. On the north and west are the great depressions of the Amazon and Paraguay rivers which comprise large areas of flood-plains and swamps, heavily wooded, and almost uninhabitable. The interior of the country is a high plateau with a general elevation of 1,000 to 3,000 feet, irregularly ridged by mountains and deeply cut by large rivers. The mountainous ranges of the maritime system form the eastern margin of this plateau. Brazil possesses three great river-systems—the Amazon, Plata, and San Francisco. The Amazon and its tributaries drain fully half of the country. The Plata system drains nearly one-fifth of the country through its three branches—the Paraguay, Parana, and Uruguay. Only the first of these is freely navigable for a long distance.

Government. The United States of Brazil constitute a federal republic, having a general resemblance to the constitution of the United States of America, but with one notable difference. The Brazilian states have severally the right of levying export duties—a concession to local sentiment. The country is divided into twenty states, one national territory, and one federal district, which includes the capital. The president is elected for four years by direct popular vote. The chamber of deputies contains 212 members; elected for three years. The 63 senators, three for each state and three for the federal district, are elected for nine years, one-third retiring every three years.

Commerce and Industry. Agriculture continues to hold first place in Brazil and the industries are related closely to agriculture. Brazil is the chief **coffee** producer of the world and the next natural product is **rubber.** Rice, cotton, sugar, tobacco, Paraguay tea and cacao are important products. Textiles amount to about forty per cent of the total manufactured articles. Both the forests and mines of Brazil are important. Gold is found and the greater part of the world's supply of monazite comes from Brazil. There has been lumber development in recent years. Pine has become an important export. Other exports are mica and talc, copper ore, platinum and rock crystal. The metric system of weights and measures is compulsory, but nevertheless certain local units are still used.

Communications. About 20,000 miles of railways are open for traffic. While many of these are short lines connecting the several ports with towns in the interior, the entire system now joins the railways of Brazil with those of Uruguay, Argentina and Paraguay. The republic has over 10,000 miles of navigable waterways open to river steamers and ocean-going vessels and 20,000 miles additional which are navigable for light-draft and flat-bottom boats only.

Principal Towns. Rio de Janeiro, the capital; São Paulo, Bahia, Pernambuco, Para (Belem), Porto Alegre, Manaos and Parahiba.

BRITISH EMPIRE
BRITISH ISLES
AND DEPENDENCIES IN EUROPE

The Countries. The British Isles comprise the United Kingdom, Northern Ireland and the Irish Free State. The governmental functions of Northern Ireland and the Irish Free State are treated under these respective headings. The Kingdom of Great Britain and the Irish Free State have an area of 121,633 square miles. Within the small compass of the islands there is a considerable variety of topography. *Ireland* is largely an ill-drained plain, dotted with lakes and peat-bogs, and crossed by the

sluggish Shannon. In the north-west and south-west respectively lie the mountains of Donegal and Kerry, while to the east lie the Wicklow Mountains, and the basalt plateau of Antrim. In Scotland three well-marked divisions stand out: the highlands, the southern uplands and between these two the central lowlands, into which four-fifths of the population is crowded. The lowlands contain the richest agricultural land, as well as the coal-fields. They are penetrated by three great estuaries, the Firths of Tay and Forth on the east, and of Clyde on the west, so that communication coast-wise or over-seas is everywhere easy. The *Welsh* upland is flanked to north and east by small coal-fields, but the greatest field, rich in steam coal and anthracite, lies to the south. A belt of limestone running from Bill of Portland to Tees Bay, and bearing at many points valuable iron ores, serves as a rough boundary of industrial *England*, for to the south and east of it, apart from the metropolis, agricultural interests predominate. Lying to the west of the limestone band, is the Devon-Cornwall peninsula, where great bosses of granite and slate build the famous moors. The Channel Islands, lying across the English Channel off the coast of Normandy, and the Scilly Islands, lying south-west of Land's End, enjoy an almost complete freedom from frost and severe weather.

Government. The government is vested in crown and parliament. **England** is united with Wales in a system of local government, for the purposes of which the country is divided into fifty administrative counties, in each of which the crown is represented by a local lord-lieutenant. County affairs are administered by justices of the peace and county councils. In certain matters, for instance, education, Wales and Monmouthshire have a distinct organization. There is also a Welsh board of health with headquarters at Cardiff. The **Isle of Man** has a governor appointed by the Crown and its own laws and government. For the general control of Scottish affairs by the government, there is a secretary for **Scotland,** who does not rank as a secretary of state. Certain British state departments, e.g., the home office and board of trade, have authority in Scotland, but for other branches of public work there are separate Scottish departments, these including education, agriculture, and health.

Commerce and Industry. The kingdom owes to its mineral wealth the basis of its prosperity. **Soft coal** of the finest quality underlies central England and Wales; **iron** abounds in the same regions, and in Scotland and Ireland; tin has been mined in Cornwall since pre-historic times, and zinc, copper, gold and silver, with a large range of non-metallic minerals, are also present. Fisheries are conducted on an extensive scale and furnish a large proportion of the food of the people. The climate favors the breeding of horses, cattle and sheep, and the development of certain breeds has greatly improved the livestock of the world. About half of the total area is devoted to agriculture but the total product is insufficient for home demands. The vast supplies of coal, the geographical situation, and the deficiency in agricultural resources, have combined to favor and force an industrial development. Great Britain maintains supremacy in ship-building and naval equipment and ranges among the greatest producers of iron and steel, machinery, metallic goods, textiles and leather goods. The majority of the population is employed in these industries, for which markets are found in all parts of the world.

British Empire—Continued—

Communications. There are about 24,000 miles of railways, and 4,700 miles of canals. The Manchester Ship Canal, opened in 1894, is $35\frac{1}{2}$ miles in length and 28 feet in depth. The canal is in direct communication with all the principal railway systems and barge canals of the Kingdom.

Principal Towns. London, the capital, is the largest city of Europe; Edinburgh, the capital of Scotland; Dublin, capital of the Irish Free State; Glasgow, famous for its shipbuilding, general manufactures and great shipping trade; Manchester, the great cotton manufacturing center, connected with the great port of Liverpool by a ship-canal. Birmingham, Sheffield, and Wolverhampton, manufacturing centers for machinery, cutlery and hardware; Belfast, the capital of Northern Ireland, is the seat of the Irish linen trade and of shipbuilding interests; Leeds and Bradford, woolen centers; Bristol a manufacturing and commercial port; Hull and Dundee, important fishing centers; Newcastle and the Tyne ports, coal exporters; Nottingham, noted for laces, curtains, boots and shoes; Cardiff and Swansea, the chief Welsh ports, exporting immense quantities of coal and ore.

DEPENDENCIES

The Countries. Consist of the Island of Malta in the Mediterranean and Gibraltar.

Government. Malta has a legislature for local affairs, consisting of 32 members and a senate of 17 members, while Gibraltar is administered by a governor who is commander-in-chief and exercises all functions of civil government and legislation.

Malta. An island south of Sicily, with an area of $91\frac{1}{2}$ square miles; total area with the neighboring dependent island 118 square miles. Chief products: wheat, barley, potatoes and fruit. Considerable fishing industry. Chief town and port, Valletta.

Gibraltar. A naval base commanding the entrance to the Mediterranean from the Atlantic Ocean and position of great importance. Area $1\frac{1}{2}$ square miles. The trade is chiefly transit trade.

BRITISH DEPENDENCIES IN AFRICA

The Countries. Consist of a number of colonies, protectorates, provinces, territories, islands and groups of islands, the chartered territory of Rhodesia, the self-governing Union of South Africa. The last and the independent kingdom of Egypt are described under their own headings.

Government. Constitution of British Empire is largely unwritten, but administration is based on three principles: self-government, wherever and whenever practicable, self-support and self-defence. The dependencies in Africa, apart from the self-governing Union of South Africa, are administered:

1. By legislative assembly, partly or entirely elected, and an executive council nominated by the crown, e.g., Mauritius.

2. By a governor with executive and (or) legislative councils nominated by the Crown, e.g., Gambia, Sierra Leone, Gold Coast, Seychelles.

3. By a governor alone, e.g., St. Helena, Bechuanaland, Basutoland.

4. By governors or commissioners under the Colonial Office, with nominated advisory or executive councils, e.g.,

Nigeria, Kenya, Togoland, Tanganyika, Uganda, Zanzibar, Nyasaland, Somaliland, Swaziland.

In the protectorates and colonies native kings and chiefs are encouraged to govern their own people, and native laws and customs are respected unless they conflict with justice or morality. Rhodesia is under the administration of the British South Africa Company; the British government is represented by a resident commissioner who acts on behalf of the high commissioner of South Africa. Southern Rhodesia is presided over by an administrator assisted by an executive council.

Anglo-Egyptian Sudan. Consists of fifteen provinces under military governors. Area about 1,014,000 square miles. Principal source of world supply of gum arabic and ivory. Cotton growing important. Principal Towns: Khartum, the capital; Omdurman, Meroe, Suakin, El-Obeid.

Ascension Island in South Atlantic, under control of British Admiralty. Area, 34 square miles. Garrison station, Georgetown.

Basutoland (Territory). Area 11,716 square miles. Produces cattle, wool, wheat, maize and Kaffir corn. Capital, Maseru.

Bechuanaland (Protectorate). Area about 275,000 square miles. Administered by Union of South Africa. Cattle rearing is principal industry. Headquarters of administration at Mafeking, Transvaal. Principal Towns: Serowe, Francistown.

Gambia (Colony and Protectorate). Area of colony proper, St. Mary Island, four square miles. Protectorate, 4,500 square miles. Capital, Bathurst.

Gold Coast (Colony) with *Ashanti* and *Northern Territories*. Area about 80,000 square miles. Chief products, cocoa (about half world's supply), gold, palm oil and kernels, kola nuts, manganese and timber. Akkra is centre of government. Other important towns, Kumassi, Cape Coast-Castle, Sekondi and Axim.

Kamerun (Colony) formerly German Protectorate. Area 191,300 square miles, divided into French and British spheres. British sphere, a strip of 28,000 square miles, on Nigerian eastern border. Rich in forest produce. Capital, Buea.

Kenya (Crown Colony and Protectorate). Area, 245,060 square miles. Rice, corn, cassava, cocoanuts and other tropical products grown on lowlands; wheat, sheep, ostrich and dairy farming thrive on highlands. Forests contain many valuable species of wood. Chief port, Mombasa, capital, with fine harbor. Other towns, Nairobi, Kismayu and Lamu.

Mauritius, with dependencies *Rodriguez, Diego Garcia* and seven other islands in Indian Ocean, east of Madagascar. Area about 809 square miles. Produces sugar, fibre, cocoanut oil. Capital, Port Louis.

Nigeria (Colony and Protectorate). Area about 336,000 square miles. Chief products, palm oil, palm kernels, ground nuts, cocoa, rubber, cotton, hides. Tin fields (about 9,000 square miles in Northern Provinces). Large coal fields. Lagos is seat of government. Other trade centers are Kano, Wari, and Opobo.

Nyasaland Protectorate. Formerly British Central Africa. Area about 39,573 square miles. Produces cotton, tobacco, ground nuts and tea. Principal Towns: Zomba, the seat of government; Blantyre, Kotakota and Fort Johnston.

Rhodesia. Area about 440,000 square miles, extending from the Union of South Africa to the Belgian Kongo.

British Empire—Continued—

Principal products: Great mineral wealth, including gold, silver, copper, chrome iron, lead and coal. Corn, tobacco, and oranges are grown. Principal Towns: Livingstone, the capital of Northern Rhodesia; Salisbury, the capital of Southern Rhodesia; Bulawayo, Hartley, Gatooma and Victoria.

St. Helena, solitary island in South Atlantic, 1,200 miles from west coast of Africa. Area, 47 square miles. Industry, flax. Capital, Jamestown.

Seychelles, about 90 islands in Indian Ocean. Total area estimated at 156 square miles. Chief products, cocoanuts, vanilla and cinnamon.

Sierra Leone (Crown Colony and Protectorate). Area about 31,000 square miles. Produces palm kernels, palm oil, ginger, kola nuts and piassaba. Principal Town: Freetown, capital and greatest seaport in West Africa.

Somaliland Protectorate. Area about 68,000 square miles. Exports, hides, gums, cattle and sheep. Principal Town: Berbera.

Swaziland (Protectorate). Area, 6,678 square miles. Excellent grazing grounds, and large cattle ranches. Sheep brought in large numbers from Transvaal for winter grazing. Rich mineral deposits; tin exported. Gold, coal, and copper also exist.

Tanganyika Territory (formerly German East Africa), divided between British and Belgians. Area estimated at 365,000 square miles. Native products as in Kenya. European planters grow rubber, sisal, coffee, cotton, rice, sugar, etc. Chief ports, Dar-es-Salaam (capital), Tanga, Bagamoyo, Kilwa Kivinje, Ujiji.

Togo (Colony), formerly German, now under joint Franco-British administration. Total area about 33,700 square miles, of which 12,500 square miles on Gold Coast borders is British. Abundantly cultivated; products similar to those of Gold Coast. Capital, Lome.

Uganda (Protectorate). Area 109,119 square miles. Chief products, cotton, coffee, oil seeds, ivory and hides. British headquarters, Entebbe.

Zanzibar (Protectorate) and **Pemba.** Two coralline islands, area 640 square miles and 380 square miles, respectively. Under a sultan and British commissioner. Clove industry is practically a world monopoly. Cocoanut industry also of great importance. Zanzibar is one of the finest ports in Africa.

BRITISH DEPENDENCIES IN AMERICA

The Countries. In addition to Canada, described separately, the British dependencies in America consist of the Archipelago of West Indies, Bermuda, Falkland Islands, British Guiana, British Honduras and Newfoundland with Labrador.

Government. All the islands and territories are crown colonies, and the crown is represented by governors. Representative government, with partially or wholly elected legislative councils or executives, exists in Bermuda, Bahamas, Barbados, Jamaica, Leeward Islands (except Antigua and Dominica), and Newfoundland. In Windward Islands each island has its own institutions, semi-elective in Grenada and by nominated council in St. Lucia and St. Vincent. Falkland Islands, British Honduras and Trinidad are ruled by governors with nominated councils. In Newfoundland the governor is assisted by an executive council, a legislative council and an elected house of assembly consisting of 36 representatives.

Bahamas. Twenty inhabited and large number of uninhabited islands. Principal island, New Providence. Area about 4,404 square miles. Chief industries, sponges and sisal, also pearls, ambergris, and fruit. Capital, Nassau.

Barbados. Area, 166 square miles. Staple products, sugar and cotton. Capital, Bridgetown.

Bermuda Islands. About 300 islands (twenty inhabited). Area, 19 square miles. Principal products are onions, potatoes, lily bulbs and garden vegetables. Capital, Hamilton.

British Guiana. Area, 89,500 square miles. Principal products are sugar cane, rice, cocoanuts, coffee, para rubber; also livestock. British Guiana is rich in gold and manganese ore and mica deposits have also been found. Capital, Georgetown.

British Honduras. Area, 8,598 square miles. Noted for mahogany and logwood production, also bananas, coffee, cocoa, etc. Capital, Belize.

Falkland Islands. East and West Falkland (about 5,300 square miles), and about one hundred small islands; total area, 6,500 square miles. Also dependencies of South Georgia (estimated 1,000 square miles), South Shetlands, South Orkneys, Sandwich group, and Graham Land (Antarctic). Principal products are whale and whale produce. Chief industries, sheep farming and horse breeding. Capital, Port Stanley.

Jamaica. Area, 4,207 square miles, with *Turks* and *Caicos Islands* (170 square miles), *Cayman Islands* (89 square miles), *Morant Cays*, and *Pedro Cays*. Principal products, sugar, bananas, rum, cocoanuts, logwood, coffee, and cocoa. Chief industry in Turks' Islands, is salt raking; in Caymans, cocoanut planting. Principal Towns: Kingston, capital; Spanish Town, Port Antonio.

Leeward Islands comprise five presidencies, as follows: *Antigua* (170 square miles), with *Barbuda* and *Redonda*. Produce sugar, cotton, and pineapples. Capital, St. John. *St. Kitts* (68 square miles) and *Nevis* (50 square miles), with *Anguilla* (35 square miles). Produce sugar, syrup, and cotton. Capital, Basseterre. *Montserrat.* Area about 32 square miles. Chief products, cotton, lime juice, sugar. Chief town, Plymouth. *Dominica,* about 305 square miles; produces limes and lime products, cocoa, cocoanuts. Chief town, Roseau. *British Virgin Islands,* about 32 of the group are British, remainder belonging to U.S.A. British area, about 58 square miles. Principal islands: Tortola, Virgin Gorda, Anegada. Chief Industry, cotton; copper mine on Virgin Gorda.

Newfoundland and **Labrador,** the latter a political dependency of the former, have a total area of 162,734 square miles. The chief occupation is fishing, dried cod being the leading commercial product, also cod-liver oil. There is a large paper-pulp industry and some mining of iron ore and copper. Principal Towns: St. Johns, the capital; Harbor Grace and Bonavista.

Trinidad. (1,863 square miles), and **Tobago** (114 square miles). Principal products are cocoa, crude petroleum, asphalt from a large asphalt lake and coconuts. Capital, Port of Spain.

Windward Islands consist of three colonies with dependencies as follows: *Grenada.* Area about 133 square miles. Chief products, sugar, rum, cocoa, nutmegs and spices. Chief town, St. George. *St. Vincent.* Area, 150 square miles. Produces fine Sea Island cotton and arrowroot; also sugar, rum, cocoa, and spices. Capital, Kingstown.

British Empire—Continued—
St. Lucia. Area, 233 square miles. Exports: sugar, cocoa, lime juice, molasses, logwood, hides, and fuel.

BRITISH DEPENDENCIES IN ASIA

The Countries. Consists of Aden, Cyprus, Ceylon, Sokotra, Bahrein Islands, British Borneo, Hong Kong, Straits Settlements, Federated Malay States, Mesopotamia and India, with the Andaman, Nicobar, and Laccadive Islands and Burma, a major province of India. India, owing to its importance is described separately.

Government. Aden and its dependencies (Perim, Lahej, Sokotra, and Kuria Muria Islands) are protectorates with political resident; Sokotra having a native sheikh. The Bahrein Islands have native sheikh under British protection. British North Borneo is a protectorate with governor under administration of British North Borneo Company. Brunei has a native sultan. Sarawak is an independent state under British protection with an English raja. British agent for North Borneo and Sarawak and high commissioner for Brunei is the governor of the Straits Settlements. Ceylon, Hong Kong and the Straits Settlements are crown colonies, with a governor and executive and legislative councils. The Federated Malay States have native rulers with British high commissioner and residents; Johore has a sultan, assisted by British adviser and executive and legislative councils. Mesopotamia is an autonomous kingdom under British mandate. Palestine is governed by a high commissioner who appoints an advisory council composed of 4 Moslems, 3 Christians, and 3 Jews.

Aden and Red Sea Territories. Aden. Area of Settlement and Protectorate about 9,000 square miles; town, 75 square miles; Perim Island, 5 square miles. Fortified coaling station; transhipment trade with adjacent coasts. *Sokotra.* Area, 1,400 square miles. Industries, pastoral. Capital, Tamareed. *Kuria Muria Islands.* Area, 29 square miles. Contain guano deposits.

Bahrein Islands. Bahrein Island is 27 miles long by 10 miles broad. *Muharrak* is 4 miles long by about half a mile wide. Pearl fishing important.

British North Borneo. Area, 31,106 square miles. Chief products, timber, rubber, tobacco, rice, sago, spices, cocoanuts, camphor. Principal Towns: Sandakan, Kudat, Tawao.

Ceylon. Area, 25,481 square miles. Ceylon produces about one-sixth of the world's tea. Principal grain is rice. Other products include cocoanuts, coffee, cinnamon, vanilla, areca-nut, tobacco. Forests yield ebony and satinwood. Pearl-fishery in the Gulf of Manar. There are about 700 miles of railways. Principal Towns: Colombo, the capital; Jaffna, Point de Galle, Kandy, Trincomali, a naval station.

Cyprus. The third largest island in the Mediterranean, 40 miles from the coast of Asia Minor. Area, 3,584 square miles. Administered by a high commissioner and an executive council. Cyprus is mainly agricultural. The chief products are wheat, barley, vetches, olives. Sponge fisheries are carried on and marble is found in abundance. The chief exports are animals, lemons and oranges, pomegranates, raisins and wine. Principal Towns: Nicosia, the capital; Larnaca and Limasol.

Federated Malay States. Area, 27,506 square miles. Exports, rubber, copra, tin and tin ore, metals, timber.

Hong Kong. Area of island 32 square miles; with *Kowloon* and *New Territories* about 391 square miles; capital, Victoria. Chief industries: sugar refining, shipbuilding and repairing, ropemaking, tin refining, manufacture of tobacco and cement, and deep-sea fishing. Large trade in sugar, flour, rice, cotton, silk, leather, wolframite, iron and steel goods, tea, oils, matches, etc.

Mesopotamia (Irak). An independent kingdom between the rivers Tigris and Euphrates, under the mandate of Great Britain. The area is 143,250 square miles. It is a land of greatest potentialities, owing to its oil wells and its rich soil, which is being developed by means of irrigation. Principal Towns: Bagdad, the capital and Basra, the seaport at the head of the Persian Gulf.

Palestine. This British mandate has the object to provide for the establishment of the Jewish National Home, without prejudicing the rights of the non-Jewish communities in Palestine. The area is about 9,000 square miles and includes only that part of Palestine which lies west of the Jordan. It is mainly an agricultural country, the principal products being raisins, wine, olives, oranges and some tobacco. Principal Towns: Jerusalem the Holy City of Jews, Moslems and Christians alike, and Yafa, the chief seaport.

Sarawak. Area about 42,000 square miles; capital, Kuching. Large deposits of coal, gold, silver, antimony, mercury; oil-fields also being developed.

Straits Settlements. Consist of *Singapore Island* with small islands adjoining at southeast point of peninsula; *Penang Island* off northwest coast; *Wellesley Province* on northwest mainland; the *Dindings*, including island of *Pangkor* and a strip on the mainland, on west; *Malacca* on southwest coast. Also *Cocos* or *Keeling Islands*, about 700 miles southwest of Sumatra, *Christmas Island*, 200 miles east of Cocos Islands and *Labuan Island*, about 43 miles from Brunei, North Borneo. Total area, 1,600 square miles. *Exports* include tin, rubber, gums, spices, copra, rattans, sago, gambier, tapioca, preserved pineapples, phosphates of lime. Singapore is chief town and seat of government for Straits Settlements and one of the greatest ports in the world.

BRITISH DEPENDENCIES IN OCEANIA

The Countries. Australian Commonwealth (with Tasmania), New Zealand and Pacific Islands. Last only dealt with here. Roughly grouped as Melanesia, Micronesia and Polynesia, they consist of colonies, protectorates and Australian territories, formerly German, with the New Hebrides and Nauru. Total estimated area of the islands discussed here about 208,000 square miles.

Government. British high commissioner for Western Pacific has jurisdiction over the islands, except those assigned by League of Nations to Australia and New Zealand. Papua has a legislative council, partly nominated by governor-general of Australia; New Guinea is administered under Commonwealth laws, as are Papuan Islands. Fiji has governor and legislative council partly elected. Tonga has legislative council on similar lines, but financial affairs are supervised by high commissioner. British policy, as in other parts of the Empire, is to encourage native administration.

Fiji. Crown colony of about 250 islands, 80 inhabited, including *Viti Levu* (area, 4,053 square miles), *Vanua Levu* (area, 2,130 square miles), *Rotuma.* Chief products: sugar, molasses, copra, rubber, bread-fruit, plantains, bananas. Capital, Suva.

British Empire—Continued—

Nauru or Pleasant Island. Formerly German, now administered by Great Britain, Australia, and New Zealand. Small coral island; has valuable deposits of phosphates.

New Britain Archipelago. Formerly Bismarck Archipelago, assigned to Australia. Native industry; cocoanut growing. Total area of islands, about 18,200 square miles.

New Hebrides. Under joint British and French administration. Area, 5,500 square miles. Chief products: copra, maize, cotton, coffee.

Papua (British New Guinea). Australian territory, consists of southeast portion of New Guinea with *D'Entrecasteaux* and *Louisiade* groups. Area, 90,540 square miles. Industries: gold and copper mining, pearlfishing, rubber, cocoanut, sisal-hemp. Trading center: Port Moresby. Northeast portion of New Guinea, formerly Kaiser Wilhelm's Land, is also Australian territory. Area, 70,000 square miles. Chief products; cocoanut, rubber, yams, bananas.

Phoenix Islands. Group of eight small islands. Area, 16 square miles.

Pitcairn Island (Colony). Area, 2 square miles. Chief products: sugar-cane, sweet potatoes, yams, pineapples, bananas, arrowroot and coffee.

Solomon Islands. British Protectorate includes *Guadalcanar, Malayta, San Cristoval, New Georgia, Choiseul, Ysabel,* and *Lord Howe.* Santa Cruz group were added in 1899. *Bougainville,* area 3,500 square miles. *Buka Island,* area 300 square miles; formerly German, assigned to Australia. Total area about 11,000 square miles. Chief products: cocoanuts, rubber, pineapples, bananas.

Tonga or Friendly Islands (Protectorate). Area 385 square miles. Products: copra, kava, green fruit, fungus, candlenuts.

Other Islands. *Gilbert Islands* (Colony), area 166 square miles, produce phosphates, cocoanuts, and pandanus fruit. *Ellice* or *Lagoon* group, area 14 square miles. *Union* or *Tokelau* group, area 7 square miles. *Fanning Island,* area 15 square miles. *Washington Island,* area, 6 square miles. *Christmas Island,* which has valuable phosphate deposits, annexed 1919. Area, about 56 square miles.

BULGARIA

The Country. A Balkan state covering an area of about 40,656 square miles. The country is hilly and well watered by numerous streams of which the Isker, Struma and Maritza are the most important.

Government. Bulgaria is a constitutional monarchy. The legislative authority is vested in a single chamber called the Sobranye or national assembly. The members of it are elected by universal suffrage. For local administration the country is divided into a number of departments, each under a prefect assisted by a departmental council and aided by several sub-prefects.

Commerce and Industry. About five-sevenths of the population are engaged in agriculture. Methods of cultivation are primitive; machinery is being gradually introduced. **Iron** is found in large quantities and the other chief mineral deposits are gold, silver, lead, manganese and copper. Chief manufactures are flour, woolen goods and cotton. **Wheat** and **live stock** are the principal *exports* of the country. The chief *imports* are metal goods, machinery, kerosene, textiles and provisions. The metric system is in general use.

Communications. There are about 1,500 miles of railway in operation in the country of which about 200 are narrow gauge. There are about 3,500 miles of telegraph and about 1,500 miles of telephone lines.

Principal Towns. Sofia, the capital; Philippopolis (Plovdiv), Rustchuk, Varna, Shumla, Slivno and Plevna (Pleven).

CANADA

The Country. The Dominion of Canada consists of Ontario and Quebec, with the maritime provinces of Nova Scotia, New Brunswick, Prince Edward Island, the three prairie provinces of Manitoba, Saskatchewan, Alberta, and British Columbia, Yukon and North-West Territories. Total area, 3,729,665 square miles (water area about 126,000 square miles).

Government. Executive authority vested in governor-general, appointed by the British crown, and executive council; legislative power in federal parliament; governor-general has power of veto, but appeal lies to privy council. Senate of 104 life members may be nominated by governor-general; present number, 96. House of commons with 235 members, to be increased to 241, elected for five years. Women have vote except in Quebec. Nine provinces have local legislatures, and control of administration under lieutenant-governor. Territory of Yukon under chief executive officer and elective council. North West Territories administered by commissioner and nominated council.

Commerce and Industry. Staple industry, agriculture; great wheat belt in prairie provinces; 55,000,000 acres under field crops. Area of land covered by timber between 500,000,000 and 600,000,000 acres. Pulp and paper production important. Mineral products include **gold, silver, nickel,** copper, cobalt, chromite, iron, zinc, lead, coal, **asbestos,** petroleum. Among the producing mines are the great nickel-copper mines of Sudbury, the chief source of the nickel supply of the world; the silver mines of Cobalt, perhaps the richest silver-bearing area of the world; the gold mines of Porcupine, which comprise three of the greatest gold mines of the world; together with important mica, feldspar and talc mines, in Ontario; the asbestos mines of Quebec, the source of most of the asbestos of the world; the coal mines of Nova Scotia and Alberta, and the coal, copper, lead and gold mines of British Columbia. Canada is the principal fur-bearing country. Other industries include fish, chiefly salmon and lobster, and canneries, fruit, wool, tobacco, maple-sugar, and agricultural implements.

Communications. Over 2,700 miles of canal, river, and lake navigation. Eight rivers over 1,000 miles in length, including Mackenzie, St. Lawrence, Nelson, and Saskatchewan. Railway mileage totals about 40,000 miles, half of which is operated by the Dominion government.

Principal Towns. Ottawa, the capital; Montreal, Toronto, Winnipeg, Vancouver, Hamilton, Quebec, Calgary, Halifax, Edmonton, St. John, London, Victoria.

CHILE

The Country. The republic of Chile occupying the western coast of South America from 18° south altitude to Cape Horn, has an area of 289,829 square miles. The average width from east to west is only ninety miles and the length of the coastline is 2,625 miles. For about two-thirds of its total length, the Andean chain borders Chilean territory. In Tierra del Fuego the loftiest peaks barely reach 7,000 ft., but the heights generally increase northwards up to Aconcagua, which exceeds 23,000 ft., the highest peak of the whole continent.

Government. Chile consists of twenty-three provinces and one territory. The administration is highly centralized, the local authorities being controlled by the executive in the capital. The franchise, being confined to property-holders and those able to read and write, is possessed only by a small minority. The president appointed by electors, rules for five years.

Commerce and Industry. The varieties of Chilean products correspond to the immense geographical range. Nitrates, iodine, **copper,** iron, silver, gold, borax and lead from the northern provinces; coal, **wheat,** fruit, wine and pastoral products from central Chile; **timber** from the southern forests; meat and **wool** from the pastures north and south of Strait of Magellan. The chief exports are minerals and pastoral products. The metric system of weights and measures is obligatory.

Communications. There are in Chile 22,000 miles of public road, 850 miles of navigable river and 497 miles of navigable lakes. The Longitudinal Railway of Chile, traversing the republic from north to south over a distance of 2,854 miles, is a government-owned line, embracing with the Arica to La Paz Railway (271 miles) an extent of 3,125 miles. There are also 2,270 miles of privately owned lines, making a total of 5,395 miles.

Principal Towns. Santiago, the capital; Valparaiso, the principal port; Concepcion, Antofagasta, Iquique, Talca and Chillan.

CHINA

The Country. The Chinese Republic comprises the eighteen provinces of China proper, and the provinces of Manchuria, Mongolia, Sinkiang and Tibet. The total area of the republic is estimated at 4,277,170 square miles. China proper is a coastal plain formed by the alluvial valleys of the Hoang, Yangtze and lesser rivers. Manchuria has a similar character, but is separated from Chosen (Korea) and the coast by mountains. Western China and Tibet are a mass of very high mountains containing the sources of all the great rivers of southern Asia.

Government. The government is composed of a president, a vice-president and a bi-cameral legislature assembling at Peking and consisting of a senate (*Tsan Yi Yuan*) of 264 members and a house of representatives (*Chung Yi Yuan*) of 596 members. Executive authority is provisionally vested in a premier nominated by the president and a cabinet of nine ministers nominated by the premier. All appointments require the sanction of both houses of parliament. The qualification for electors is based on property, education or previous official rank.

Commerce and Industry. Silk is one of the most important of Chinese industries and exports. Another famous industry which originated in China is the manufacture of porcelain. The typical native industries still flourishing are lacquer-ware and enamel and cloisonne. Tientsin has a reputation for its carpets and rugs. Fireworks, mats and matting and palm-leaf fans are manufactured. Industries on a large scale are carried on at the open ports; cotton-spinning and weaving at Shanghai, sugar-refining at Canton, iron and steel works at Hanyang, docks, ship-building and engineering works at Shanghai and Han-kau.

Next to India, China is the largest **rice** producing country in the world. Home requirements prevent the exports from being very large. **Wheat,** cotton, corn and **tea** are being cultivated on a large scale and the only food material exported from China on a large scale is the **soya-bean** and its products. In **cotton** growing, China occupies third place in the world's countries. China possesses abundance of coal, including ample quantities of coal suitable for coking, which are found in the vicinity of iron ore deposits. Iron ore is not so plentiful as coal, but although geological research in China is still in its infancy, many deposits of high-grade ore have been located capable of yielding several hundred million tons. China also possesses an abundance of antimony, zinc and lead ores, quicksilver, copper, silver and wolfram ores.

Communications. China has some 8,000 miles of railways open including the foreign system on Chinese territory but much of the internal trade is carried on by means of the numerous canals and navigable rivers.

Principal Towns. Peking, the capital; Han-kau, Shanghai, Canton.

COLOMBIA

The Country. The republic of Colombia occupies the northwestern region of South America. Alone among the South American republics, Colombia has a coastline upon both oceans, its northern shores being washed by the Caribbean Sea, its western shores by the Pacific Ocean. The country lies wholly within the tropics, the equatorial line traversing its southern region. The area is estimated at about 440,846 square miles. The dominating feature of the whole country is the gigantic mountain-system of the Andes.

Government. The president, elected by direct popular vote for a term of four years, possesses large centralised power, particularly through the exercise of official patronage. The senators are elected for four years and the deputies for two years.

Commerce and Industry. Only a small section of the country is under cultivation. Coffee is the staple product. Tobacco is also grown; cotton, cocoa, sugar, vegetable ivory, tagua (or vegetable ivory nut) and dyewoods are produced, besides wheat, corn, plantains, etc. **Banana** cultivation is increasing rapidly. The rubber tree grows wild, and its cultivation has begun. Tolu balsam is cultivated and copaiba trees are tapped but are not cultivated. Dye and cedar woods are abundant on the Magdalena river but little or no wood of any sort is exported. The **Panama hat** industry is making great strides. Colombia is rich in minerals, and gold is found in all parts. Other minerals, more or less worked, are copper, lead, mercury, cinnabar, manganese, **emeralds** and platinum. Nearly all the emeralds mined to-day come from Colombia. The iron works northeast of Bogota are important; in the immediate neighborhood of the works are coal, iron, limestone, sand, manganese and fireclay deposits. The **salt** mines north of Bogota are a government monopoly and a great source of revenue, supplying most of the interior departments. In several sections there are extensive deposits of coal and oil. The metric system of weights and measures is used.

Communications. Colombia cannot be said to possess a railroad system. The few railroads are detached lines uniting important towns to sea or river. The total length of the railroad systems is about one thousand miles. The main channel of communication to the interior is the Magdalena river, whose mouth is blocked by an impassable bar.

Principal Towns. Bogota, the capital, at an elevation of 8,600 feet above the sea; Medellin, Barranquilla, Cartagena an important mining center; Manizales and Bucaramanga, center of coffee production.

COSTA RICA

The Country. A Central American republic with an area of 23,000 square miles. Costa Rica is traversed from northwest to southeast by a chain of mountains (cordillera). The slopes of the mountains are heavily forested, much of the timber consisting of mahogany and other valuable cabinet woods.

Government. Legislative power is vested in the congress, a chamber of 43 deputies, elected by universal suffrage. The president is elected for six years.

Commerce and Industry. The principal industry is agriculture; **coffee** and **bananas** are exported in large quantities, as rosewood, cedar and mahogany; horses, pigs, sheep, and goats are raised in considerable numbers. Gold and silver are mined; and there are deposits of manganese. The metric system is in general use.

Communications. The country has about five hundred miles of railway including one through transcontinental railroad. At Limon there are excellent terminal facilities, with wharves so equipped with track facilities that loading and unloading can be carried on directly from the car to the vessel. At Puntarenas on the Pacific Ocean, the harbor has only fifteen feet of water at low tide, necessitating the handling of cargo by lighters. There are sixteen navigable rivers in the republic, the most important being the San Juan River and its tributaries, which are largely utilized for the transportation of the natural products. There are fifteen hundred miles of telephone lines in operation.

Principal Towns. San Jose, the capital; Cartago, Heredia, Limon, Puntarenas and Alajuela.

CUBA

The Country. Cuba, the largest and westernmost of the West India Islands, has an area of 44,215 square miles, its maximum length east to west is 730 miles and its width varies from 20 to 100 miles, its coast line being about 2,000 miles. It is generally mountainous, though considerable flatlands and marshy depressions extend along the south coast.

Government. Republic, modelled after the system of the United States, with a president, vice-president, senate and a house of representatives. The government of Cuba cannot make a treaty with any foreign government endangering its independence, and the United States has the right of intervention and the use of naval stations.

Commerce and Industry. The foremost crops are **tobacco** and **cane sugar**, the former producing the finest leaf for cigars in the world. Other products are coffee, cacao, cereals, potatoes, market vegetables and fruits, bananas, guavas, oranges, grapes, etc. Cattle-raising in the central and eastern districts is an ancient and extensive industry. The *exports*, largely to the United States, are **sugar, leaf tobacco, cigars,** iron ore, cattle products, forest products, and fruit. The *imports*, also largely from the United States, are meat products, iron and steel manufactures, wheat, lumber and timber products, coal and coke. Copper, iron and manganese mines are worked in the east, and limestone, clays, and asphalt occur in useful quantities.

Extensive forest lands yield mahogany, cedar and other valuable cabinet woods, dyewoods, gums, resins and other tropical forest products. Metric system of weights and measures.

Communications. Cuba has about 2,600 miles of steam railways and 250 miles of electric railways. Through trains run daily between Havana and Santiago and many branch lines from this main trunk connect the principal ports on both the north and south coasts with the interior. The railway system is being supplemented by an elaborate system of highways.

Principal Towns. Havana, the capital; Camaguey, Cienfuegos, Santiago, Guantanamo, Santa Clara, Matanzas, Manzanillo, Pinar del Rio, Sancti Spiritus, Trinidad and Cardenas. Coaling stations at Guantanamo Bay and Bahia Honda were leased to the United States.

CZECHO-SLOVAKIA

The Country. A land-locked state comprising the former Austrian states of Bohemia, Moravia and a part of Silesia, together with the former Hungarian districts of Slovakia and the semi-autonomous Carpatho-Russia or Ruthenia, with an area of 54,264 square miles and about 700 miles in length from east to west. It includes on the west the plateau of Bohemia and on the east the southern slopes of the Carpathians as far as the Danube and the Theiss. The rivers are, with two exceptions, the relatively useless upper courses, *i.e.* of the Elbe, Oder, Vistula, etc. The exceptions are the Moldau (Vltava), which is entirely Bohemian and fragments of the course of the Danube on the south of Slovakia.

Government. The National parliament, which constitutes the only legislative body for the whole of the republic, is composed of a chamber of deputies elected by universal franchise without distinction of sex, for a period of six years and containing 300 members, and of a senate comprising 150 members to be renewed every eight years. The two chambers in joint congress elect the president of the republic for seven years. The constitution safeguards racial minorities to whom it assures the maintenance of their schools.

Commerce and Industry. The principal products of the mines are **coal, lignite, iron,** gold, silver, and graphite. Manufactured products include textiles, shoes, **gloves, glass,** porcelain, sugar, metal goods, foodstuffs, **toys,** etc. Agriculture is highly developed and intensive farming is carried on. The beet-root is the foundation of an enormous sugar industry. Large quantities of fruit are exported. Forests comprise thirty-two per cent. of the whole area, the country ranking among the most richly wooded of Europe. Only metric weights and measures are used.

Communications. There are about 8,300 miles of railways, over half of which are owned by the government. There is no important continuous railway route from east to west; the majority of important lines simply cross the republic to connect German cities and ports with Vienna or Budapest. Traffic on the internationalized Danube is constantly increasing and the government is doing all in its power to develop the Danube ports. The Elbe and Oder are also internationalized and the Peace Treaty vested Czecho-Slovakia with the right to use certain terminal facilities in the German ports of Hamburg and Stettin.

Principal Towns. Prague (Praha), the capital; Brunn (Brno), Pilsen (Plzen), Pressburg (Bratislava).

DANZIG

Danzig, constituted as a Free City ("Freistaat") by the Treaty of Versailles and under the protection of the League of Nations, stands on the delta of the Vistula. The territory included within the administration of the city has an area of about 794 square miles and contains 325 localities. About three thousand steamships use the port annually. Sugar is next in importance to grain, and lumber ranks third as the commodities shipped through Danzig. The City is in fiscal union with Poland and under Polish suzerainty as regards foreign affairs, but German currency is used. Weights and measures are of the metric system.

DENMARK

The Country. Denmark occupies a peninsula and numerous islands between the North and Baltic Seas and its area, including the islands in the Baltic and Faroe Islands is 16,609 square miles. The highest elevation is the Himmelbjurg in Jutland, which is only 560 feet high.

Government. Constitutional monarchy. The *Rigsdag* or diet embraces two houses, the *Folketing* or lower house, and the *Landsting* or senate. The *Folketing*, which consists of 140 members, is elected by universal suffrage (male and female) for a term of four years. The seats allotted to Copenhagen are filled by proportional representation, the remainder, including the Faroe Islands, by simple majority, but a certain number of seats are held by non-elected candidates who have received the largest minority votes and whose parties are not proportionally represented. The *Statsraadet* or cabinet consists of twelve ministers who are individually and collectively responsible to the *Folketing*.

Commerce and Industry. The principal industries of the country have to do with agricultural pursuits. Beet-root, potatoes, barley, wheat, rye, oats and other cereals constitute the chief agricultural products of the country. The live stock and **dairying** industries, the manufacture of margarine and the fisheries are important. The principal *imports* of Denmark are: oil cake and meal, iron, steel, lumber, coal, hardware and machinery, fertilizers, paper, wheat, flour and cotton.

Communications. In the kingdom, 2,635 miles of railway are open for traffic, half of which belong to the state.

Principal Towns. Copenhagen, the capital and great clearing house for all of Scandinavia: Aarhus, Odense, Aalborg, Horsens and Randers.

Colonies. *Greenland* is the only colonial possession of Denmark. The King of Denmark is also King of Iceland, which, however, is independent of Denmark.

DOMINICAN REPUBLIC

The Country. The Dominican Republic embraces the eastern and larger portion of the Island of Haiti. It has an area of 19,332 square miles. Mt. Tina (9,420 ft.) is the highest peak in the island and in the West Indies.

Government. The Dominican Republic is nominally governed by a president elected for six years, and a national congress, consisting of a senate and a chamber of deputies, elected for four years. This system of government obtained until 1916, when the United States set up a government with naval officers at the heads of all departments. In October, 1922, plans for the withdrawal of the American Marines were completed in accordance with a proclamation of the military governor providing for ratification of the laws of American administration in the island, the pro-

visional president to further the restoration of constitutional government through general elections, free from the intervention of military government.

Commerce and Industry. The chief industry is agriculture, the products being **sugar**, tobacco, **cacao**, coffee and cotton. There are large forested tracts throughout the country, yielding enormous quantities of cedar, mahogany, satinwood and dye woods. **Cattle-raising** is extensively carried on and the minerals, although not exploited to any considerable extent, include gold, silver, platinum, quicksilver, coal, iron and rock salt.

Communications. Roads are bad in the interior and transport is difficult; there are only 153 miles of railway in use.

Principal Towns. Santo Domingo, the capital; Puerto Plata, chief north coast port, and Santiago.

ECUADOR

The Country. This South American republic is so named because the equatorial line runs through the country. Its western shores, 500 miles in extent, are washed by the Pacific Ocean. Its area is approximately 116,000 square miles including the Galapagos Islands, in the Pacific Ocean, 600 miles from Ecuador. It contains the volcanoes Chimborazo, Cotopaxi and others of great altitude. The most valuable and productive part of the country is the broad coastal plain.

Government. The president is chosen by direct popular election for four years. The 32 senators and 48 deputies are elected upon a limited franchise which is withheld from illiterates, an arrangement which secures ascendency to the inhabitants of more or less white blood.

Commerce and Industry. The staple products of Ecuador are **cacao** and ivory nuts. Coffee is grown and largely exported. Other products are rubber, **tobacco** and **sugar**. Weaving of **Panama hats** is a considerable industry. Some gold is produced in the Andes. The legal system of weights and measures is metric.

Communications. Roads of the country are mostly bridle roads only, and often impassable for half the year. A railway is open from Guayaquil to Quito, 280 miles. There are also a few short lines connecting important points. Various streams provide access from Guayaquil to a large part of the cacao-bearing region of the southern coastal strip. The lower reaches are navigated by river steamers, the upper waters by canoes and rafts. The Maranon River is navigable in its entirety.

Principal Towns. Quito, the capital; Guayaquil, chief port; Cuenca and Riobamba.

EGYPT

The Country. Area including the Libyan Desert, the region between the Nile and the Red Sea, and Sinai Peninsula, about 350,000 square miles. The Libyan Desert is part of the extensive territory.

Government. Independent sovereign state. Sultan Ahmed Fuad Pasha, proclaimed king March 14, 1922, with cabinet and legislative assembly. The British government proclaimed Egypt a sovereign state, having no connection with the British Empire, and enjoying the same status as any other sovereign state in the world. The British reservations, announced coincident with the withdrawal of the protectorate were: The security of British imperial communication; the defense of Egypt against attack; protection of foreign interests, and retention of Britain's interests in the Sudan.

Commerce and Industry. Chief industry: agriculture. The cultivable area is estimated at about 13,000 square miles. Grain, cotton and sugar are important products. Where, as in Lower Egypt, irrigation is perennial, two and sometimes three crops are secured each year. The date palm is an important growth, and limes, bananas, melons, and olives are cultivated. Oil and tobacco are being exploited, and building stones, clays, gypsum, gold, manganese ores, natron, phosphate of lime, salt, alum, magnesia, and others developed commercially. The leading *exports* are textiles and yarns, cereals and vegetables, and tobacco.

Communications. The Nile is the great highway, and much travelling is done by boat. Exclusive of the Sudan military railway to Khartum, the state-owned railways have over 2,311 miles of track; private companies own over 720 miles of light railways. Since 1918 there has been direct railway communication between Cairo and Palestine. Length of Suez Canal, including approach channels, is 103 miles.

Principal Towns. Cairo, the capital; Alexandria, Port Said, and Ismailia, Tanta, Assiout, Damanhur, Medinet-el-Faiyum, Zagazig, El Minya, Suez and Damietta.

ESTHONIA

The Country. Esthonia comprises the former Russian province of Esthonia, the northern part of Livonia, the northwestern portion of the Pskof government and the Islands Osel (Ezel) and Dago in the Baltic Sea. Its area is 23,160 square miles. Except in the southeast which is hilly, the mainland lies low, much of which is swampy. There are many lakes and about half of Peipus Lake lies within it.

Government. According to the constitution of the republic, the sovereign power is assured to the people by means of the elections to the legislative assembly (*Riigikogu*, the state assembly), the referendum and the right of initiating legislation. The state assembly is composed of 100 members elected for three years on the basis of proportional representation and by universal suffrage. The executive power consists of the state head (*Riigiwanem*, state elder), and ministers who form the government.

Commerce and Industry. Agriculture is the chief occupation of Esthonia. Flax is one of the principal products and the live stock industry is flourishing. Oil-shale in rich quality is plentiful. Principal *exports* are timber, meat, potatoes, flax, and paper. Manufactures include iron, steel, machinery, cotton, paper, wood pulp, and spirits. Principal *imports* are salt, coal, fertilizers and sugar. Metric weights and measures.

Communications. Reval is an important port for the transit of Russian imports and exports. It is also the nearest winter port for Siberian produce. When Petrograd is closed by ice, most of that trade passes through Reval.

Principal Towns. Reval (Tallinn), the capital; Dorpat (Yurief), the university town; Pernau, the port on the Gulf of Riga, and Ivangorod (Narva), manufacturing town.

FINLAND

The Country. Finland comprises the former Grand-Duchy of Finland to which was added through treaty with the Soviet government of Russia, the territory of Petsamo, giving outlet to the Arctic Ocean. The Aland Islands were awarded to Finland by the League of Nations. The total area of Finland is 149,586 square miles. The country consists of a great plateau, the southern half of which has about 25 per cent. of its area occupied by thousands of shallow lakes, many of them linked by short natural and artificial channels.

Government. Republic. The president is elected for six years and the cabinet consists of twelve members, and the house of representatives chosen by direct and proportional election. The suffrage is possessed, with the usual exceptions, by every Finnish citizen (man or woman) who has reached his or her twenty-fourth year. Every citizen entitled to vote is eligible to the house of representatives, which is elected for three years.

Commerce and Industry. Agriculture is the chief occupation of the people, although the cultivated area covers less than 9 per cent. of the land. A considerable part of the population along the coast gains its livelihood from fishing and considerable quantities of **salt fish** are exported to neighboring Baltic countries. **Lumber** is the main industry and the principal basis of the general prosperity of the country. **Butter** is also being exported extensively. Manufactures are well developed, mainly by help of water power. They include engineering, machine and shipbuilding, pulp and paper making, cotton goods and tanning. Metric weights and measures are used.

Communications. The southern half of the country is well served by railways which are linked with those of Russia and those of Sweden, total mileage being about 2,700. Most of the railways are owned by the state. Numerous canals connect the lake districts in the interior with the coast.

Principal Towns. Helsingfors, the capital; Tammerfors (Tampere), Abo (Turku), Viborg and Uleaborg.

FIUME

The Country. This Adriatic seaport was created an independent state by the Treaty of Rapallo (1920), between Italy and the Kingdom of Serbs, Croats, and Slovenes (Jugo-Slavia). Area 8 square miles. Practically all the shipping trade of Hungary passes through its port, and the fisheries are of great importance. Long a small center of coastwise trade, it came into prominence only when the Budapest-Zagreb-Fiume Railway was built. The town possesses distilleries, oil refineries, and mills, while there is trade in fruit, barrels, staves, furniture, tobacco, paper, chemicals, fertilisers and soap.

FRANCE

The Country. France is a republic of western Europe with an area, including Corsica, of 212,659 square miles. The total length of the coastline is about 2,000 miles. The surface is diversified, but most of it is lowland, with a few level plains. In the center is a triangular plateau called the Auvergne Mountains, with a height of something over 3,000 feet. The Cevennes form the eastern edge of this plateau and from them to the Vosges, the tableland continues. There is a mountainous area in Brittany, but the greatest heights are on the frontiers, the Jura separating France from Switzerland, the Pyrenees separating it from Spain, and the Alps separating it from Italy. The Ardennes in the northeast are less lofty. France has few lakes, but in the southwest, there are numerous lagoons. The Seine drains the north, the Loire and the Garonne the west, and the Rhone the east and south.

Government. France is governed by a president and a council of ministers who are responsible to a parliament of two houses called the national assembly. The president is elected by the assembly for seven years. He chooses the ministers, but his functions approximate rather to those of the English king than of the prime minister, although on ceremonial occasions he presides over meetings of the council of ministers. The ministers are the responsible heads of the various departments and it is not necessary for them to be members of the assembly for they can attend and speak in either house when necessary. They are responsible to the parliament and also for all the acts of the president. Their responsibility is collective. Their head is the prime minister who presides over their ordinary deliberations. The senate, or upper house, consists of 314 members. Of these 225 are chosen by indirect election, for nine years, one-third retiring every three years. The remaining 75 are chosen from among the other senators and sit for life. The senate sits in important cases as a high court of justice. The lower house or chamber of deputies, consists of persons directly elected by universal manhood suffrage. They are chosen for four years.

Commerce and Industry. First among the industries of France are fine textile products and the French have a worldwide reputation for fine silks, fine linens, and fine cloths. **Manufactured silk** is by far the largest export and raw silk figures high up in the list. Wine, is of course, prominent, but much more is imported than exported. French coal mines, of which the most productive are in the north, do not yield sufficient for the manufacturers' needs. The making of soap, cheese, and beet-sugar are important industries. The state maintains manufacturing and industrial monopolies in tobacco and matches. Certain explosives, but not dynamite or nitro-glycerine, are state products and the artistic manufactures of **Sevres** porcelain and **Gobelin** and Beauvais tapestries are famed for a higher quality than are the first-named monopolies. Iron ore, lead, zinc and silver are the chief mineral products. Fisheries and oyster culture form a large item in the wealth of the coast population. Agriculture is distinguished by thoroughness of cultivation, the land being divided into a multitude of small holdings. Only metric weights and measures are legal.

Communications. The total length of railways is about 26,000 miles of which about 6,000 miles are operated by the state. The canals of France are a most valuable auxiliary to the railways and are used regularly for transporting merchandise. There are over 3,600 miles of them actually navigated out of 3,620 miles in existence. French roads are excellent. Those of the first class, national roads, are looked after by the state. In the second class come the departmental roads, kept up by the local government authorities; and in the third class, district roads under the district councils.

Principal Towns. Paris, the capital and metropolis; Marseille, the chief Mediterranean port; Lyon, a leading industrial and commercial center; Bordeaux, and important port and coaling station on the Garonne River with a large export trade; Lille, center of important coal fields; Strasbourg, an important Rhine port in Alsace; Nantes, an important port on the Loire; Toulouse, a large manufacturing and market town; St. Etienne, a mining and manufacturing center; Nice, pleasure and health resort on the Riviera; Havre, an important port on the English Channel.

Colonies, Mandates, and Dependencies. France has the second greatest colonial empire of the world. Its colonies, dependencies, protectorates and mandates in all parts of the world, from which it derives a great part of its wealth and power, cover a total area of about 5,000,000 square miles. The French colonies and dependencies in Africa are: *French Equatorial Africa* with 982,049 sq. m.; *French West Africa* with 1,800,000 sq. m.; *Madagascar* with 228,000 sq. m.; *Mayotte* with 790 sq. m.; *Morocco* with 231,500 sq. m.; *Reunion* with 970 sq. m.; *Sahara* with 1,544,000 sq. m.; *Somali Coast* with 5,790 sq. m.; *French Togo* with 31,000 sq. m.; *Tunis* with 50,000 sq. m.; *French Kamerun* with 160,000 sq. m.; and *Algeria* with 222,180 sq. m. which, however, has not the status of a colony, but is politically an integral part of France proper.

The Colonial possessions and mandates in Asia embrace *Syria* with an area of 106,700 sq. m.; *Anam* with 52,100 sq. m.; *Cambodia* with 45,000 sq. m.; *Cochin China* with 20,000 sq. m.; *French India* with 196 sq. m.; *Kwang-chauwan* with 190 sq. m.; *Laos* with 98,000 sq. m.; and *Tongking* with 46,400 sq. m.

The insular possessions in America are represented by *Guadeloupe* with an area of 722 sq. m.; *Guiana* with an area of 32,000 sq. m.; *Martinique* with an area of 385 sq. m.; and *St. Pierre and Miquelon* with an area of 93 sq. m.

The principal possessions in Oceania are *New Caledonia* with an area of 7,650 sq. m. and *Tahiti* and many other small islands with an area of 9,194 sq. m.

GERMANY

The Country. The largest state of Central Europe with an area of 183,381 square miles. The greater part of the country is flat. Throughout the northern districts, the plain is scarcely broken; in the south there are several systems of hills and regions of great beauty. On the Bavarian border the highest point is 9,710 feet and there are many peaks between 4,000 and 8,000 feet. The rivers, in order of importance, are the Rhine, Elbe, Weser and Oder.

Government. Republic. The president according to the constitution is elected by direct vote of all citizens and holds office for seven years. Though the head of the German State is not, like the American president, also the chief executive, that post being held by the chancellor, who, like the British and French premiers, gets his support from a majority of the reichstag, he is the commander-in-chief of the military and naval forces, and can at will dissolve the reichstag. He can also refuse to approve laws passed by the reichstag and have them submitted to a popular referendum. The legislature of Germany (the reichstag) and of each of the constituent republics is elected on the proportional system by the universal, equal, direct and secret votes of all voters of both sexes. Declarations of war and peace must be by legal enactment.

Commerce and Industry. About 90 per cent. of the area of Germany is agriculturally productive, the principal crops being wheat, rye, barley, oats, potatoes and beets. Forestry is an important industry, conducted by scientific methods under governmental supervision. Rye is the cereal chiefly grown. Potatoes are produced in enormous quantities and sugar beets also. Vines are cultivated in many parts and the wines have a world-wide fame. **Coal, iron,** copper, zinc, lead and **potash** are mined. **Textiles** are largely manufactured in Saxony, Silesia and Westphalia. The chemical industry is of special importance. Metric weights and measures.

Communications. The total railway mileage is 38,000 of which nearly four per cent is narrow-gauge. The lines are fairly evenly distributed in proportion to area, among the constituent states. Germany is well served by north and south waterways. The Rhine, Ems, Weser, Elbe and Oder form natural highways for water transport, all of which have been canalized to bring the inland areas into connection by barge with the North Sea and Baltic ports. From Magdeburg on the Elbe, a valuable system of east-west canals extends east to the Oder, near Frankfort, and to the Vistula at Bromberg, Poland. The Kiel Canal carries as much traffic as the Rhine. The Oder has been canalized to Breslau.

Principal Towns. Berlin, the capital and one of the great railway centers of Europe; Hamburg, chief of the German Hansa ports; Munich, capital of Bavaria, with the famous academy of arts; Leipzig, chief city in the publishing trade; Dresden, capital of Saxony, noted for its picture galleries; Cologne, an important river port and center of coal fields and textile areas of the north; Breslau, an important market town at the head of the barge traffic on the Oder; Frankfort (on-the-Main), a financial center; Dusseldorf, the river port for the industrial area of the Westphalia coal fields; Nuremberg (Nurnberg), the chief railway center of Bavaria; Hanover, a market town and industrial center; Essen, with the Krupp works.

GREECE

The Country. Greece lies in the south of the Balkan peninsula, with a very long coastline on the Aegean and Ionian Seas, and a large number of islands. The area of Greece is estimated at about 42,000 square miles. It is generally mountainous. The mountains, though not very high, divide the country into a number of small districts between which communication is difficult. It is the sea which links up the different regions of Greece.

Government. The government is a limited monarchy. There is only one legislative chamber, the *Boule* or chamber to which each 16,000 inhabitants return one member. They are elected for four years. The chamber must be in session for at least three months every year and cannot transact business unless one third of its members are present. There is a council of state, but its functions are judicial, not legislative.

Commerce and Industry. The forests are gradually disappearing, there is little pasture land, and the area available for cereals is small. Although wheat, corn, and barley are grown, the chief crop, especially in the west, is the **currant**, with which Greece supplies the world. Olives, to-bacco, oranges, lemons, **figs** and nuts are important products. Rice is grown near Saloniki. Ores of manganese, iron and emery are mined.

Communications. There are only about 1,700 miles of railways open for traffic. All the lines are state-owned and state-controlled. There are good steamer services on the long coastline.

Principal Towns. Athens, the capital and ancient city, now an important railway center; Saloniki, a great port near the mouth of the Vardar; Piraeus, the port of Athens and an important manufacturing center; Candia, chief town and former capital of Crete.

GUATEMALA

The Country. A Central American republic with a long coastline on the Pacific and a short coastline on the Caribbean Sea. It has a total area of 48,290 square miles. The surface is mountainous, except near the northeast coast where it is low-lying and marshy forest land. Several mountain ranges, mainly belonging to the Antillean system, traverse the country. The coastline is unbroken on the Pacific side and the only indentation on the Atlantic side is the Gulf of Amatique, an extension of the Gulf of Honduras.

Government. The legislative power is vested in a national assembly, consisting of representatives (one for every 20,000 inhabitants) chosen by universal suffrage for four years and a council of state of 13 members partly elected by the national assembly, partly appointed by the president of the republic. The president is elected for six years.

Commerce and Industry. The most important crops are coffee, plantains, **bananas, corn,** rice and potatoes. The cotton-growing industry is being developed. On the plateau horses, mules, **cattle,** sheep, goats, and pigs are reared in large numbers. Gold, silver, coal, lignite, manganese, copper, tin, lead, cinnabar, slate, alum, antimony, marble, alabaster, plumbago, asbestos, bitumen, porphyry, zinc and chalk are found, and opals and other precious stones also exist. The forests abound in valuable trees, producing mahogany, dyewoods, oak, pine and spruce wood. Metric weights and measures.

Communications. There are about 500 miles of railways. One trans-continental line and several minor lines are in operation. Most of the traffic is borne by mules.

Principal Towns. New Guatemala, the capital; Quezaltenango, an industrial center and Coban, center of a coffee district.

HAITI

The Country. The republic of Haiti, occupying the western portion of an island of the same name, has an area of 10,204 square miles. It is a land of mountains and valleys. The coast line is greatly indented on the west by the Gulf of Gonaive or Leogane. Several islands lying off the coast are subject to this republic. Torrid heat prevails on the lowlands but the climate is more equable in the higher regions.

Government. The legislative power is vested in a chamber of deputies whose members are chosen for two years by direct vote, and in a senate of 15 members elected for 6 years, likewise by direct vote of the people. All citizens over 21 enjoy the franchise. The president is elected for four years by the two chambers in joint session. The United States maintains a protectorate over the republic.

Commerce and Industry. Nearly all the trade is with the United States. Logwood from the forests, excellent **coffee,** some cotton and cocoa are exported. Most of the people depend on agriculture. Many minerals, gold, iron, copper, etc., are known to occur, but are little worked. Officially, metric weights and measures have been adopted.

Communications. Port au Prince is connected with Cap Haitien by a road 169 miles long and with Mirebalais and Las Cahobas by a road 33 miles long. A light railway has been constructed from Port au Prince to Lake Assuei (28 miles) but the traffic is small.

Principal Towns. Port au Prince, the capital with a large shipping trade; Cap Haitien, with considerable export trade.

HEJAZ

The kingdom of Hejaz which obtained its independence during the course of the great war, has an estimated area of 170,000 square miles. It has a frontage on the Red Sea of about 700 miles. It is barren or semi-barren in its entire area. Lacking perennial rivers, the land is fertile only in its few valleys. It owes its importance to the holy cities of Mekka and Medina, from the latter of which the Hejaz railway runs north to Damascus, a distance of 1,105 miles. Besides Mekka and Medina, the towns of the Hejaz are Jidda and Yanbo, the ports respectively of these two cities and Taif, in the south. In these cities and towns live the greater number of the population of the country.

HONDURAS

The Country. A Central American republic with an area of 44,275 square miles. The surface is mainly mountainous, especially in the west and southeast, interspersed with elevated plateaus, plains and valleys. The coastal regions are low-lying and swampy. The loftiest peaks are found in the volcanic ranges on the Nicaraguan boundary, rising to nearly 10,000 feet. Most of the rivers are difficult of navigation. The Gulf of Fonseca on the south coast, contains numerous islands.

Government. At the head of the government is the president, who, assisted by an executive council of five members, serves for four years. Legislative power is vested in a congress of deputies, also serving for four years, who are elected at the ratio of one per 10,000 inhabitants.

Commerce and Industry. Stock-raising is extensively engaged in. The chief agricultural product is **bananas.** Lemons, oranges, corn, rice, tobacco and coffee are also produced. The minerals include gold, silver, lead and copper, but the mining industry has not yet been extensively developed. Metric weights and measures.

Communications. There are about 500 miles of railways on the north coast. In general, travelling and transport are accomplished by means of mules and ox-carts, but the number of automobiles for mail service is increasing. Boats of 20 feet draft ply on the Ulua River. The government owns and operates the telephone and telegraph lines.

Principal Towns. Tegucigalpa, the capital and mining center; La Esperanza and Santa Rosa.

HUNGARY

The Country. Hungary is one of the states of Europe formed out of the old Austro-Hungarian Empire. It has an area of 35,654 square miles. It is almost entirely lowland. The shallow Lake Balaton is fed by springs, has brackish waters, and drains into the Danube.

Government. The titular head of Hungary is styled officially Protector of the Magyar State or regent; the state is to be regarded as a monarchy and the word royal is officially retained.

Commerce and Industry. The cultivation of the soil is the chief industry of Hungary. Except for lignite, there are no minerals and there are none but local industries. The Magyars still retain the bulk of the agricultural land, the products of which made Hungary the chief granary of the old dual empire. **Corn** and **wheat** are the chief cereals, although barley and oats are grown. **Horses** are reared in large numbers, and great efforts have been made to improve the breeds of cattle. Metric weights and measures.

Communications. Hungarian railways radiate from Budapest, the total mileage being 4,372.

Principal Towns. Budapest, the capital and great railway center; Szegedin, important trading center; Debreczin, chief city of the northeast; Kecskemet, an important agricultural and cattle market; Hodmezo-Vasarhely, an agricultural center.

ICELAND

The Country. An island of the north Atlantic, with an area of about 39,709 square miles. Iceland is a great tableland averaging 2,000 feet above sea-level, of which a large portion is covered with lava fields or with enormous glaciers. Of its whole area barely a quarter is habitable. The surface is dotted by over 100 volcanic peaks. There are many boiling springs, and the geysers are world famous.

Government. The King of Denmark is also King of Iceland. It is however independent of Denmark which is represented by a minister at Reykjavik. Denmark also takes charge of the foreign affairs of Iceland. The legislative body is the *Althing,* composed of a senate of 14 and a house of representatives of 26 members.

Commerce and Industry. Apart from sheep and cattle-raising, the principal industry is **fishing.** Herring abound, but the chief wealth of Icelandic waters consists of cod. Finbacked whales are hunted by the Icelanders and seals are numerous. Large quantities of **eider-down** and feathers are exported annually. The only minerals are lignite, sulphur and Iceland spar.

Communications. There are no railways in Iceland.

Principal Town. Reykjavik, the capital and largest city.

INDIA

The Country. The term British India includes the districts subject to British law, the area of which is 1,093,-074 square miles. The Indian States or Agencies having political relations with the Indian Government have an area of 709,555 square miles, thus making the total area of India and Dependencies 1,802,629 square miles. The whole northern portion is mountainous, and includes the Himalayas, the loftiest mountains in the world, with Mt. Everest (29,002 ft.) and several others exceeding 25,000 feet. An extension of the western coast uplands crosses central India and forms the western and eastern Ghats. The Malay peninsula is formed by mountain ranges with broad lowlands along the coast.

Government. The sovereign of the United Kingdom is emperor of India. The chief authority is the secretary of state for India, who is a member of the cabinet of the United Kingdom, and is responsible to parliament. He has a council composed of twelve members representing Indians. In political and secret matters he can act without them. In India the government is committed to the governor-general-in-council, who has also the title of viceroy. He and the eight members of his council are appointed by the crown. The Indian legislature consists of a council of state and a legislative assembly, the majority of the members of both being directly elected by various constituencies such as the Mahomedans, Sikhs and Europeans. Each house also has appointed members in order that government may be directly represented, for some of these have to be non-officials. Each of the large provinces, except Burma, is governed by a governor who is advised by a council, while ministers look after the departments of state. *Burma* is under a lieutenant-governor. In each province there is also a legislative council.

Commerce and Industry. Minerals of every sort occur in the mountains, and coal is abundant in east central parts. The aggregate output of gold is very great and constantly increasing, while the gem mines of Burma yield the greater part of the world's supply of rubies and similar precious stones. The tin and oil of upper Burma, and lead and copper in the Himalayas, are also important. The most valuable forest product is teak. Several breeds of cattle have been domesticated from wild stock. The fisheries supply a notable proportion of the food of the common people. Five sevenths of the people are engaged in agricultural pursuits, and irrigation is extensively developed. Rice, corn, wheat, millet and sugar cane, are the chief food-crops; of these rice and wheat are *exported*. Cotton, jute, opium, tea, tobacco, indigo and oil-yielding seeds are also grown for export. Cattle are largely raised in the northwest, whence hides form a valuable item of export; camels, asses and horses in the northwestern plains, and sheep, goats and yaks among the northern mountains. The manufactures are mainly yarns and cheap cottons, silks, largely from tussar (wild silk), cocoons, sugar, paper, rugs and blankets. Shipbuilding is extensively carried on. India *imports* manufactured articles, chief of which are cotton goods, metals, sugar, silk, woolen goods, machinery, railway equipment and oils.

Communications. There are about 40,000 miles of railways open. There are good metalled roads over most of India. Inland steam navigation is well established on the lower courses of the main rivers.

Principal Towns. Calcutta, the principal port of the east coast; Madras, the great cotton manufacturing and shipping port of the south; Bombay, the principal financial center; Delhi, the capital; Karachi, the port of the western region There are twenty-five other towns exceeding 100,000 inhabitants, and fifty-two more with over 50,000 inhabitants each. Important towns, including several native capitals, are Hyderabad, Lucknow, Rangoon, the port of Burma, Benares, Lahore, Cawnpur, Agra, Ahmadabad, Mandalay, the capital of Burma, Allahabad, Amritsar, Jaipur, Bangalore, Howrah, opposite Calcutta, Poona, Patna, Bareli (Bareilly), Nagpur, Srinagar, the capital of Kashmir, Surat, Meerut, Madura, Trichinopoli and Baroda.

IRELAND, NORTHERN

The Country. The present Ulster border was determined by the Government of Ireland Act in 1920, which contemplated the division of Ireland between a nationalist south and a unionist north. For centuries Ireland had been geographically divided into four provinces, Ulster, Munster, Leinster and Connaught, of which the first is predominatingly unionist, and the remainder nationalist, the latter term being used to include Sinn Fein. But upon closer examination the framers of the act discovered that three of the counties of Ulster, namely, Donegal, Monaghan and Cavan, contained a population with a considerable majority of nationalists. These counties were therefore included in Southern Ireland, and the Ulster border became the lines circumscribing the remaining six counties of Ulster. Area of Northern Ireland 8,613 square miles.

Government. Under the Act of 1920 the government of the territory comprising the six counties of Down, Antrim, Londonderry, Armagh, Tyrone and Fermanagh is intrusted to a parliament "consisting of His Majesty, the senate of Northern Ireland, and the house of commons of Northern Ireland." The powers of the parliament and government of Northern Ireland are wholly domestic. The ministry of commerce of Northern Ireland assists in the development of new markets and encouragement of export trade. So far as foreign policy and affairs are concerned Ulster remains essentially a part of the British unit. Therefore her foreign credit remains on a par with that of Great Britain. Her representatives abroad are the British representatives.

For description of physical features, principal towns etc., see under British Isles.

IRISH FREE STATE

The Country. For demarcation of territory see under Northern Ireland; for physical features see under British Isles. Area of Irish Free State 23,973 square miles.

Government. The constitution of the Irish Free State gives the people those powers to govern themselves possessed by the peoples of Canada, Australia, South Africa and New Zealand. Unlike the cases of these self-governing dominions, however, the constitution of the Swiss Republic rather than that of Great Britain was used as a model in framing the organization through which these powers are to be exercised. The British and dominion system of government by a cabinet composed exclusively of members of the dominant party in parliament is replaced by intrusting the carrying out of the will of the elected majority to a federal council, in which only a minority of the members are drawn from the ranks of politicians. The similarity to the Swiss constitution extends also to an arrangement included whereby legislation can be initiated by referendum. Article XI says: "The rights of the state in and to natural resources, the use of which is of national importance, shall not be alienated. Their exploitation by private individuals or associations shall be permitted only under state supervision and in accordance with the conditions and regulations approved by legislation." Another important point is the immunity Ireland is to enjoy from embroilment in British quarrels. Article 48 provides that, save in case of actual invasion, the Irish Free State "shall not be committed to active participation in any war," without the assent of the Free State parliament.

For description of principal towns see under British Isles.

ITALY

The Country. Italy consists of the Italic peninsula, the peninsula of Istria and the islands of Sicily and Sardinia. The area including the new territories added to the kingdom, comprises about 117,982 square miles. The Apennines, extending southward from the Alps, form the backbone of the peninsula, the southern and western parts of which have been subjected to volcanic eruptions and Vesuvius, Etna and Stromboli are still active volcanoes. The Alpine lakes are long and narrow and the lakes of central Italy are in the craters or pipes of extinct volcanoes. The principal rivers are the Adige, 230 miles in length, the Arno, 150 miles, the Po, 420 miles and the Tiber, 250 miles.

Government. Constitutional monarchy; the executive power is vested in the king, but is exercised through responsible ministers. Law-making power is the joint prerogative of king and parliament, the latter consisting of a senate and a chamber of deputies. The king nominates the senators for life, the deputies are elected on a universal manhood suffrage.

Commerce and Industry. Italy is predominantly agricultural; one fifth of the area is forested and many portions of the lowlands cannot be cultivated on account of the prevalence of malaria. The chief food products are wheat, **wine** and **olives.** Corn, beans and oats come next in importance; then potatoes, sugar beets, barley and rice. Silk culture is general, but of special importance in the north. The chief minerals are **sulphur,** marble and iron. The chief *imports* are wheat, coal, raw cotton, iron goods and woolens. The prime *exports* are raw silk, cotton and silk goods, hemp, **wine** and **motor-cars.** Metric weights and measures.

Communications. There are nearly 12,000 miles of railways, three fourths of which belong to the state. The merchant fleet numbers about eight hundred steamships and five times as many sailing vessels.

Principal Towns. Naples, the most important port; Milan, great railway and industrial center; Rome, the capital; Turin, manufacturing center; Palermo on the island of Sicily and the center of a great fruit producing industry; Genoa, the port on the Ligurian coast and headquarters of the iron trade.

Colonies and Dependencies. Italy has in Africa a colonial empire of 591,230 square miles, consisting of *Eritrea* with 45,800 square miles; *Italian Somaliland* with 139,430 square miles, and *Tripoli* and *Cyrenaica* with an area of 406,000 square miles. In addition to those it has in Asia, a concession in Tientsin.

JAPAN

The Country. The Japanese Empire comprises five large and numerous small islands together with the peninsula of Chosen (Korea), the southern part of the Sakhalin Island and the leased territory on the Asiatic coast Kwantung. In addition, it exercises a mandate of the League of Nations over the former German colonies in the Pacific, north of the equator. The area of the mainland and adjacent islands is 148,756 square miles. Bays and inlets are numerous and there are many natural harbors, especially on the Pacific side. The chief feature of the Empire is its mountainous character, for each island has a mountainous backbone. Among the higher mountains, several extend above the snow line. Fuji Yama, the sacred mountain of Japan, is the highest and reaches 12,245 feet. The Yoda, one of the longest streams, empties into the Bay of Osaka. One of the most notable physical features is the Inland Sea or Japanese Mediterranean which reproduces on a smaller scale, the same features as the larger Sea of Japan. It is almost entirely landlocked and surrounded by chains of volcanoes of which few are now active. The climate is temperate and healthful with abundant rainfall.

Government. The government is in the hands of the emperor. He is assisted by cabinet ministers whom he appoints and who are responsible to him. There is a privy council which is consulted on important occasions but the executive power rests with the emperor. Laws are made under his sanction by the imperial diet which consists of two houses, a house of peers which has 373 members and a house of representatives of 381 members, elected by a restricted suffrage.

Commerce and Industry. Agriculture is the chief industry, but only about 20,000 square miles of Japan proper can be cultivated; of this 57 per cent is under **rice,** and 33 per cent under wheat. **Tea** plants are produced on nearly 500 square miles. Over 3,000,000 households are occupied with the production of **silk,** the yield of raw silk equalling that of the whole of Europe and about 75 per cent. of the silk is exported. Tobacco, soya beans and fruit are extensively produced. Over 2,000,000 men are engaged in fishing. Coal, copper, phosphate, and zinc are mined. Chief manufactures are textiles, silk, earthenware, glass, lacquered goods, matting and hemp. Trade in matches and paper is important. A large amount of timber is produced. *Imports* are chiefly raw cotton from the United States, India and China.

Communications. The whole country is covered with a network of railways with a total length of nearly 8,000 miles, and it is possible to travel from the extreme north of Hokkaido (Yezzo) to the extreme south of Kiushiu without once leaving a railway station except to cross the Straits of Tsugaru and Shimonseki, where special steam ferries are provided. The Japanese government subsidizes shipping companies for foreign trade and Japanese vessels run on four great routes to Europe, North America, South America and Australia.

Principal Towns. Tokyo, the capital and great industrial center; Osaka, seaport and textile manufacturing city; Kobe, seaport and extensive shipbuilding; Kyoto with silk, porcelain and lacquer goods factories; Nagoya, port with large textile industries; Yokohama, port of Tokyo; Nagasaki, a seaport and winter resort.

Dependencies. The most important of Japan's dependencies are *Chosen (Korea)*, with an area of 84,738 square miles, from which Japan takes the surplus rice crop and the bulk of the raw cotton; the island *Formosa (Taiwan)* with 13,944 square miles; the southern part of *Sakhalin (Karafuto)* with 13,253 square miles; and the former German colonies in Oceania awarded by the League of Nations as mandates to Japan, viz: *Caroline Islands, Mariana Islands, Marshall Islands* and *Pelew Islands* with a total area of 1,520 square miles.

JUGO-SLAVIA

The Country. Jugo-Slavia or the Kingdom of the Serbs, Croats and Slovenes, occupies the northwest corner of the Balkan peninsula. It combines the old kingdoms of Serbia and Montenegro, the former Austro-Hungarian territories of Bosnia and Herzegovina, the former Hungarian provinces of Croatia-Slavonia and parts of the Banat and Bacska, and portions of Styria, Carniola and Dalmatia, former Austrian provinces. It consists essentially of a mountainous core, most of which is over 3,000 feet in elevation which stretches from the Dinaric Alps in the northwest to the Balkan Mountains on the Bulgarian frontier. The only valley which cuts the mountains and forms a passage way is that of the Morava which, with that of the Vardar, leads from Belgrade to Saloniki. Beyond the Save-Danube, as far as the northern boundary, the land is low, swampy near the rivers, with a few minor elevations. The chief concentrations of people are round Zagreb (Agram) and near Belgrade. The area is 95,620 square miles.

Government. Jugo-Slavia is a limited nonarchy, with a two-chamber parliament in which the senate is an advisory chamber. Parliament is elected for four years on the basis of one deputy for every 40,000 inhabitants. The senate consists of 100 members and is elected for nine years though one third of its membership is renewed every three years.

Commerce and Industry. Agriculture is the chief industry. Mediterranean fruits, chiefly plums, and tobacco, are successfully grown. **Swine** are reared in the oak and beech forests; **cattle,** sheep and goats are also reared. Some wheat is grown. Small quantities of iron ore are mined. Coal occurs near Sarajevo and Banjaluka. Lead, iron and coal are mined in Serbia. Quicksilver is extensively mined. The principal *imports* are textiles, agricultural products, animal products, chemicals, leather and leather goods, metals and machinery. *Exports:* Corn, wheat and oats, cattle and other animals, **fruits,** timber and timber goods. Metric system of weights and measures.

Communications. Jugo-Slavia has about 6,000 miles of railway, mostly state-owned. Total length of waterways, principally the Danube and the Save, 1,322 miles.

Principal Towns. Belgrade, the capital; Zagreb (Agram) the university city; Sarajevo, former capital of Bosnia; Monastir, trade center near the Greek frontier; Uskup on the Vardar, and Nish, an important railway center.

LATVIA

The Country. Latvia, a republic on the Baltic Sea, was formerly part of the Russian Empire. Its area is about 24,440 square miles. It has about 340 miles of sea coast. The land is flat and low-lying, and is watered by many rivers, the chief of which is the Dvina. There are many marshy tracts and lakes; a quarter of the country is covered with forests.

Government. At the head of the republic stands a president elected for 5 years on the basis of universal suffrage. War can only be declared by a vote of the legislature. Parliament consists of one chamber of 100 members, elected for three years.

Commerce and Industry. Agriculture is the principal industry, and includes dairy farming, the raising of live stock and beekeeping. The soil is moderately fertile, but is highly cultivated, producing good crops of **barley,** oats, **flax** and potatoes. The fisheries are of considerable value. Manufactures comprise metals, minerals, chemicals, textiles, timber and spirits. *Exports* are timber, cereals, flax, dairy products and fish. Metric system of weights and measures.

Communications. Latvia has about 1,700 miles of railroads. Three of the Russian main lines verge on Latvian ports.

Principal Towns. Riga, the capital and chief seaport; Libau (Libava), an important port on the Baltic Sea; Mitau (Mitava), formerly the capital of Courland with tanneries and textile industries.

LIBERIA

The Country. Liberia is an independent negro republic, with an area of 40,000 square miles. It occupies about 350 miles of the west African coast and extends inland 200 miles at its widest part. Many rivers are navigable in stretches. The interior rises into mountains of from 2,000 to 6,000 feet in height.

Government. The constitution of the republic is modelled on that of the United States. The executive power is vested in a president and a council of 6 ministers and the legislative power in a parliament of two houses called the senate and the house of representatives. Electors must be of negro blood and owners of land.

Commerce and Industry. The *exports* include **rubber,** palm oil, palm kernels, piassava fibre from the rafia palm, **coffee,** cocoa, ginger, chillies, ivory, annatto seed, dye, and camwood—a hard dyewood. The chief *imports* are rice, textiles, tobacco, building timber, galvanized roofing iron, ready-made clothing and dried and preserved fish.

Communications. There are no railways or vehicular means of transport in the country except ox-carts and a motor road of about 20 miles.

Principal Towns. Monrovia, the capital and chief port; Robertsport and Marshall.

LIECHTENSTEIN

Liechtenstein, a small independent principality, extending along the right bank of the Rhine, opposite the Swiss canton of St. Gallen and the Austrian land of Vorarlberg. It has an area of 65 square miles. The industries include agriculture, weaving and embroidery. It is governed by a diet of fifteen members. It has a customs treaty with Switzerland which includes administration by Switzerland of the post and telegraph lines. Vaduz is the capital and principal town.

LITHUANIA

The Country. Lithuania is a republic carved out of the former Russian Empire. It has an estimated area of 22,520 square miles and a narrow frontage on the Baltic Sea. The country is flat and low-lying. It has numerous lakes and marshes and many rivers, the largest being the Niemen. About 25 per cent of the land is forest.

Government. The constituent assembly makes laws, ratifies treaties with other states, approves the budget and superintends the execution of the laws. The executive power is placed in the hands of the president of the republic and of the cabinet of ministers. The president is elected by the constituent assembly.

Commerce and Industry. The chief articles of *export* are corn, cattle, hams, poultry, eggs, butter, **timber, flax,** linseed, hides and wool. The *imports* are mainly manufactured articles, fertilizers and agricultural machinery. About seventy per cent of the population is engaged in agriculture, the products being cereals, potatoes, flax and **linseed.** Poultry farming, particularly of geese, is a considerable industry.

Communications. Lithuania has about 1,600 miles of railways. There are about 120 miles of streams navigable for steamboats. The Niemen is navigable for about 270 days in the year.

Principal Towns. Kovno (Kaunas), provisional capital and an important grain market; Vilna, the historical capital; Grodno, an important manufacturing center.

LUXEMBURG

The Country. A Grand Duchy surrounded by France, Germany and Belgium. It has an area of about 998 square miles. The great wealth of the country lies in its **iron ore.** Three fifths of the area is cultivated; wheat, rye, oats and potatoes are the main crops. The vine is grown in the Moselle valley; horses and cattle are reared. The government is in the hands of a council of state and a chamber of deputies. Luxemburg is in customs union with Belgium.

Principal Towns. Luxemburg, the capital; Esch, center of mining district.

MEXICO

The Country. Mexico has an area of 767,198 square miles. Two mountain chains traverse the republic, forming between them a number of valleys and plateaus. The plateau of Anahuac, on which the capital is situated, is the largest and most important. The eastern edge of the plateau is formed by the Sierra Madre Oriental. On the western edge of the plateau, the Sierra Madre Occidental shows a steep front and narrow ridges broken by canyons; in both Sierras the highest peaks are about 10,000 feet. At the southern edge of the plateau, confused ranges of mountains fall sharply to the Isthmus of Tehuantepec, where the lowest point on the watershed between the Atlantic and Pacific is a little over 700 feet. The physical divisions eastward of the Isthmus of Tehuantepec include the highlands of Chiapas, and the narrow low plain of Soconusco on the Pacific side. These highlands range from 6,000 to 8,000 feet in extreme elevation. Northeast of them is the peninsula of Yucatan.

Government. Mexico is a federative republic, divided into states, each of which has a right to manage its own local affairs, while the whole are bound together in one body politic by fundamental and constitutional laws. The powers of the supreme government are divided into the legislative, executive and judicial. The legislative power is vested in a congress consisting of a house of representatives and a senate and the executive power in a president. Representatives are elected for two years by universal suffrage. The senate consists of fifty eight members, two for each state, and are elected in the same manner as the deputies. Mexico is divided into twenty eight states, one federal district and two territories.

Commerce and Industry. Mexico is a country of immense natural wealth, with its **oil fields,** its gold, **silver, copper,** iron and other minerals and the great variety of vegetable products determined by the wide range of elevation and climate. Among these last may be specially mentioned hemp, bananas, logwood, and other tropical forest products of the southeast; coffee, tobacco and cotton of more northerly localities, with a variety of fruit and all usual grain crops. The most interesting development in resources of Mexico in recent years has occurred in the oil industry. In spite of inadequate transportation facilities, the Mexican oil fields have been able to take a high place among the petroleum-producing territories of the world. Its vast oil reservoirs have scarcely been tapped. Coal is mined in the state of Coahuila. Large quantities of sugar, molasses and spirits are also produced.

Communications. Mexico has in operation about 16,000 miles of railways, most of which are run by the government. Through connections to the United States can be made at the following five border points: Nogales, Ariz., El Paso, Tex., Laredo, Tex., Eagle Pass, Tex. and Brownsville, Tex. A railway service from Vera Cruz and Mexico City to the frontier of Guatemala has also been completed. Puerto Mexico, on the Atlantic and Salina Cruz on the Pacific are connected by the Tehuantepec railroad.

Principal Towns. Mexico (city), the capital and chief commercial center; Guadalajara, an agricultural and manufacturing center; Puebla, with cotton-spinning and other manufactures; San Luis Potosi, an agricultural and mining center; Leon, a mining and manufacturing town; Vera Cruz, principal port; Tampico, principal oil port.

MONACO

This principality, the smallest state of Europe, situated on the Mediterranean coast, has an area of 8 square miles and is encircled by the French department of Alpes Maritimes and the Mediterranean Sea. The government is carried out under the authority of the prince by a ministry assisted by a council of state. The legislative power is exercised by the prince and the national council which consists of 21 members elected for four years. About one thousand of the inhabitants are employed in the rooms of the celebrated gambling-house known as the "Casino." The climate is very mild. Revenue is derived chiefly from the gambling tables.

NETHERLANDS

The Country. The area of the country, about 15,760 square miles, is for the most part flat, much of it lying below the level of the water, salt and fresh. Along the canals, the meadows are often ten or twelve feet below the water-line, and between the land and sea at high tide, there may be a difference of twenty-five feet or more. The land is protected by embankments and dikes and it may be pictured as a great trough, the floor of which slopes down from east and southeast toward the North Sea in the west and north. The rivers which flow across this country from the higher continent beyond, are, at their mouths, frequently below the level of the sea into which they have to be lifted by canals and locks across the dams or dikes. At all times the precarious river levels threaten internal floods.

Government. Constitutional monarchy. The executive power is vested in the sovereign with nine ministers in council, the legislative authority being the sovereign and states-general, which consists of two chambers, the first of 50 members elected for nine years and the second of 100 deputies elected for four years. There are eleven provinces, sub-divided into communes.

Commerce and Industry. The chief *exports* are **dairy** produce, vegetables and bulbs, flax, **fish,** sugar-beets, and colonial wares. Ship-building is an important industry. Textiles are extensively manufactured. Chief *imports* are oil and raw cotton. One-third of the land is permanent pasture, and intensive methods are largely used in horticulture as well as in agriculture. Metric weights and measures.

Communications. Total length of railroads in operation is about 2,500 miles. Total extent of canals is about 2,000 miles.

Principal Towns. Amsterdam, the metropolis and second seaport; Rotterdam, chief port with a large foreign trade; The Hague ('s Gravenhage), the capital; Utrecht, university city; Groningen, chief city of the north; Haarlem, famous for horticulture and center of the bulb trade; Arnhem on the Rhine near the German frontier; Leiden, the famous university town; Nijmegen, a historic fortified city on the Waal.

Dependencies. The Netherlands have a large colonial empire of about 782,000 square miles in Asia and America, the population of which is many times larger than the population of the Netherlands. The principal colonies are the large islands in the Indian Ocean, the *Dutch East Indies*, consisting of *Bali* and *Lombok* with 4,065 sq. m., *Banka* with 4,446 sq. m., *Billiton* with 1,863 sq. m., *Borneo, South* and *East* with 156,912 sq. m., *Borneo, West* with 55,825 sq. m., *Celebes Island* with 72,070 sq. m., *Java* and *Madura* with 50,557 sq. m., and the capital, Batavia, *Molucca Island* with *Dutch New Guinea*, with 195,653 sq. m., *Riou Linga Archipelago* with 16,301 sq. m., *Sumatra* with 159,739 sq. m., *Timor Archipelago* with 17,698 sq. m.

These colonies are governed by a governor-general who has the right of passing laws and regulations for the administration of the colony, so far as his power is not reserved to the legislature of the mother country. The principal products of Dutch East Indies are sago, corn, tapioca, coffee, tobacco, tea, copra, and oil-seed.

The *Dutch West Indies* are *Curacao*, with 210 square miles, lying just off the mainland of Venezuela, South America and *Dutch Guiana*, with 40,060 square miles, on the north coast of South America, producing coffee, cacao, bananas and balata.

NEW ZEALAND

The Country. New Zealand is a British Dominion in the South Seas. Politically it embraces the two main islands, north and south, the small Stewart Island separated from the south end of South Island by Foveaux Strait, and many islands in the neighboring seas. Area, 104,751 square miles. South Island consists of a great mountain range, the Southern Alps, alpine in magnitude. North Island consists of a highland reaching from Cook Strait in the south to East Cape in the northeast, and two peninsulas.

Government. The Dominion is governed by a governor-general and a general assembly, consisting of a legislative council of thirty-seven paid members and a house of eighty paid representatives, upon a system of constitutional cabinet government.

Commerce and Industry. The dominant industry is sheep-raising. Dairy farming, mainly for the production of butter and cheese, is of growing importance. Crops of wheat, oats, and barley are grown for local consumption. **Kauri gum** is dug in the Auckland peninsula. **Coal** is mined on the western coast of South Island, and **gold** in the Thames peninsula; some alluvial gold is dredged. The principal *exports* are **wool, frozen meat,** butter, cheese, tallow, hides, skins and flax.

Communications. Communication is maintained by a growing railway system connecting the chief towns and supplemented by a coastal steamer service. Total railway mileage about 3,200. The government telegraph system comprises 14,000 miles of line and a government telephone system is very generally used.

Principal Towns. Wellington, the capital; Auckland, Christchurch, Dunedin, Hamilton, Gisborne and Napier.

Dependencies. New Zealand exercises the mandate over those of the Samoan Islands which formerly belonged to Germany. Their total area is about 1,250 square miles.

NICARAGUA

The Country. Nicaragua, a Central American republic, has an area of 49,200 square miles. The east coast is backed by an alluvial plain, beyond which lie the central mountains, which rise to 7,000 feet. From the Gulf of Fonseca on the northwest coast a depression extends south-east across the state, comprising the basins of Lakes Managua and Nicaragua and the San Juan River. Between the lakes and the Pacific Coast is a range of low mountains the chief center of volcanic activity in the country.

Government. Executive power is vested in the president, appointed for four years. Legislative power is vested in a congress of two houses consisting of 40 deputies elected for four years by universal suffrage, and 13 senators elected for six years.

Commerce and Industry. The **banana** is the principal agricultural product in the east. Cocoanuts are also of some importance and a few plantains, oranges and pineapples and some yucca are raised. Rice is grown to a small extent and some wheat in the hilly districts, while tobacco is cultivated round Masaya. The most important products of the western half are **coffee,** sugar-cane, cacao, corn and beans. Extensive forests yield mahogany, cedar, gums, and medicinal plants. Over a million **cattle** provide hides for export. Gold and silver are mined. Metric weights and measures.

Communications. The total railway mileage of the republic is about 200 miles. The principal line runs from Corinto to Grenada.

Principal Towns. Managua, the capital; Leon, largest city; San Juan del Norte (Greytown), chief seaport.

NORWAY

The Country. Norway, occupying the western half of the Scandinavian peninsula, has an area of about 125,000 square miles. It is 1,160 miles in length and the coastline, excluding minor indentations, is over 2,100 miles long. It is separated from Sweden by the Kjolen Mountains, which form the backbone of the peninsula. These mountains rise in many parts to over 6,000 feet, the highest peaks being over 8,000 feet. Norway's long coastline facing the Atlantic is edged with lofty cliffs and seamed with deep fiords. Islands, countless in number, fringe the coast. These archipelagoes cover a total area of no less than 8,600 square miles. Seventy per cent of Norway's area is barren land—mountain, moor, or glacier—uninhabitable by man. Of the whole area of 125,000 square miles only 3,500 square miles are fit for agriculture and nearly 3,000 square miles are water. The rivers are short and torrential, but provide the finest salmon fishing in Europe. Its comparatively mild climate is due entirely to the influence of the ocean. *Spitzbergen* and adjacent islands, with total area of 25,000 square miles and rich coal fields, is under the sovereignty of Norway.

Government. Parliament, called the *Storting*, consists of an upper and a lower house, having in all 123 members, one-quarter forming the *Lagting* or senate, three-fourths the *Odelsting* or house of commons. Questions relating to the laws are considered by each house separately, but if the two houses do not agree they resolve themselves into a common sitting for discussion and a two-thirds vote is then required for decision. Members are chosen by universal suffrage, without distinction of sex.

Commerce and Industry. Soil and climate are not very favorable to agriculture. The chief crop is oats; barley, rye, and potatoes are also cultivated. The hay harvest is large and important. Dairy farming on cooperative lines is making great progress; butter and tinned milk are exported. **Fishing** is the principal occupation. Norway claims a four-mile instead of a three-mile territorial limit and so many of the coastal fishing grounds are under her sovereignty. The **cod fishing** is the most important. Silver, copper, iron and feldspar are mined. The **timber** industry is important, especially in the south. Metric weights and measures.

Communications. The total railroad mileage is about 2,000 miles. Important trunk lines join Christiania with Bergen, and four lines run into Sweden. Coastwise steamers serve all ports.

Principal Towns. Christiania, the capital; Bergen, an important seaport with fishing and ship-building industry; Trondhjem and Stavanger.

OMAN

An independent state in southeastern Arabia whose integrity has been guaranteed by Great Britain and France. It has an area of 82,000 square miles. The chief products are dates and other fruit. Maskat is the capital.

PANAMA

The Country. Panama, formerly a department of the republic of Colombia, has an area of 32,380 square miles. It occupies the narrowest portion of the connecting link between North and South America, known as the Isthmus of Panama. The interior is elevated and is drained by short rapid streams to both coasts. The peninsula of Azuero projects into the Pacific Ocean.

Government. The constitution provides for a chamber of deputies of 33 members, and for a president of the republic, elected by direct vote for four years and not eligible for the succeeding term. There are three vice-presidents and a cabinet of five ministers.

Commerce and Industry. The most important product is the **banana**. Rubber is collected by the Indians of the mountains, or is obtained from trees planted by Europeans near the coast. **Coffee** is grown near the Costa Rican frontier. Other products are coconuts, mahogany, and other woods, copaiba, sarsaparilla and ipecacuanha. The country has great timber resources. Cattle raising is carried on successfully and **hides** form an important article of export. Pearl fishing is carried on at the Pearl Islands in the Gulf of Panama and at Coiba Island. **Turtle-shell** is also exported to a considerable amount. Metric weights and measures.

Communications. The U. S. government railroad between Colon and Panama, 48 miles in length, with a branch line 3 miles to Balboa, the Pacific entrance to the canal, is the most important transportation route of the isthmus. There are also other railroad lines of minor importance.

Principal Towns. Panama, the capital and chief port of the Pacific; Colon, the chief port on the Caribbean.

PARAGUAY

The Country. Paraguay, one of the two inland countries of South America, has an area of about 97,722 square miles. An area officially stated to be 100,000 square miles in extent, lying between the rivers Paraguay and Pilcomayo, known as the Chaco, is claimed by Paraguay, whose rights, however, are disputed by Bolivia.

Government. The legislative authority is vested in a congress of two houses, a senate and a chamber of deputies elected by the people, the executive power being entrusted to a president, elected for a term of four years, with five ministers. There is also a non-active vice-president who is at the same time president of the senate.

Commerce and Industry. Excellent grazing land is abundant and pastoral industries have made great advance in recent years. The chief *exports* are **hides, yerba mate** (Paraguay tea), oranges, tobacco, timber, meat, cattle and quebracho (tannin) extract. Chief *imports* are textiles, provisions, hardware and fancy goods.

Communications. Total railroad mileage is less than 300 miles. Asuncion, the capital, is now in direct communication with Buenos Aires. The main channel of communication is the navigable system of the Plata. Large river steamers and small sea-going ships penetrate as far as Asuncion. Thence north, the Paraguay is navigable by smaller steamers throughout the limits of the republic. Metric weights and measures.

Principal Towns. Asuncion, the capital and chief river port; Villa Rica, the center of tobacco growing; Villa Concepcion, a trading center on the Paraguay River.

PERSIA

The Country. Persia, country of Asia called Iran by the Persians and Arabs, has an area of about 628,000 square miles. Most of the country is a plateau, from 2,500 feet to 3,500 feet above the sea, surrounded by mountain chains, except in the east, where are the huge salt deserts. An extension, locally known as the Khorasan Mountains of the Hindu Kush, enters on the northeast from Afghanistan and merges into the Elburz range south of the Caspian, the highest peak being Mt. Demavend, 19,400 feet.

Government. The Shah of Persia divides his power with a cabinet and a national assembly or *"Majlis."* The empire is divided into provinces ruled by governors-general directly responsible to the crown, and these are again divided into districts, cities, and their dependencies.

Commerce and Industry. Deposits of coal and iron in the Elburz Mountains, copper, lead and other metallic ores in Kerman Desert, copper and turquoise in Khorasan and rock salt near the Persian Gulf, are known but have been but little exploited. **Petroleum** is being obtained in increasing quantity. The chief *exports* are petroleum, opium fruit, animals, raw cotton, rice, wool and carpets.

Communications. Traffic is by camels and cart caravans, merchants combining together for protection against robbers who in some parts are well-armed and numerous. Small steamers ply on the Karun as high as Ahwaz. With the exception of a small line (six miles) at Teheran and a branch of the Trans-Caspian Railway to Tabriz, there are no railways.

Principal Towns. Teheran, the capital; Tabriz, manufacturing and chief commercial center; Ispahan, the former capital; Meshed, principal city of the northeast.

PERU

The Country. A South American republic with an area of 709,871 square miles. The Cordilleras of the Andes divide Peru into three natural divisions. The first lies between the coast and the Maritime Cordillera, and consists for the most part of desert. By means of irrigation, much of this desert is now cultivated. The second lies between the Maritime and Central Cordillera, and consists of grass-clad uplands, suitable for the rearing of cattle and sheep. Further east in the mountainous regions between the Central and Real Cordilleras, there are huge mineral resources, untapped for the most part.

Government. The legislative power is vested in a senate of 35 members and a house of representatives of 110 members elected by direct vote and renewed totally every five years. The executive power is entrusted to the president, elected for five years and not re-eligible until after another five years. The president exercises his executive functions through a cabinet of six ministers.

Commerce and Industry. The mineral deposits which are found in the mountainous regions of the east, consist of gold, silver, **copper**, iron, lead, zinc, sulphur, petroleum and various valuable earths. **Cotton, sugar** and **corn** are the principal productions; coffee, cacao and coca (from which cocaine is made) are also cultivated. Cinchona, sarsaparilla, copaiba are produced in large quantities. Rubber which is now an important product is found in the basin of the Amazon. The *exports* consist chiefly of minerals, sugar, cotton and **rubber**. The principal imports are manufactured goods and machinery. Metric weights and measures.

Communications. The Andean plateau has access to the sea by two mountain railways. One of these, the Callao-Oroya line, traverses the western Cordillera and is linked by a north extension to the great copper mines of Pasco. The Southern Railway mounts over the west Cordillera to the north shore of Lake Titicaca at Puno whence steamers connect it with the Bolivian railway system. These two mountain railways with their extensions, together traverse about 900 miles. But much of the transport in the mountains is still carried by troops of llamas driven by Indians. The river port of Iquitos, 2,300 miles from the Atlantic, is visited by ocean steamers. Large river steamers navigate great stretches of the Amazonian affluents. Metric weights and measures.

Principal Towns. Lima, the capital with manufactures of glass, furniture, etc.; Callao, the principal port; Cuzco, the ancient capital of the Incas; Arequipa, a cathedral town.

POLAND

The Country. Poland, whose independence has been re-established as the result of the war, consists of the Polish territories formerly incorporated into Russia, Austria and Prussia. The largest area was recovered from Russia, the so-called "Congress" Poland; from Austria, Poland recovered Galicia, with the valuable oil and salt mines and from Germany, Posen, West Prussia, and the necessary territory for an outlet to the Baltic Sea. It has an estimated area of about 150,000 square miles. It consists essentially of the basins of the Vistula and the Warthe (a tributary of the Oder), and stretches from the Carpathian Mountains towards the Baltic Sea. Only by a narrow corridor does it reach the shore, and the Free City of Danzig, at the head of this corridor, lying outside of the Republic, is the port of Poland.

Government. There are two chambers, a diet and a senate, both elected by universal suffrage of both sexes. The president, elected for a term of seven years by the diet and senate united in a national assembly, is the supreme commander of the army, and can make treaties with foreign powers.

Commerce and Industry. In the production of **coal**, Poland ranks third among the European countries. It occupies fifth place among the **petroleum** producing countries of the world. Iron ore, copper, lead and rock salt are extensively mined. Rye is the chief cereal. Fruits, wheat, potatoes and sugar beets are important crops. Flax and wool, obtained locally and imported cotton are worked into textile goods.

Communications. Poland has about 8,000 miles of railways, all of which are the property of the state. There are about 2,000 miles of navigable waterways of which 300 miles are accessible for vessels of over 400 tons. The most important canal is the former German Bromberg Canal from the Vistula to the Netze.

Principal Towns. Warsaw, the capital; Lodz, a great textile industry center; Lemberg (Lwow), Krakow, the old capital of Poland; Posen (Poznan), Bialystok, a railway center with manufactures of linens, etc.

PORTUGAL

The Country. Portugal, a republic in the extreme southwest of Europe, has an area of 34,254 square miles. Including, however, the Azores and Madeira Islands in the Atlantic Ocean, which politically form an integral part of the republic, the area is 35,490 square miles. The length of Portugal from north to south is approximately 300 miles and its average width is a little less than 100 miles. Physically, Portugal is an integral part of the Iberian peninsula, its mountains and rivers being mainly prolongations of those of Spain. The longest river rising in Portugal is the Mondego. The chief rivers are the Minho, which forms part of the northern boundary; the Guadiana, which forms part of the southeastern frontier; the Duero and the Tagus.

Government. There are two chambers, viz.: the national council and the second or upper chamber. The former consists of 164 members elected for three years by direct suffrage; the latter is composed of 71 members, elected by all the municipal councils and is renewable as to one half of the members every three years. The president is elected by both chambers, his term of office being for four years; he may not be re-elected. He appoints the ministers of state, who are responsible to parliament.

Commerce and Industry. The vine is the most generally cultivated plant, and **wine** the most important product. In the mountainous regions, rye is grown and sheep and goats are reared; in the north, corn and cattle are raised; in the south, wheat and swine. **Olive** trees cover nearly 1,000,000 acres; figs, tomatoes, potatoes, **oranges**, nuts, etc. are grown. Fish, especially **sardines** and **tunny** fish are caught, cured and tinned for exportation. Cotton-spinning ranks next after fishing. Articles manufactured of **cork** are largely exported. Other industries are silk, leather, glass, paper, and gold and silver filigree manufactures. Salt, gypsum and marble are exported.

Communications. About 2,000 miles of railroads are in operation, of which nearly half are state-owned.

Principal Towns. Lisbon, the capital and chief seaport; Oporto, with extensive port wine trade; Setubal, noted for its sardine fisheries and export of fruit and salt; Braga, noted for its manufactures of firearms; Coimbra, an inland city with a famous university.

Colonies and Dependencies. Portugal has a large colonial empire in Africa totaling 927,292 square miles and minor possessions in Asia, extending over 8,972 square miles. Thus the total area of the colonies is 936,264 square miles.

In *Africa* the colonies are: *Cape Verde Islands,* 1,480 square miles, with the capital, Porto Praya; *Guinea* on the coast of Senegal, with 13,940 square miles; *Principe and St.*

Thomas Islands with 360 square miles; *Angola* (Portuguese West Africa) with 484,800 square miles and a coast line of 1,000 miles; capital, Loanda; and *Mozambique* (Portuguese East Africa) with an area of 428,132 square miles; capital, Lourenco Marques.

In *Asia* the possessions are *Goa*, 1,469 square miles; *Diu*, 169 square miles; and *Timor*, 7,330 square miles, in India; and *Macao*, 4 square miles, in China.

RUMANIA

The Country. Rumania, which now has an area of 122,-282 square miles, consisted in 1914, of the two principalities of Walachia and Moldavia, together with the Dobruja on the other side of the Danube. To these were added after the great war, Bessarabia to the east and Bukowina to the north of Moldavia, along with Transylvania and part of the Hungarian plain. The physical structure of Rumania is comparatively simple. Walachia is bordered on the north and Moldavia on the west by the great arc of the Carpathians. On the south and east this range passes into a region of hills which in Walachia has an extreme breadth of fifty miles. The Dobruja, situated between the Black Sea and the Danube in its northward course, is hilly in the north, plateau-like in the south and marshy along the coast, especially in the deltaic land of the northeast. Bessarabia, in soil and climate, belongs essentially to the steppe lands of Russia. Transylvania, is, on the whole, a mountainous country; on the east and south lie the Carpathians, while within the great curve formed by them is a high tableland, relieved by various ranges and deeply dissected by river valleys. To the southwest of Transylvania lies the Banat, much of which has been ceded to Rumania.

Government. Constitutional monarchy. No act of the king can become effective until it has been countersigned by the minister of state. The executive power which belongs to the crown is generally exercised by the council of ministers appointed and dismissed by the king. Parliament consists of two houses, a chamber of deputies and a senate. All citizens of twenty-one years, paying taxes, are electors.

Commerce and Industry. About 80 per cent. of the population are engaged in agriculture. **Wheat** is the chief crop cultivated, but corn and other cereals, the mulberry, tobacco and vines are also grown. Principal mining products are oil, salt, lignite, iron and copper ore. Metric weights and measures.

Communications. About 7,500 miles of railway and a navigation service on the Danube and Black Sea are all under government control.

Principal Towns. Bukharest (Bucuresti), the capital; Jassy; Galatz, chief port on the Danube; Ismail, a river port in Bessarabia; Kishenef, a trading center in Bessarabia.

RUSSIA

The Country. The former Russian empire extended from the Baltic Sea to the Pacific Ocean and from the Black Sea to the Arctic Ocean, stretching nearly half way around the globe and including an area of 8,500,000 square miles. Of this area it lost about 300,000 square miles to Finland, Poland, Latvia, Lithuania, Esthonia, which have been recognized as independent countries and Bessarabia, which was annexed by Rumania. The official name of Russia is now:

Russian Socialist Federated Soviet Republic and is a federation of fourteen autonomous Soviet Republics, the most important of which are Azerbaijan, Armenia and Georgia in the Caucasus, the Soviet Republic of Ukraine on the Black Sea and Siberia. The western coast of Russia consists only of a narrow section at the head of the Gulf of Finland. Russia is mostly a plain and nowhere does the land rise to heights exceeding 1,200 feet; only in the fringing Caucasus, Crimean heights and Urals are there peaks exceeding 5,000 feet; for roughly 200 miles north of the Caspian Sea, the land is below sea level. Nearly all the most useful rivers radiate from the Valdai Hills, the central boss. Of them the greatest is the Volga, which flows east to Kasan and then south to the Caspian, receiving the Kama set of tributaries from the Urals. The Don and the Dnieper flow to the Black Sea, the Dvina to the Baltic Sea across Latvia and the Volkhof to Lake Ladoga which drains by the Neva to the Gulf of Finland.

Government. The government of the peoples and nationalities inhabiting the territory of Russia is vested in local, regional, and central *Soviets* or councils of workers and soldiers delegates. Only those have qualifications for franchise who are earning a livelihood by productive labor. The central power is in the hands of the peoples commissars elected by the All-Russian soviet congress convened periodically in Moscow. Local affairs are settled by the local or regional soviets, but matters pertaining to war, foreign affairs, foreign trade, etc. are in the hands of the central government. Many of the largest industries have been socialized and are run by the government, though smaller industries are run by private owners.

Commerce and Industry. Under normal conditions Russia is the world's greatest grower of **rye** and **barley,** and was second only to the United States in the production of **oats** and **wheat.** Less than a quarter of these grain crops were exported. **Skins, hides** and **furs** are also largely exported under normal conditions. **Flax** and hemp are products of the wet soils of the west; sugar beets are cultivated in the southwest, near the Dnieper; and tobacco, vines, mulberry trees and cotton are produced in the warm south. The forests yield **timber,** wood pulp, wood-pitch and turpentine, and the tundra yields furs. **Coal** is mined west of the Urals, south of Moscow and in the valley of the Donetz; iron is mined in the first two coal fields, in the neighborhood of Krivoi Rog, 100 miles northeast of Kherson and near Kertch in the Crimea.

Communications. In October 1917 the length of railways was 34,000 miles. There are over 20,000 miles of rivers, canals, and lakes navigable for steamers.

Principal Towns. Moscow, the capital; Petrograd, the former capital; Odessa, a great port on the Black Sea; Kief, the ancient capital and present capital of Ukraine; Kharhof, important industrial center.

Russia in Asia and **Dependencies.** *Siberia* forms an integral part of Soviet Russia, *Turkestan* is a federated soviet republic. Allied to Soviet Russia, without forming, however, an integral part of it are the former vassal states of the Russian Empire, and at present independent soviet republics:

Bokhara, with an area of 83,000 square miles. It produces mostly cotton and raw silk; wheat, hemp, tobacco, and fruit trees are extensively cultivated, and sheep, camels, and horses are bred in the steppes. Gold, alum, salt, and sulphur are found. The principal towns are Bokhara, Kermineh, Karshi, and Charjui.

Khiva, on the Sea of Aral. Its area is about 24,000 square miles. It consists mainly of sandy deserts, the only fertile part being the Amu-Daria delta. Here wheat, barley, millet, rice, and fruit, especially melons, are cultivated. The chief industries are pottery, silk and textile fabrics. Khiva is the capital.

SALVADOR

The Country. Salvador, the smallest of the American republics and the only one of the Central American states lying wholly on the Pacific, has an area of 13,253 square miles. The Pacific coast plain is narrow, and is backed by the coast range of mountains, which rise above 7,000 feet, and contain many volcanoes. The chief river is the Lempa.

Government. The administrative affairs of the republic are carried on, under the president, by a ministry of four members, having charge of the departments. Every citizen over eighteen years of age not only has the right, but is compelled to vote.

Commerce and Industry. Population is largely engaged in agriculture. **Coffee** is the chief crop and the chief *export;* cacao, sugar, indigo and tobacco are grown. **Cattle** are numerous. Gold, **silver,** copper, iron and mercury occur. Metric weights and measures.

Communications. Total railroad mileage is 213 miles.

Principal Towns. San Salvador, the capital; Santa Ana, center of the sugar-growing district, and San Miguel, an agricultural center.

SAN MARINO

The Country. One of the oldest states in Europe and one of the smallest republics in the world, entirely surrounded by Italian territory. The frontier is 24 miles long and encloses an area of 38 square miles. The state is hilly, embracing spurs of the Apennines. Authority rests in the council of 60 popularly elected members; a third of whom are renewable every three years, and from whom two selected councillors act as regents for a period of six months. Wine, cattle and stone are exported. The capital, whose name is also San Marino, is situated on the Mt. Titano.

SIAM

The Country. An independent kingdom of southeastern Asia in the Indo-Chinese peninsula, occupying an area of 198,900 square miles. The climate is hot, but not unhealthy and the country is mountainous and forest-covered.

Government. Siam is nominally a constitutional, but practically an absolute monarchy. The king, assisted by a cabinet of 12 ministers with crown nominees, form a legislative council.

Commerce and Industry. Rice is the staple crop and the main export. Other produce includes pepper, sesamum, cardamoms, areca nut, gamboge and tobacco. **Teak** is the chief commercial product of the forests. The mineral resources are extensive and varied, including **tin**, tungsten, wolfram, coal and iron, zinc, manganese and antimony.

Communications. About 1,500 miles of railway are in operation. It is now possible to travel by train to Bangkok, *via* Penang (Georgetown) to Singapore. The Menam is navigable by deep-draught launches during flood for 275 miles.

Principal Towns. Bangkok, the capital, principal port and trading center; Ayuthia, trading center on the Menam River.

SPAIN

The Country. Spain, a kingdom in the southwest of Europe, occupying about five-sixths of the Iberian Peninsula, has an area of 194,783 square miles. The Balearic Islands and the Canary Islands form two of its forty-nine provinces; the province of Cadiz includes Ceuta, a fortified station on the north coast of Morocco. A greater part of the surface is a tableland ranging in height from 2,000 feet to 3,000 feet above sea level. This great table land is enclosed by the Cantabrian Mountains and the Pyrenees on the north and the Sierra Morena on the south. Outside the plateau lie the highest summits of the whole country, the Pic de Nethou in the Pyrenees being over 11,000 feet. The plateau itself is traversed by four mountain-ranges which separate the valley of the Ebro from that of the Duero. All the considerable rivers except the Ebro flow westward to the Atlantic.

Government. Spain is a constitutional monarchy and legislation is vested in the king and the cortes (senate and congress). The senate consists of not more than 360 members and congress of deputies in the proportion of one to every 50,000 of the population.

Commerce and Industry. Spain is largely an agricultural country. Wheat, barley, maize, rye, oats and rice are the chief crops; the annual production of grape-juice exceeds 500,000,000 gallons and of olive oil 385,000 tons. Silk culture and stock raising are important branches of industry. Coal, **iron, copper,** lead, zinc, mercury, iron pyrites, and lignite are mined. The chief *imports* are raw cotton, machinery, coal and coke, chemical products and fish; the chief *exports* are metals and **mineral ores, wine, olive oil, oranges,** cotton and manufactures and **cork.**

Communications. Total length of railways is about 10,000 miles, owned by private companies.

Principal Towns. Madrid, the capital; Barcelona, the chief seaport, on the Mediterranean; Valencia, important center of tobacco and pottery; Seville, a thriving port and chief city of Andalusia; Malaga, an important seaport and health resort; Saragossa, capital of the former kingdom of Aragon; Cartagena, fortified seaport on the Mediterranean.

Colonies and Dependencies. The former great colonial empire of Spain is now considerably reduced. All colonies are in Africa and occupy a total area of 128,149 square miles. They consist of *Spanish Morocco* with 7,700 sq. miles, with the fortified towns of Ceuta and Melilla; *Ifni,* 965 sq. miles; *Rio de Oro,* 109,200 sq. miles; and *Spanish Guinea,* including *Fernando Po* and other small islands, 10,284 sq. miles.

SWEDEN

The Country. Sweden, occupying the eastern and larger portion of the Scandinavian peninsula, has an area of 173,035 square miles. The length is nearly 1,000 miles and it has a coast line of over 1,500 miles. Besides the large number of small islands which fringe the coast, Sweden includes the two large Baltic islands of Gotland and Oland. Her islands cover an area of 3,000 sq. miles. The whole country is a tableland sloping from the Kjolen range to the Baltic. No less than 8 per cent of the surface of Sweden is water, the immense number of lakes covering 14,000 square miles. The two largest are Wenner and Wetter. in the southern portion of the country and are connected by an excellent system of canals.

Government. Sweden is a constitutional monarchy, the king's power being exercised in conjunction with a council of state and a diet. There are two chambers, the first of 150 members and the second of 230.

Commerce and Industry. Principal crops are oats, potatoes, barley, rye and wheat. **Live stock** are produced in great number. A large amount of butter is exported. Forests of pine, fir and larch cover more than half of the area and her output of **timber** and **paper pulp** is very large. The mining of iron ore and the production of **iron** and **steel** is of utmost importance. Cream separators, **matches**, lighthouse apparatus, telephone supplies, motors and many kinds of electrical machinery are among the highly specialized products of industry. Porcelain factories and the glass factories produce wares that have achieved a high reputation in the markets of the world. About 3,500,000 H.P. are available for hydroelectric development, of which 800,000 are being used. Metric weights and measurements.

Communications. Sweden has about 10,000 miles of railway supplemented by an excellent system of canals. Steamer communication is kept up on the internal waterways along the coast during the open season.

Principal Towns. Stockholm, the capital; Gottenborg the chief seaport; Malmo, a seaport opposite Copenhagen; Norrkoping, an important manufacturing town.

SWITZERLAND

The Country. Switzerland, an inland mountainous country in the central portion of the Alps, has an area of 15,976 square miles. The northwest of the country bounding France and Germany consists of some of the parallel ridges and valleys of the Jura Mountains. Between Lake Constance on the Rhine and the Lake of Geneva on the Rhone are the Lakes Neuchatel, Zurich, Lucerne, Brienz, Bienne, etc., which all drain to the Aar. Lake Geneva and Lake Constance each exceed 200 square miles in area; Lake Neuchatel covers 93 square miles. Owing to its elevation, much of Switzerland is under permanent snow.

Government. Switzerland is a confederate republic of twenty-five cantons. The parliament consists of the state council (44 members) and the national council (189 members). The federal assembly which consists of both chambers, is the supreme authority. The referendum is used when legislative measures are submitted directly to the people. The separate cantons have an independent system of local government.

Commerce and Industry. The thousands of tourists who visit Switzerland have made hotel-keeping one of the principal industries of the country. **Silk,** cotton and **textile** mills employ thousands, the manufacture of machinery, **clocks** and **watches,** and dairy farming are the most important economic factors of Switzerland. Large quantities of milk are consumed in **chocolate** factories and **milk-condensing** concerns, and in the manufacture of cheese for export. Metric weights and measures.

Communications. About 4,000 miles of railways are in operation, a large portion of which is electrified.

Principal Towns. Zurich, great industrial center; Basel, manufacture of silk ribbons; Bern, the capital; St. Gall (St. Gallen), industrial center south of Lake Constance; Lausanne, educational center; Geneva, headquarters of the League of Nations, and noted for its watches; Lucerne, great tourist center.

TURKEY

The Country. Turkey, now reduced in size to about 174,900 square miles, comprises a portion of Thrace adjacent to Constantinople and is now mainly confined to Asia Minor, a peninsula of southwestern Asia. This peninsula from north to south varies in length from three hundred to four hundred miles and from east to west is about 800 miles. Much of the district is an elevated plateau, the altitude varying from 6,000 to 2,500 feet above the sea. Among the chief mountains are the Taurus Chains, stretching across the south of the country from the southwest shore of the Aegean to the the north of Syria, their principal peaks reaching from 7,000 feet to 10,000 feet; the Bulgar Mountains are upwards of 10,000 feet and the Ala Mountains, north of Adana, are 8,000 to 10,000 feet high. Between the mountains on the north and on the south are several chains, from one of which —near Kaisarieh, soars Mount Argaeus, 13,100 feet and the highest peak in Asia Minor. Flowing into the Black Sea are the Chorok, the Yeshil Irmak, the Kizil Irmak (Halys) and the Sakaria. Into the Mediterranean flow the Sihun and the Jihun. In the east of Asia Minor are the headwaters of both the Euphrates and the Tigris as well as of the Aras (Araxes). The lakes are the Tuz, 60 miles long; the Kirili, 30 miles long; the Eyerdir, 30 miles long in Anatolia; and Lake Van 80 miles long.

Government. Hereditary monarchy limited by constitution proclaimed in Angora. The parliament consists of only one chamber elected by the people. This parliament has the supreme legislative and executive power.

Commerce and Industry. Agriculture is primitive, but the soil, where cultivable, is fertile and produces considerable crops of wheat, **barley,** cotton, **tobacco,** nuts, **figs,** olives, grapes and other fruits. A large quantity of opium is grown. The *exports* include cereals, cotton, fruit, olive oil, tobacco, carpets and wool. Asia Minor is rich in minerals, which, however, are only slightly worked.

Communications. About 1,500 miles of railways are in operation. The so-called Bagdad railroad extends from the Bosphorus via Adana and Aleppo to Nisibin.

Principal Towns. Constantinople, the capital; Smyrna, an important seaport; Brusa, the ancient capital and center of silk manufacture; Sivas, a mining center; Angora, the provisional capital.

UNION OF SOUTH AFRICA

The Country. The Union of South Africa is a self-governing dominion of the British Empire; area 473,089 square miles. The Union of South Africa consists of the four provinces, the Cape of Good Hope, Natal, Transvaal and Orange Free State. South Africa is a vast tableland with a lofty rim to the east and south, represented by the Drakensberg and other mountains. The main drainage is carried west by the Orange and Vaal Rivers. The Cape region has a vegetation of evergreen trees, shrubs and heaths; the well-watered eastern terraces are clothed with a rich wooded savannah, with palms on the coastal belt; over vast acres of the eastern tableland there is an almost treeless grassland, the veldt, which merges westwards into scrub and bush, composed of thorn bushes and other drought-resisting plants. In the north the grassland is wooded, and is known as the bush veldt. *Southwest Africa,* formerly German, with an area of 322,400 square miles, is now administered by the Union under a mandate from the League of Nations.

Government. Under the act constituting the Union, the sovereign appoints a governor-general, who, with an executive council, administers the executive government of the Union. Departments of state have been established, the governor-general appointing officers to administer them. Legislative power is vested in a parliament consisting of the king, a senate and a house of assembly. The senate may not be dissolved within ten years of the establishment of the Union. There must be a session of parliament every year.

Commerce and Industry. The most important cereal crop is **corn.** Tobacco is widely grown. The leading pastoral occupation is **sheep** raising. Dairy farming is very successful in Natal on the higher and cooler eastern terraces and in similarly situated parts of the Cape province. **Ostriches** are reared. The mineral wealth is enormous; of this, **gold** represents considerably more than half. Ranking second to the gold mines as regards the monetary value of their output are the **diamond** mines. Coal is mined in the Transvaal and Orange Free State. Among metals of secondary importance are **copper** and **tin.** The Union is now the world's largest producer of **corundum,** and has valuable asbestos mines. As regards manufactures, the products include biscuits, jams and preserves, beer, cement, soap, candles, matches, furniture, leather, boots and shoes, explosives, chemicals, **tobacco,** vehicles and so forth.

Communications. The whole transport system of South Africa—railways, ports and harbors—is owned and managed by the State. There are nearly 10,000 miles of railway.

Principal Towns. Johannesburg, the center of the densely populated gold mining region; Cape Town, the premier port of South Africa; Durban ranks second, and is the principal port for Johannesburg; the nearest port to the latter city is, however, Delagoa Bay (Lourenco Marques), which takes a certain portion of the Transvaal trade; Pretoria, Port Elizabeth and East London.

UNITED STATES OF AMERICA

The Country. Area of the contiguous territory of continental United States is 3,026,791 square miles. Length from north to south is 1,780 miles, width from east to west 3,100 miles, coastline 21,354 miles. Mountains and highlands cover the eastern and western borders; the Rocky Mountains in the west, the Appalachians in the east. Short slopes and coastal plains drained eastward by the Hudson, Delaware, Susquehanna, Potomac and other rivers, and westward by the Columbia and Colorado, extend from the mountains to the sea-boards. Between the mountain-systems is the great central valley of the Ohio-Missouri-Mississippi river system. Waterfalls, chief of which is Niagara, are features along many of the rivers. The climates vary in different regions, owing to the size of the country. Its northern regions are in a zone where winters are long and severe; its southern extremities lie near the tropics. But for the most part the country is temperate, though the summers are much hotter and the winters colder than in western Europe. The prevailing winds of the northwest are from the Pacific Ocean; they give the western coast a mild and fairly uniform climate. In Florida and Texas there are regions where tropical vegetation flourishes; in California and the states along the Gulf of Mexico and the Atlantic, as far north as Virginia, subtropical plants are found.

Government. The country, a federal republic of forty-eight sovereign states, is bound together by the pact of 1787, put in force in 1789. The Federal Government, from its seat at Washington, deals with only such matters as the states have delegated to it, and each state retains complete authority over all unenumerated categories. The government looks after foreign relations, army and navy, and dependencies, and controls interstate trade, customs, post office, currency, bankruptcy and patents. The ordinary civil and criminal law are state matters, but income tax, suits between residents of different states, prohibition, and the majority of banks are under the control of Washington. The president and vice-president are elected every four years. The vice-president presides over senate, and, in case the president dies, fills out his term. The president is commander-in-chief of the army and navy, and until it comes to treaty-making, is supreme in foreign affairs. He can, within ten days of its passage, veto any bill. The senate, representing the states as sovereign entities, has two members from each state, regardless of its importance; the house has state delegations proportionate to their population. Senators sit for six years, and, as one third retire every second year, the life of the senate is never interrupted and is periodically renewed. Congressmen are elected for two years, a general election being held every presidential year and again two years later.

Commerce and Industry. The mineral supply is one of the chief natural sources of wealth of the country, which exceeds every other in its output of **coal, iron, oil** and silver. The deposits of gold, quick-silver, lead and copper also are extensive. In the west and northeast are dense forests of pine, spruce, birch and maple; in the southeast the cedar, pine, and many valuable hard woods abound; in the east-central part grow oak, maple, hickory, elm, and other useful trees, while in California are found the giant sequoia trees. The great agricultural region, raising three fourths of the **corn** and **wheat** crop of the world, is in the northern and central part of the Mississippi Valley. Three fourths of the **cotton** supply of the world, and half the tobacco crop, together with corn, rice, and tropical fruits, grow luxuriantly in the south; grains, vegetables, fruits, including grapes, are cultivated extensively in California. The raising of cattle, sheep, hogs and poultry, are important industries, yielding an immense product for export.

Communications. Total railway mileage 270,000. Total tonnage of American shipping about 7,000,000. The New York Barge Canal from Buffalo on Lake Erie to Troy on the Hudson River is 352 miles long, to which its Oswego and Cayuga-Seneca tributaries add another 100 miles. The Great Lakes are connected with each other and by canals with the Atlantic Ocean, Saint Lawrence River and the Mississippi River. There are over 290 streams in the country used to a substantial degree for navigation, with an approximate navigable mileage of 26,400.

Principal Towns. New York City, Chicago, Philadelphia, Detroit, Cleveland, St. Louis, Boston, Baltimore, Pittsburgh, Los Angeles, Buffalo, San Francisco, Milwaukee, Washington, the capital.

Dependencies. The total area of Dependencies and non-contiguous territory of the United States is 716,740 square miles divided as follows: On the Continent of America, *Alaska,* with an area of 590,884 square miles, forms a territory of the United States, governed conjointly by Congress at Washington and by the local legislative assembly consisting of 8 senators and 16 representatives. The seat of government and largest town is Juneau. Other dependencies in America are the *Panama Canal Zone*, with an area of about 500 square miles, the *Virgin Islands*, with an area of 132 square miles, (formerly Danish West Indies), and its capital, St. Thomas, and the island of *Porto Rico*, with an area of 3,425 square miles and its capital, San Juan.

In the Pacific Ocean is the most important dependency, the *Philippine Islands*, with a total area of 114,400 square miles and the capital, Manila. A governor-general, appointed by the president of the United States, administers the islands in conjunction with the local legislative body, consisting of two houses, the senate and a house of representatives. Other dependencies in Oceania are the islands of *Guam*, with an area of 225 square miles; *Hawaii*, with an area of 6,449 square miles with the capital Honolulu, and American *Samoa*, with an area of 102 square miles.

URUGUAY

The Country. Uruguay has an area of 72,153 square miles. The most notable feature of Uruguay is its long rolling plains, comprising almost the entire length of the country, occasionally broken by low mountain ranges and copiously watered by numerous streams. The Uruguay River, forms the western boundary with its chief tributary the Negro, draining the entire central portion of the republic. The climate is generally moderate and healthy.

Government. The executive is divided between the president and a national administrative council. The president is elected for four years by direct vote and may be re-elected after an interval of eight years. The national administrative council consists of nine members, six of the majority party and three of the largest minority party; three retiring every two years. The election is by direct popular vote. The president appoints the ministers of foreign affairs, of war and marine and of the interior and has supreme control of these departments; the other ministers are appointed by the council. The legislative power is-vested in a parliament of two houses. the senate and the chamber of representatives, which meet in annual session. In the interval of the session, a permanent committee of two senators and five members of the lower house assumes the control of the executive power. The representatives are chosen for three years. The senators are chosen for six years by an electoral college whose members are directly elected by the people.

Commerce and Industry. Sheep and cattle raising are the principal industry. Agriculture is also practiced to a considerable extent, nearly all of the cereals being grown. Wine is produced in considerable quantities, and tobacco and olives are cultivated. In the northern department,

gold mines are worked. Silver, copper, lead, magnesia and lignite coal are found. The *exports* consist almost entirely of **animal products**. Metric weights and measures.

Communications. River transport is very extensive. The Uruguay affords the principal means of communications, while railways of a total length of nearly 1,600 miles link up the ports with the chief centers of commerce.

Principal Towns. Montevideo, the capital and chief seaport; Paysandu, seaport on the Uruguay, with meat packing interests; Salto, also on the Uruguay, with large trade in hides.

VENEZUELA

The Country. Venezuela has an area of 398,594 square miles. It comprises roughly the basin of the Orinoco and the district surrounding the Gulf of Maracaibo. The country is divided geographically into three distinct zones, viz., the extensive plains and river valleys, known as llanos, affording excellent pasturage for cattle; the mountain section, formed by three mountain ranges; and the tablelands. This variety of physical features yields an equal variety of climate, products and soil.

Government. Legislative authority of the republic is vested in a congress of two chambers, the senate and the chamber of deputies. The former consists of forty members elected for three years, two for each state. The latter is constituted by direct election for three years. The executive power is exercised by the president in conjunction with the cabinet ministers through whom he acts. The president is elected by congress for seven years; there is no restriction as to re-election.

Commerce and Industry. **Coffee** and **cacao** are largely grown and exported and wheat and other cereals thrive. The mountains are heavily wooded and many useful trees and plants are found. The mines produce **gold**, silver, copper and lead; the various asphalt lakes yield the best quality of **asphalt**; along the coast pearls are obtained. Metric weights and measures.

Communications. Total railway mileage is about 700 miles. The waterways of Venezuela form important means of communication and transportation, there being no less than 70 navigable rivers in the country with a total navigable length of over 6,000 miles of which the Orinoco, with its tributaries, furnishes nearly 4,000 miles. A regular steamship service is maintained on the Orinoco, between Ciudad Bolivar and the interior, as well as points along the coast. Ocean-going vessels enter Lake Maracaibo which is navigable in its entirety.

Principal Towns. Caracas, the capital; Maracaibo, the city with extensive export trade in coffee, cocoa and rubber; Ciudad Bolivar, on the right bank of the Orinoco, with export trade of coffee, hides, etc.; Puerto Cabello, and La Guaira, seaports.

DISTANCES BETWEEN THE LARGER CITIES OF THE UNITED STATES

The distances are by the shortest usually traveled railroad routes. Compiled from the War Department's official table of distances.

From / To	New York	Chicago	Philadelphia	St. Louis	Boston	Baltimore	Cleveland	Buffalo	San Francisco	Pittsburg	Cincinnati	Milwaukee	New Orleans	Washington	Minneapolis
	Mls.	Mls.	Mls.	Mls.	Mls.	Mls.	Mls.	Mls.	Mls.	Mls.	Mls.	Mls.	Mls.	Mls.	Mls.
Albany	145	832	236	1,028	202	333	480	297	3,106	567	724	917	1,517	373	1,252
Atlanta	876	733	785	611	1,106	688	736	919	2,805	805	492	818	496	648	1,153
Baltimore	188	802	97	934	418	....	474	398	3,076	334	593	887	1,184	40	1,222
Boston	217	1,034	321	1,230	....	418	682	499	3,308	674	926	1,119	1,602	458	1,454
Buffalo	442	525	416	731	499	398	183	....	2,799	270	427	610	1,256	438	945
Chicago	912	....	821	284	1,034	802	357	525	2,274	468	298	85	912	790	420
Cincinnati	757	298	666	341	926	593	244	427	2,572	313	....	383	829	553	718
Cleveland	584	357	493	548	682	474	....	183	2,631	135	244	442	1,073	437	777
Columbus, O	637	314	546	428	820	511	138	321	2,588	193	116	399	935	471	734
Denver	1,934	1,022	1,843	916	2,056	1,850	1,379	1,537	1,371	1,490	1,257	1,107	1,347	1,810	884
Detroit	693	272	669	488	750	649	173	251	2,546	321	263	357	1,092	655	692
Duluth	1,391	479	1,300	728	1,513	1,281	701	1,004	2,238	947	777	422	1,447	1,269	162
El Paso	2,310	1,465	2,219	1,245	2,414	2,179	1,703	1,915	1,287	1,866	1,586	1,550	1,195	2,139	1,521
Galveston	1,792	1,144	1,691	860	2,012	1,594	1,408	1,591	2,157	1,481	1,157	1,229	410	1,554	1,340
GrandRapids,Mich.	821	178	815	462	878	796	332	379	2,452	462	308	263	1,090	764	598
Helena	2,452	1,540	2,361	1,549	2,574	2,342	1,897	2,065	1,250	2,008	1,838	1,455	2,152	2,320	1,119
Indianapolis	825	183	734	240	965	704	283	466	2,457	381	111	268	888	664	603
Jacksonville, Fla.	983	1,097	892	975	1,213	795	1,085	1,193	3,098	1,057	841	1,182	616	755	1,517
Kansas City	1,342	458	1,251	277	1,466	1,211	755	967	1,981	898	618	543	880	1,171	573
Los Angeles	3,149	2,265	3,058	2,084	3,273	3,018	2,562	2,774	475	2,705	2,425	2,350	2,007	2,978	2,301
Louisville	871	304	780	274	1,040	703	358	541	2,468	427	114	389	778	663	727
Memphis	1,157	527	1,066	311	1,387	939	738	921	2,439	807	494	612	396	929	894
Milwaukee	997	85	906	369	1,141	887	442	610	2,359	553	383	....	997	875	335
Minneapolis	1,332	420	1,241	586	1,454	1,222	777	945	2,096	888	718	335	1,285	1,210	....
Mobile	1,231	929	1,140	647	1,461	1,043	1,029	1,212	2,623	1,098	785	1,014	141	1,003	1,233
Montreal	386	841	477	1,051	330	574	623	434	3,115	704	826	926	1,655	614	1,125
Newark, N. J	9	903	82	1,056	226	179	575	405	3,177	435	748	988	1,363	219	1,323
New Haven	76	980	167	1,141	140	264	628	445	3,254	520	833	1,065	1,448	304	1,400
New Orleans	1,372	912	1,281	699	1,602	1,184	1,073	1,256	2,482	1,142	829	997	....	1,144	1,285
New York	....	912	91	1,065	217	188	584	442	3,186	444	757	997	1,372	228	1,332
Ogden	2,496	1,494	2,315	1,414	2,528	2,296	1,851	2,019	780	1,962	1,792	1,579	1,891	2,284	1,316
Omaha	1,405	493	1,314	413	1,527	1,295	1,750	1,018	1,781	961	791	578	1,080	1,283	381
Philadelphia	91	821	....	974	321	97	493	416	3,095	353	666	906	1,281	137	1,241
Pittsburg	444	468	353	621	674	334	135	270	2,742	....	313	553	1,142	302	888
Portland, Me.	332	1,149	436	1,345	115	533	797	614	3,423	789	1,041	1,234	1,717	573	1,569
Portland, Ore.	3,204	2,292	3,113	2,212	3,326	3,094	2,649	2,817	772	2,760	2,590	2,378	2,746	3,082	2,042
Providence	190	1,034	281	1,230	45	378	682	499	3,308	634	926	1,119	1,562	418	1,454
Quebec	530	1,013	621	1,343	402	718	795	612	3,287	876	1,039	1,098	1,827	786	1,433
Richmond, Va.	343	879	252	918	573	155	553	553	3,153	417	581	964	1,046	115	1,299
Rochester, N. Y.	373	603	361	799	430	354	251	68	2,877	338	495	688	1,324	394	1,023
St. Joseph, Mo.	1,392	470	1,301	327	1,474	1,261	875	1,058	1,867	948	668	555	941	1,221	485
St. Louis	1,065	284	974	....	1,230	934	548	731	2,194	621	341	369	699	894	586
St. Paul	1,322	410	1,231	576	1,444	1,212	767	935	2,086	878	708	325	1,275	1,200	10
San Antonio	1,943	1,204	1,852	920	2,150	1,755	1,468	1,651	1,911	1,541	1,217	1,289	571	1,715	1,320
San Francisco	3,186	2,274	3,095	2,194	3,308	3,076	2,631	2,799	...	2,742	2,572	2,359	2,482	3,064	2,096
Seattle	3,151	2,239	3,060	2,332	3,273	2,941	2,596	2,764	957	2,707	2,537	2,154	2,931	3,029	1,818
Spokane	2,812	1,900	2,721	1,932	2,934	2,702	2,257	2,425	1,205	2,368	2,198	1,815	2,535	2,690	1,479
Springfield, Mass.	139	935	230	1,131	99	327	583	400	3,209	583	827	1,020	1,511	367	1,355
Tampa, Fla.	1,195	1,309	1,104	1,187	1,425	1,007	1,297	1,405	3,310	1,269	1,053	1,394	828	967	1,729
Toledo	705	244	615	437	795	595	113	296	2,518	261	203	329	1,032	595	664
Washington	228	790	137	894	458	40	437	438	3,064	302	553	875	1,144	....	1,210

AREAS OF THE EARTH

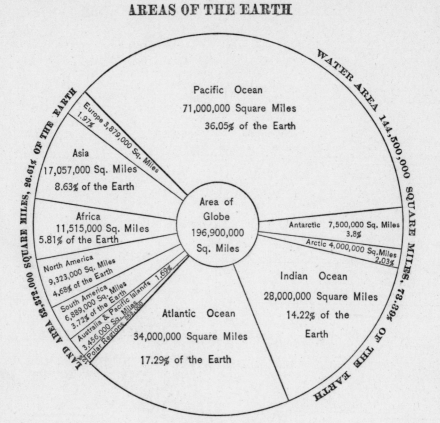

WATER AREA 144,500,000 SQUARE MILES, 73.39% OF THE EARTH

LAND AREA 52,372,000 SQUARE MILES, 26.61% OF THE EARTH

Pacific Ocean
71,000,000 Square Miles
36.05% of the Earth

Europe 3,879,000 Sq. Miles 1.97%

Asia
17,057,000 Sq. Miles
8.63% of the Earth

Africa
11,515,000 Sq. Miles
5.81% of the Earth

North America
9,323,000 Sq. Miles
4.68% of the Earth

South America
6,889,000 Sq. Miles
3.72% of the Earth

Australia & Pacific Islands 1.69%
3,456,000 Sq. Miles
Polar Regions 258,000

Area of
Globe
196,900,000
Sq. Miles

Antarctic 7,500,000 Sq. Miles 3.8%

Arctic 4,000,000 Sq. Miles 2.03%

Indian Ocean
28,000,000 Square Miles
14.22% of the
Earth

Atlantic Ocean
34,000,000 Square Miles
17.29% of the Earth

PRINCIPAL RELIGIONS
OF THE WORLD

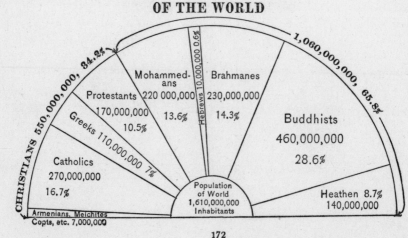

CHRISTIANS 550,000,000, 34.2%

1,060,000,000, 65.8%

Mohammed-
ans
220 000,000
13.6%

Brahmanes
230,000,000
14.3%

Protestants
170,000,000
10.5%

Hebrews 10,000,000 0.6%

Greeks 110,000,000 7%

Buddhists
460,000,000
28.6%

Catholics
270,000,000
16.7%

Population
of World
1,610,000,000
Inhabitants

Heathen 8.7%
140,000,000

Armenians, Melchites
Copts, etc. 7,000,000

172

CHARACTER OF LAND OF THE EARTH

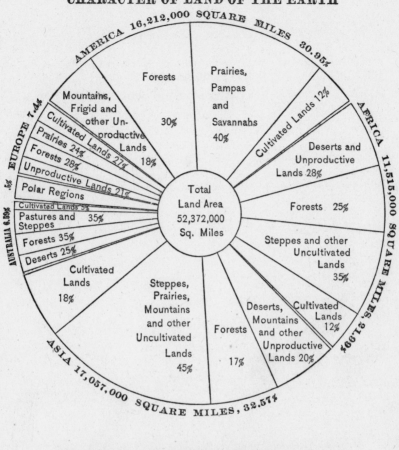

AMERICA 16,212,000 SQUARE MILES 30.95%

Forests 30%

Prairies, Pampas and Savannahs 40%

Mountains, Frigid and other Unproductive Lands 18%

EUROPE 7.44%

Cultivated Lands 27%

Prairies 24%

Forests 28%

Unproductive Lands 21%

AUSTRALIA 6.59%

Polar Regions

Cultivated Lands 5%

Pastures and Steppes 35%

Forests 35%

Deserts 25%

Cultivated Lands 18%

Total Land Area 52,372,000 Sq. Miles

Cultivated Lands 12%

AFRICA 11,515,000 SQUARE MILES 21.99%

Deserts and Unproductive Lands 28%

Forests 25%

Steppes and other Uncultivated Lands 35%

Cultivated Lands 12%

Deserts, Mountains and other Unproductive Lands 20%

Forests 17%

Steppes, Prairies, Mountains and other Uncultivated Lands 45%

ASIA 17,057,000 SQUARE MILES, 32.57%

PRINCIPAL RELIGIOUS DENOMINATIONS OF THE UNITED STATES

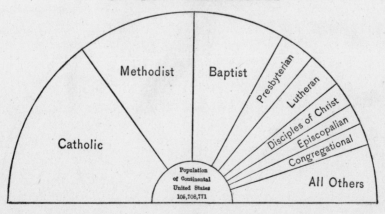

Catholic

Methodist

Baptist

Presbyterian

Lutheran

Disciples of Christ

Episcopalian

Congregational

All Others

Population of Continental United States 105,708,771

173

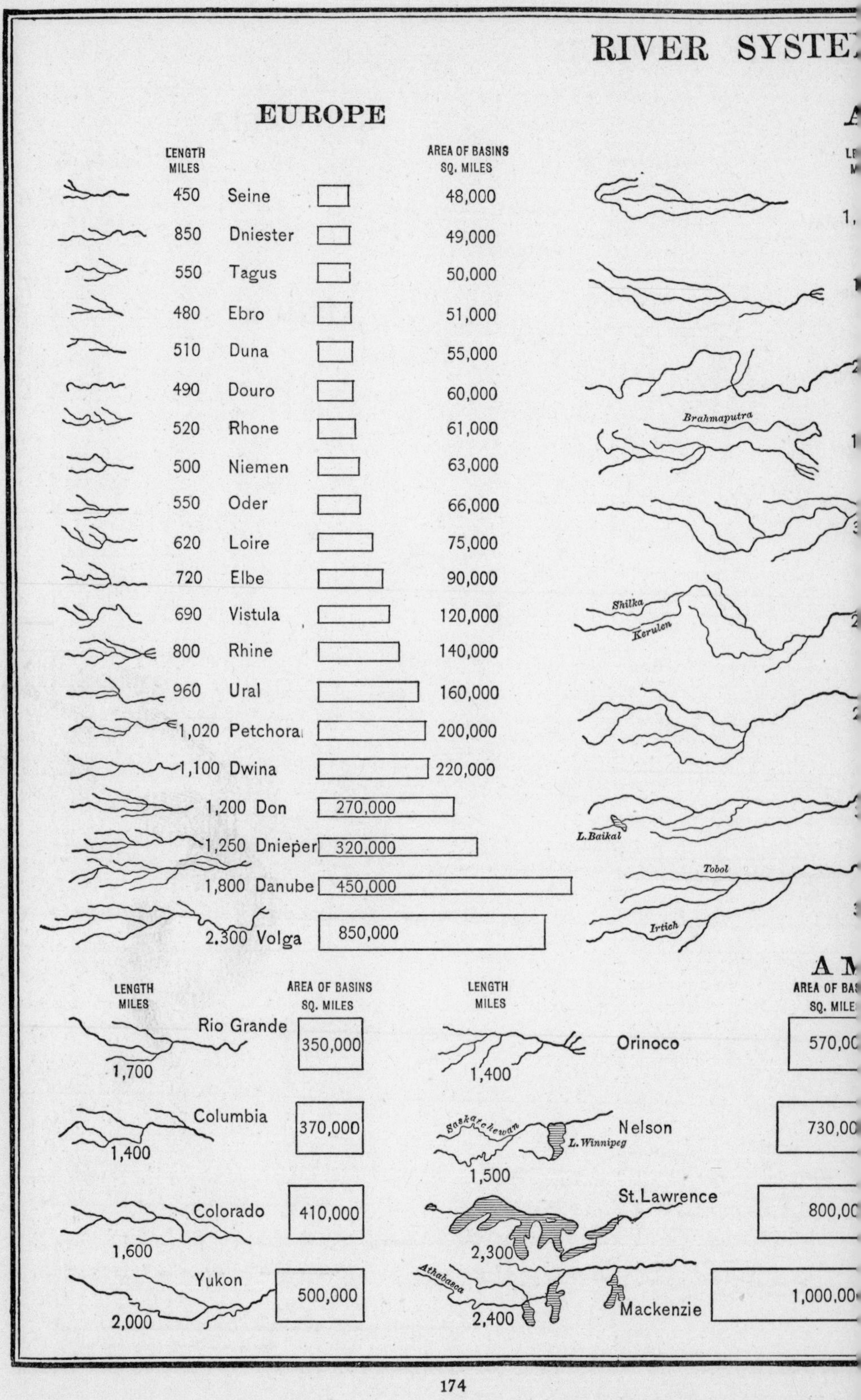

EUROPE

LENGTH MILES			AREA OF BASINS SQ. MILES
450	Seine		48,000
850	Dniester		49,000
550	Tagus		50,000
480	Ebro		51,000
510	Duna		55,000
490	Douro		60,000
520	Rhone		61,000
500	Niemen		63,000
550	Oder		66,000
620	Loire		75,000
720	Elbe		90,000
690	Vistula		120,000
800	Rhine		140,000
960	Ural		160,000
1,020	Petchora		200,000
1,100	Dwina		220,000
1,200	Don	270,000	
1,250	Dnieper	320,000	
1,800	Danube	450,000	
2,300	Volga	850,000	

Brahmaputra

Shilka

Kerulen

L. Baikal

Tobol

Irtich

LENGTH MILES		AREA OF BASINS SQ. MILES	LENGTH MILES		AREA OF BASINS SQ. MILES
	Rio Grande	350,000		Orinoco	570,00
1,700			1,400		
	Columbia	370,000		Nelson	730,00
1,400			1,500	Saskatchewan L. Winnipeg	
	Colorado	410,000		St. Lawrence	800,00
1,600			2,300		
	Yukon	500,000	Athabasca	Mackenzie	1,000,00
2,000			2,400		

A M

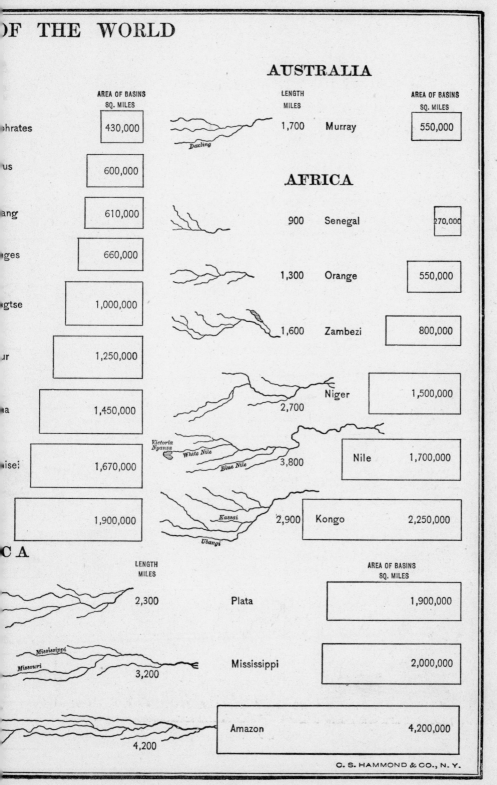

AUSTRALIA

AREA OF BASINS SQ. MILES		LENGTH MILES		AREA OF BASINS SQ. MILES
ohrates	430,000	1,700	Murray	550,000

AFRICA

us	600,000			
ang	610,000	900	Senegal	270,000
ges	660,000	1,300	Orange	550,000
gtse	1,000,000	1,600	Zambezi	800,000
ur	1,250,000			
a	1,450,000	2,700	Niger	1,500,000
ise	1,670,000	3,800	Nile	1,700,000
	1,900,000	2,900	Kongo	2,250,000

Victoria Nyanza · White Nile · Blue Nile · Kassai · Ubangi · Dazling

C A	LENGTH MILES		AREA OF BASINS SQ. MILES
	2,300	Plata	1,900,000
	3,200	Mississippi	2,000,000
	4,200	Amazon	4,200,000

Mississippi · Missouri

176